NORTH-SOUTH
DIVIDE

Jim Lewis is lecturer in Geography at the University of Durham. He has studied and taught about regional development in the UK for over ten years. His work has been primarily concerned with the geography of industrial and social change in Europe, but he has also conducted research in Africa, Australia and Asia. He has published numerous articles, book chapters and was an editor of *Regions in Crisis* (Croom Helm, 1980), *Regional Planning in Europe* (Pion, 1982) and *Uneven Development in Southern Europe* (Methuen, 1985).

Alan Townsend, Reader in Geography at the University of Durham, has specialised in questions of the location of employment growth and decline. He has practical experience of UK regional development through his work for government departments in North West England and Scotland, and for consultants on urban development in North East England. He was director of the North-East Area Study at the University of Durham, and is Co-Director of the National Online Manpower Information System. He has authored or co-authored 46 articles or book chapters, and is the author of *The Impact of Recession: on industry, employment and the regions* (Croom Helm 1982 and 1983).

THE
NORTH-SOUTH DIVIDE

Regional Change in Britain in the 1980s

Edited by
JIM LEWIS
and ALAN TOWNSEND

P·C·P
Paul Chapman
Publishing Ltd

Copyright © 1989. Introduction © Jim Lewis and Alan Townsend
Other material © 1989 Paul Chapman Publishing

Published 1989 by
Paul Chapman Publishing Ltd
144 Liverpool Road
London N1 1LA

British Library Cataloguing in Publication Data

North south divide: regional change in Britain
   in the 1980s.
   1. Great Britain. Regional economic
   development
   I. Lewis, J.R. II. Townsend, Alan R.
   330.941'0858
ISBN 1-85396-042-X

Typeset by Burns & Smith, Derby
Printed and bound by St Edmundsbury Press

To the memory of David Lewis (1913–88)
and Peggy Lewis (1907–88)

CONTENTS

LIST OF CONTRIBUTORS

Michael Bradford completed four years of postgraduate research at the University of Wisconsin, Madison, and the University of Cambridge. Since 1971 he has been a lecturer at the University of Manchester, where he is a founder member of the Centre of Urban Policy Studies (CUPS). His research interests include education, housing and marketing.

Frank Burdett was an undergraduate and postgraduate at the University of Manchester. He was a lecturer at Bath College of Higher Education from 1983 to 1988, when he became the Adviser to Higher Education for Acorn Computers. His research interests include education, local-authority policy-making and organization theory.

Tony Champion is Lecturer in Geography at the University of Newcastle upon Tyne. He is currently researching population deconcentration in Britain, migration between London and the rest of Britain, the variation in local house prices and their relationship to labour-market conditions and the monitoring of local economic performance in Britain.

Sarah Curtis is a lecturer in geography at Queen Mary College, London. Her main research interests are in public service provision and inequalities in health in Britain and France. She is the author of *The Geography of Public Service Provision* (Routledge, 1989).

Anne Green is currently a research fellow at the Institute for Employment Research, University of Warwick. She was formerly a research associate at the Centre for Urban and Regional Development Studies, University of Newcastle upon Tyne. Her research interests include spatial variations in employment, unemployment and population change, indices of local prosperity and migration.

Chris Hamnett is a senior lecturer in the Social Sciences Faculty of the Open University where he is Head of the Urban and Regional Research Group. In 1986 he was awarded the Banneker Research Professorship at the Center for Washington Area Studies, George Washington University, Washington, DC. In 1984–5 he was a member and research director of the Nugee Committee of Inquiry. The committee's report received all-party support and led to the Landlord and Tenant Act 1987. He has published widely on housing and urban social problems. His latest book co-authored with Bill Randolph is *Cities, Housing and Profits* (Hutchinson, London, 1988).

R.J. Johnston is Professor of Geography at the University of Sheffield. He has published widely on the geography of elections, including *The Geography of English Politics: The 1983 General Election* (Croom Helm, Beckenham, 1985) and – with C.J. Pattie and J.G. Allsopp – *A Nation Dividing? The Electoral Map of Great Britain 1979–1987* (Longman,London, 1988).

Andrew Leyshon is a research officer in the Department of Geography at the University of Bristol. He is an expert on financial services.

Ron Martin is a lecturer in Economic and Political Geography at the University of Cambridge, and Fellow and Research Tutor at St Catharine's College. His research interests include regional economic development, government policy and State intervention, and the geography of labour-market problems. His publications include *Regional Wage Inflation and Unemployment* (Pion, London, 1981), *The Geography of De-industrialisation* (with R. Rowthorn, Macmillan, London, 1988), *Rethinking Human Geography* (with G.E. Smith and D.J. Gregory, Macmillan, London, 1989), *The Political Economy of Space: A New Economic Geography* (with S. Corbridge and D. Reeve, Macmillan, London, 1989).

John Mohan is Lecturer in Geography at Queen Mary College, London, where he previously held an ESRC Postdoctoral Research Fellowship. His main research interests are in spatial aspects of restructuring and privatization in the British health sector. He is the editor of *The Political Geography of Contemporary Britain* (Macmillan, London, 1989).

Charles Pattie is Research Fellow in the Department of Geography at the University of Sheffield, working on an ESRC-financed project concerned with the changing electoral geography of Great Britain since 1955. He has recently completed a PhD thesis on urban politics and has carried out research on education policy and youth employment.

Nigel Thrift is a reader in the Department of Geography at the University of Bristol and Director of the Centre for the Study of Britain and the World Economy. He is the author or editor of ten books and more than seventy articles.

H.D. Watts is Senior Lecturer in Geography at the University of Sheffield with research interests in the impact of the behaviour of large organizations on urban and regional economies. Publications include *The Large Industrial Enterprise* (Croom Helm, Beckenham, 1980), *The Branch Plant Economy* (Longman, London, 1981) *Industrial Geography* (Longman, London, 1987).

PREFACE

Until recently, different parts of Britain appeared to have become more and more similar in terms of economic, political and social life. Expressions of regional distinctiveness – even in accents, beer or clothing – seemed to be disappearing in the face of a mass-consumption society and the departure of many local economies from their dependence on the industrial staples of the 19th century. With greater personal mobility, caricatures of the Surrey stockbroker or the canny Geordie had more to do with comedy shows than actual people you could meet in Woking or Newcastle. There were still exceptions to these trends – most notably in Northern Ireland and Scotland with their separate educational, legal and media systems – but Britain in the 1970s was a great deal more homogeneous than it had been in 1945.

At the end of the 1980s, such a claim would be almost unbelievable. Instead, numerous newspapers and television programmes, politicians and market researchers announce that the country is divided between a poor north and a rich south. The evidence to support – or, more rarely, contest – this finding is provided by government statistics on employment and income, building-society figures on house-price trends, investigative reports comparing living conditions in different towns and increasing polarization in the electoral support of the main political parties. A north-south divide is now presented as one of the distinctive characteristics of Britain in the 1980s. It is thought to be a feature that affects the lives of ordinary people, as well as the fortunes of politicians. It raises vital questions about efficiency and equity in the country today.

Clearly, contemporary geographical research has a great deal to say about the validity – or otherwise – of such views. In order to focus attention on this single aspect of regional change in Britain, we agreed to convene a joint meeting of the Industrial Activity and Area Development Study Group and the Social and Cultural Geography Study Group on the theme 'North versus South?'. It was held during the Annual Conference of the Institute of British Geographers at Loughborough University of Technology in January 1988.

This collection is based on the presentations to that meeting, all of which have been improved as a result of the discussion that took place there. As we also chair these study groups, we are particularly grateful to the contributors for allowing the bulk of the royalties from this publication to go to promote the study groups' activities. Not all of the papers presented in Loughborough were available for publication here – a matter for regret, especially as it means that there are now no contributors currently working outside England. Those who have contributed, however, work in all parts of England – at universities in Bristol, Cambridge, Coventry, Durham, London, Manchester, Milton Keynes, Newcastle upon Tyne and Sheffield – so that we hope to have avoided compounding the Anglocentric view by adding any strong northern, or southern, bias to the collection. We have been fortunate in receiving two additional contributions (Chapters 7 and 8) that broaden the scope of the book in other important ways.

Several of the ideas that led to the organization of the initial meeting and that appear in our Introduction arose from our involvement in the research initiative on the 'Changing Urban and Regional System of the UK', so we gratefully acknowledge the financial support provided to us and our colleagues in Durham by the Economic and Social Research Council (under Grant D04250018) during 1985–7. We should also like to thank Dorothy Trotter for her part in the preparation of the manuscript, David Cowton for drawing the majority of the figures, and Hope Page for indexing work.

Jim Lewis
Alan Townsend
Durham, 1988

ACKNOWLEDGEMENTS

The editors and publishers wish to thank the following who have kindly given permission for the use of copyright material.

The Institute of British Geographers, for Chapter 2. This is a revised version of the paper presented at the Annual Conference of the Institute of British Geographers, held at Loughborough University, 5-8 January 1988. The paper has previously appeared in *Transactions, Institute of British Geographers*, New Series, Vol. 13, pp. 389-418, and is reproduced with permission of the Institute of British Geographers.

The Conservative Research Department, for permission to use material from Iain MacLeod (1952) *One Nation*.

The Financial Times for material by Hamilton Fazey (1987) *Financial and Professional Services: Centre of Gravity in Manchester Financial Times Survey: Northwest England,* 2 October p.3, (1987) *Financial and Professional Services: A Remarkable Growth of Strategic Importance, Financial Times Survey, Yorkshire and Humberside*, 29 July p.5, and also for J Rogaly (1987) *Divided They Stand*, 31 March.

Martin Secker & Warburg, for material from I. Jack (1987) *Before the Oil Ran Out: Britain 1977-87.*

Times Newspapers Ltd, for material from the *Sunday Times* by P. Wilsher and J. Cassidy (1987) *Two Nations: The False Frontier.*

Chatto and Windus/The Hogarth Press, for material by P. Jenkins (1987) *Mrs Thatcher's Revolution: The Ending of the Socialist Era* (pp. 375-6).

Business, for material from *Across the North-South Divide*, September 1987, pp. 48 and 58.

1

INTRODUCTION

Jim Lewis and Alan Townsend

The emergence of an issue

The 1980s have been remarkable years in Britain. They have seen national economic growth at rates higher than the other large European nations, as the country recovered from the 1979–81 recession and rose to fifth position amongst the world's oil producers. There have been social changes – both highly visible, such as the arrival of the 'yuppie' and the impact of the 'lager lout', and more subtle, like the 'greying' of the population. They have been years of dramatic conflict, with a war against Argentina, continuing unrest in Northern Ireland and the violence of inner-city riots or the picket line. Politically, the domestic electoral scene has been dominated by the Conservative Party, whose Leader, Mrs Thatcher, became the first Prime Minister this century to win three consecutive elections.

The decade has also been remarkable for the extent to which such trends are seen as having changed the basic regional patterns of Britain. In particular, attention is increasingly drawn to the differences between an apparently impoverished, Labour-voting north of the country and an affluent, Conservative, south. Comments on the significance of a line drawn between the Rivers Tees and Exe, as the division between 'Highland' and 'Lowland' Britain, are being replaced in geography classrooms by discussion of a possible line from the River Severn at Bristol to the Wash, as the key division between northern and southern parts of the country. Regional variations in house prices are now not only the staple of conversation at middle-class dinner parties but also a recognized constraint on workers' mobility. On their visits to the north, southern football fans, flaunting their 'loadsamoney' and chanting 'You'll never work again', express their view of the differences in living standards without needing to refer to *Regional Trends*. Opposition politicians – of whatever party – have found the contrast between under-investment in the north and the over-congestion in the south to be a valuable stick with which to beat Mrs Thatcher's government. Political commentators have also become more aware of the polarization in voting behaviour and in election results between different parts of the country.

Recognition of a growing divergence between north and south in recent years has been encouraged by media presentations. The most dramatic of these, involving films of northern and southern families exchanging places, are reminiscent of American TV programmes in the 1960s on differences between the experiences of white people and black people. Journalists have also found powerful phrases to describe division, as in Ian Jack's observations (1987, p. ix) that

> Money has always tended to move south in Britain, as though it were obeying some immutable Newtonian law, but now it is not just the cream off the top, a case of Bradford profit being spent in Bond Street. The actual generation of wealth has moved south, as well as the spending of it... ninety-four per cent of net jobs lost since 1979 were north of a line drawn between the Wash and the Bristol Channel. This is a new frontier, a successor to Hadrian's Wall and the Highland Line. Above it, wealth and the population dwindle; beneath it, both expand.

The emergence of the north-south divide as an issue in Britain in the second half of the 1980s owed much to such analyses in the press (see also Chesshyre, 1987) or on television. However, by the time of the 1987 General Election, a recognition of the ways in which the country was rapidly becoming the 'Disunited Kingdom' was not confined to Channel 4 or the writings of 'disaffected' British journalists in *The Observer* or the *Guardian*. *The Financial Times* summarized its view of the disparity between north and south in the simple headline 'The gap widens' (Duffy, 1987). When *The Economist* turned to an American for an outsider's view of Britain, he too commented

> Roughly, with pockets of prosperity and blight on both sides, Britain is split by a north-south divide running from Bristol to the Wash. The victims of decaying smokestack industry live in the north; the beneficiaries of new high-tech, finance, scientific and service industries, plus London's cultural and political elite are in the south. Cross the divide, going north, and visibly the cars get fewer, the clothes shabbier, the people chattier.
> (Crichfield, 1987, p.4)

If there is a widening north-south divide, as these journalists and most of the contributors to this book suggest, it raises other issues that are important for the future of the country as a whole. Regional variations in employment opportunities, housing markets and educational provision combine to reduce national efficiency and increase social inequality in ways that are examined in detail in the chapters that follow. Politically, too, the north-south divide now raises questions broader than those of governmental devolution, or the damaging effects of southern growth on its countryside and transport infrastructure. In his analysis of the future of Mrs Thatcher's revolution, Peter Jenkins argued that the achievement of her aims of 'killing socialism' and the Labour Party are now dependent on spreading her political vision to the north. As he put it (1987, pp. 375-6),

> Between 1979 and 1987 she [Mrs Thatcher] constructed a new majority in the land, an anti-socialist coalition involving the prosperous working classes of the south and Midlands... . Yet for as long as Britain's electoral system remains Labour *can* win and

if Labour is what she means by socialism her revolution cannot be secure... . So what does she have in mind? The application of Thatcherism to the cities in order to destroy these last bastions of socialist Britain... . She was motivated in this latest enterprise... by a new determination to prove that what her enemies called 'Thatcherism' was the moral and intellectual superior of what she called 'socialism' and was as relevant to the cities as to the suburbs and the shires. By this means she would reinstate the Conservative Party in the great cities of the north. The south would move north. Tory Britain would invade and conquer Labour Britain. Her revolution would be complete.

Given the political significance that is thus now attached to claims about patterns of inequalities within the country, it is not surprising that the sorts of view of division and divergence presented above have been challenged. Mrs Thatcher herself frequently denies that there are divisions between north and south, as in this response to a parliamentary question: 'You are quite wrong in trying to give any impression that the North of England is down and out when very many parts of it are very prosperous. The road systems are excellent...the hospitals are excellent, in many places the airports are excellent, the railways are running' (Thatcher, 1987, col. 734).

Almost as often, journalists visiting one of the garden festivals or new shopping complexes in the north file stories on northern prosperity and southern suffering – showing that 'Glasgow has Porsches and London poverty' (Jack, 1987, p.ix) as a way of challenging a simple notion of a north-south divide.

A good example is 'Two nations: the false frontier' (Wilsher and Cassidy, 1987, p. 25) that ran:

> The main Porsche dealer in Newcastle upon Tyne, where the decline of shipbuilding has virtually wiped out the city's staple job creator, sold 150 cars last year, at an average price of £30,000 apiece, and 47% of the company's total UK sales were in what they define as 'the North'... . Unemployment in Middlesbrough, at 21.2% on the latest count, is amongst the highest in the country and its neighbours, Stockton on Tees, at 18.3%, and Darlington, at 14.2%, are hardly flourishing. But just beyond their town limits, in places like Yarm, Stokesley and the ICI strongholds north of Billingham, is the land of motorised golf trolleys and timeshares in the Algarve... .
>
> This is not to deny that Britain, when it comes to prosperity, is an increasingly divided nation. But the main split is not geographical but social. There is no Severn-Wash line separating the haves from the have-nots. The poor, predominantly recruited from young, ill-educated, often black males, unskilled over-50-year-olds and the growing army of unmarried mothers are certainly concentrated in the old, one-industry towns and decaying inner cities of the North. But they represent an equally intractable and numerically even larger problem in the boroughs at the heart of London. Meanwhile the relatively affluent majority, those enjoying jobs, cars, home-ownership, videos and regular foreign holidays, are to be found almost everywhere.

In a similar vein, *The Financial Times* (Rogaly, 1987, p. 14) argued that

> There is certainly greater inequality of income and possibly even of wealth than there was in 1979. There are specific areas of need and hardship. There are disgruntled communities, some of them smouldering with potential violence... .
>
> But it is important to set the context: Britain's principal division is in the mind. On the one side is a collection of minorities that cannot be expected to share the *weltanschauung* of Thatcherism... who feel that it is somehow wrong to accept a world-outlook that denies the warm comforts of the 1960s and 1970s and demands responsibility from individuals, cohesiveness of families, and a contribution from the able-bodied to

their own well-being.

On the other side those who feel that it is just this collection of characteristics that is required if Britain is to survive, let alone prosper as a modern economy.

It is this division in the mind that leads to so much confusion about the real divisions on the ground. One of the most confused notions is that of the 'north-south' divide. It implies that virtually all the wealth is in the south, or even the south-east, while the rest of the country is a zone of unrelieved devastation.

The truth is that there is an archipelago of wealth in the north, just as there is an archipelago of poverty in the south. For example, parts of Brixton or some of the council estates around King's Cross in London are as depressing as their counterparts in, say, Manchester.

These journalists' observations are borne out by research evidence but their conclusions are not justifiable. Both the chapters here by Champion and Green (Chapter 3) and Leyshon and Thrift (Chapter 5) and previously-published work – such as Breheny, Hall and Hart (1987) or Champion and Green (1985) – confirm that there are significant intra-regional variations in economic well-being. In searching for Rogaly's archipelagos, Table 3.11 (p. 91) shows, it is hoped, that the north does contain prosperous places like Northallerton (N. Yorks.), Kendal (Cumbria) or Hawick (Borders), just as the south includes depressed areas such as Deal (Kent), Lowestoft (Suffolk) and Redruth (Corn.). It is clearly important to bear this kind of information in mind, as it suggests that the geographical causes of differences in socio-economic conditions between regions as a whole are not purely physical ones, such as climatic conditions or distance from London.

However, it is not the basis of a convincing argument against the evidence that north and south are divided. If both contain pockets of prosperity and poverty, a lower average figure on a measure of living conditions for one area means that its better-off places are outweighed by much worse conditions in its poorer parts. Returning to the example from Table 3.11, the low median scores on an index of local economic prosperity for northern regions mean that the better the conditions in high-scoring places like Northallerton, the worse must be conditions in Mexborough (S. Yorks.), Consett (Co. Dur.) and the like.

Furthermore, there is as much of a danger of obscuring the causes of Britain's growing divisions in dismissing differences between north and south, as there is in considering them on their own. The concentrations of the poor in 'the old, one-industry towns and decaying inner-cities of the North' – *and* 'in the boroughs at the heart of London' – are partly a product of a geographical immobility, which is nowadays reinforced by increasing spatial variations in housing availability. Massive unemployment and growing labour shortages have both been features of Britain in the 1980s, not just because of a mismatch of skills but also because new jobs are not always accessible to those looking for work. Even if the key division in Britain is one between different attitudes, opinion polls and electoral behaviour show that people's views are affected by where they live (as Johnston and Pattie illustrate for the 1987 General Election in Chapter 9). The problems of a north-south divide are thus not ones that can be ignored: in this case, too, 'the geography of a society has important effects on the way the society works' (Massey, 1988, p. 13).

Of course, there are problems other than those raised by the north-south divide facing Mrs Thatcher, the government and the country; other divisions between people of different class, race and sex that are actually more fundamental than those of location. Between locations, there are still fundamental differential trends in rural and urban areas, just as major differences can be found in conditions in inner-cities, genteel suburbs, outer estates and commuter villages. Yet the metaphor of the north-south divide is the one that has gained the greatest currency in discussions of Britain's inequalities in the 1980s. It has come to serve as a shorthand in which 'northern' is equivalent to backward, dependent, industrial, public sector, Labour and poor; while 'southern' means successful, enterprising, service, private sector, Conservative and rich – wherever these characteristics occur.

Our aims in this book are to show how far these features really do distinguish the geographical north of Britain from the south, and to explain the processes that are reshaping the regional divisions of the country. In the following sections of this introductory chapter, we place the more-detailed studies of our contributors in context. This is done by first explaining why regional imbalance is an important issue and then by summarizing the key evidence and explanations put forward elsewhere.

For these purposes, we have excluded Northern Ireland from consideration (largely for lack of comparable data) and recognize the popular view of a Severn-Wash line as a dividing line between north and south. We, and most of our contributors, have grouped the standard regions of the North, North West, Scotland, Wales, West Midlands and Yorkshire & Humberside as the north, and treated East Anglia, East Midlands, South East and South West as the south. There are obvious limitations in using such large areal units as building blocks and our contributors have often tested or supplemented analysis at the level of these standard regions with finer-grained approaches.

The implications of regional imbalance

Variations between one part of a country and another are neither surprising nor new. The history of Britain would be impossible to understand without an awareness of regional differences in economy, culture, society and polity. Elsewhere, too, patterns of regional difference and the processes that produce them have been seen as important elements in any analysis of that country. By comparing these patterns and processes, social scientists have produced a number of models of the ways in which regional change occurs and the best known of these all stress the ways in which one region's initial advantage becomes reinforced.

Myrdal (1957) sets this out in terms of a process of 'cumulative causation', whereby a region that is growing more rapidly than the rest of the country tends to attract further growth, through both the movement of people to it and the investment of capital in it. These sorts of flow, combined with trade in goods and services, create what he called 'backwash' on the other regions – they lose part of whatever growth they may have had because the most able people are the ones who migrate to the emerging core region, and their capital takes the more profitable investment opportunities there too. There are a number of possible counter-balancing flows, or 'spread', such as the demand created by the growing core for products like foodstuffs from elsewhere, or investments located in the peripheral areas to avoid the mounting costs (e.g. of land or labour) of producing in the core. Myrdal, however, was clear in his view that spread would not outweigh backwash without government intervention, so he concluded that 'the play of the forces in the market normally tends to increase, rather than to decrease, the inequalities between regions' (*ibid.* p. 26). Other authors have refined this kind of analysis (for example, by adding in the advantage of innovations usually being introduced in the core) and there are those, such as Hirschman (1958), who argue that sufficient spread – or 'trickle-down' – does happen to reduce regional imbalance with only modest governmental corrective action (for opposing views of these arguments, see Hansen, 1981, and Stöhr, 1981). By the start of the 1980s, the dominant international view on these possibilities could be summarized thus: 'It is now widely accepted that initial patterns of regional income inequality contain the seeds of continued growth of disparities in the future', (Bennett, 1980, p. 43).

There are many reasons for democratic governments to wish to reduce regional inequality, involving some, or all, of the elements of economic efficiency, social equity, national security and electoral strategy. This means that they need to intervene in the process of cumulative causation to strengthen spread effects and/or weaken the backwash effects. Certainly in Britain, all governments from 1945 to 1979 have accepted this view. They have involved themselves, both consciously and unconsciously, in the regional distribution of population and resources. Through a range of measures, including Regional Policy, Regional Plans, the Rate Support Grant (which helped to finance local government) and public expenditure on physical and social infrastructure, governments have tried to tackle regional imbalance.

Why, then, should so much attention have been directed at current patterns of regional imbalance? Much of the answer is to be found in the analysis of the political debate on the north-south divide given by Martin in Chapter 2 (pp. 20–61) and in the examination of the recent electoral trends by Johnston and Pattie (Chapter 9). Both stress the re-emergence of regional divergence as a trigger to both the political interest in regional imbalance, and changes in voters' perceptions of their future.

In itself, an increase in the scale of regional inequality in Britain need not have much material effect, since the amount of variation around the national average is actually relatively small. *The Economist* (1987a, p. 63) put this simply in the comment that 'Glasgow – let alone Manchester – has more in common with London than Paris with Marseilles or Turin with Palermo'. In more precise terms, average personal income per capita in the north in 1986 at £4,247 was only £637 below that of the south, northern unemployment rates in 1988 were but 4.9 per cent higher than in the south and levels of ownership of common consumer goods, like colour TVs, are effectively uniform (Tables 1.5, 1.6, 1.7).

Comparing the regional differences of the whole UK with those of other European Community (EC) states underlines the relative homogeneity of the country. The coefficient of variation of Gross Domestic Product (GDP) per capita for the regions of the UK in 1978 was 0.097, indicating less disparity than in FR Germany (0.206), France (0.212) or Italy (0.266) (Jensen-Butler, 1987). Using the more recent EC 'synthetic index' of the intensity of regional problems in the early 1980s, the range for British regions – excluding Northern Ireland – was from 74 to 122 (in relation to a Community of 12 average of 100). Italian regions had values from 49 to 133, French ones ranged from 97 to 152 and even FR Germany had greater diversity, with index values between 104 and 159 (Commission of the European Communities, 1987).

What has changed in the 1980s to attract renewed attention is thus not the relative scale of regional imbalance but the general trend, and increases in absolute levels of problems (especially unemployment). In Britain – and many other northern European countries (see Molle, van Holst and Smit, 1980) – the 1960s and 1970s were a period in which regional imbalance was generally reduced. In part, this reflected the use of national and, later, EC regional policies and it was also due to the spontaneous shift of people and economic activities away from the great cities. The widening gaps of the 1980s have thus come as something of a shock. Evidence of the broad convergence of regional unemployment rates in Britain is given by Marshall (1987), who averages out cyclical fluctuations to show that rates were becoming more alike from 1961 to 1976. Employment data for a similar period show a reduction in the rate at which the south gained more jobs than the north, and this was especially marked in the early 1970s. More generally, Damesick (1987, p. 20) claimed that 'from about 1963, it is possible to identify a marked improvement in the employment performance of the problem regions of the North [of England], Scotland, Wales and Northern Ireland...[which] persisted until the recession in the mid-1970s'. Output data, such as GDP, show a similar trend for those parts of the north receiving government assistance. Rhodes (1986, p.142) noted that, from 1966, the 'Assisted Area regions taken together experienced a growth rate in GDP slightly better than the national average until 1978, after which it became slightly worse'. The exact reasons for this convergence in Britain are still not established – though the relative decline of industrial activity in the conurbations, led by London (e.g. Fothergill and Gudgin, 1982) and higher rates of job creation in the publicly-assisted regions (e.g. Moore, Rhodes and Tyler, 1986) seem to have dominated. However, there appeared to be sufficient evidence at the time to question whether regional policy was 'still the best framework for tackling spatial social disparities in Britain' (Keeble, 1977, p. 5).

The election of a Conservative government with Mrs Thatcher as Prime Minister in 1979 turned this question into a matter of political priorities. Successive official reviews of regional policy (summarized by Hudson and Williams, 1986; Townsend, 1987) have both redefined its objectives and coverage and cut its annual expenditure in real terms to some £700 million. Even though the early years of the 1980s were marked by increasing regional imbalance (discussed in the next section) and there were political risks of a resurgence in the nationalist movements in Wales and Scotland, the British government did not react by intervention at the regional scale, but rather by schemes for inner-city areas and/or local self-help. Despite the continued interest in regional development by the Commission of the EC, reversing the general trends towards greater regional inequality was given a low priority.

This was partly a reaction arising from the overall philosophy and political strategy of the government but it also reflected the significant increase in social and economic problems at a national level. The rising absolute levels of unemployment, in particular, concentrated attention on the effects of international pressures and government policies across the country. Yet it was still clear that certain parts of the country were being affected more profoundly than others. Pockets of persistent unemployment at levels not known since the 1930s were to be found in many parts of the country by 1983, but above all they were to be found in the north. The speed with which ex-company towns and parts of the great industrial cities in the north were becoming wastelands provided the political opposition parties – and internal opponents – with a lively issue on which to attack a government that could see 'no alternative'. Moreover, the issue of regional inequality was one that encapsulated other features of an 'uncaring' government and did so in a way that the media could readily capture. Thus, by the time of the 1987 General Election, regional imbalance was once again an issue in Britain.

Measuring the north-south divide

Accurate measurements of regional variations and their trends over time are seldom easy. Our contributors provide a range of attempts to do this for the north-south divide, both in aggregate terms (Chapters 2 and 3) or for specific elements, such as house prices (Chapter 4), ill-health (Chapter 7) and voting behaviour (Chapter 9). Hence we consider here only some of the more widely-available official statistics by way of context for the substantive chapters. Given their importance in heightening awareness of regional inequality, we start by focusing attention on employment trends and then turn to the evidence of north-south divergence in income and expenditure.

The underlying reasons for the north-south division in employment performance during the 1980s are not hard to find. Prime amongst them is the structural disadvantage of the older, industrial economy of the north. Most British coalfields and conurbations – the *loci* of 19th and early 20th-century industrialization – are in the north and Martin (Chapter 2) shows how their share of national industrial and economic activity has been falling from 1921.

This process accelerated in the early 1980s recession, when the adoption of a policy of high interest rates had a most searching effect on industry's costs and even threatened the survival of exporting companies. Other government policies accentuated this effect – most obviously the closure of loss-making plants in the (northern) nationalized industries, such as the British Steel Corporation. Within the larger private companies, there was also a tendency to close northern branch plants before the others (Townsend and Peck, 1985). Thus, for all the variety of industrial restructuring strategies that can be identified as constituting the 'anatomy of job loss' (Massey and Meegan, 1982), the net results during the early 1980s were predominantly higher rates of employment reductions in the north.

The initial structure of employment in an area was one of the principal factors governing its economic prosperity during this period. A high proportion of service activities normally guaranteed relative prosperity; a heavy dependence on manufacturing made a disproportionate increase in unemployment more likely. With 56.2 per cent of the country's manufacturing employment in the six standard regions of the north in 1979, the 29.0 per cent reduction in manufacturing jobs by 1987 hit there harder. Table 1.1 shows the overall effect of this in terms of employment estimates for 1979–87: a clear pattern of net job gain in all component regions of the south and job loss at rates of 5 per cent or more throughout the north (see also the similar evidence and slightly different interpretation of MacInnes, 1988, for the period 1975–87).

Table 1.1   Change in total employment, 1979–87 (June) (thousands, employees plus self-employed)

Region	1979	1987	Change, 1979–87	
			Nos.	%
South East	8,124	8,480	+ 356	+ 4.4
East Anglia	781	922	+ 141	+ 18.1
South West	1,744	1,870	+ 126	+ 7.2
East Midlands	1,671	1,717	+ 46	+ 2.8
Sub-total, 'south'	12,320	12,989	+ 669	+ 5.4
West Midlands	2,382	2,260	− 122	− 5.1
Yorkshire & Humberside	2,145	2,038	− 107	− 5.0
North West	2,890	2,541	− 349	− 12.1
North	1,325	1,198	− 127	− 9.6
Wales	1,157	1,011	− 146	− 12.6
Scotland	2,262	2,080	− 182	− 8.1
Sub-total, 'north'	12,161	11,128	− 1,033	− 8.5
Great Britain	24,481	24,117	− 364	− 1.5

(*Sources: Employment Gazette*, 1988, March, p. 162; May, Table 1.5; Historical Supplement no. 1, pp. 28–40.)

These results can be largely predicted statistically, based on the initial structure of employment. If we assume that industries in all places expand or contract their employees at their national rate, applying these rates to the detailed mix of sectors of industry in each region allows a prediction that is within 1 per cent of the actual job changes in the north. This kind of 'shift-share' analysis provides a similarly accurate prediction based on structure for the earlier period 1971–8 and the two statistical phases of the recession, 1978–81 and 1981–4.

The effects of the composition of the manufacturing sector can be seen further in Table 1.2. Metal manufacturing, chemicals and metal-using industries lost one third of their jobs nationally between 1979 and 1987 but the concentration of the worst-hit branches of iron- and steel-making, motor vehicles and industrial plant in northern regions means that the percentage rates of loss were higher there. Put another way, the initial mix of industries within the manufacturing sector can be used in a 'shift-share' analysis at minimum list-heading level to account for 747,800 of the 804,900 manufacturing jobs lost in the north, 1978–81: only 57,100 job losses need be attributed to a worse-than-average 'performance' by northern firms.

In terms of employment, the apparent decline of the north is thus a result of acceleration in the national trend away from manufacturing (accentuated by a

Table 1.2   Change in industrial employees across the 'north-south' divide, 1979–87 (June) (thousands)

Area	Metal manufacturing and chemicals	Metal goods, engineering and vehicles	Other manufacturing	Manufacturing (total)	Energy and water supply
'South', nos.	−52.0	−424.0	−222.0	− 698.0	−59.0
'South', %	−14.7	−28.0	−17.8	−22.4	−22.7
'North', nos.	−322.0	−677.0	−373.0	−1,374.0	−162.0
'North', %	−41.6	−37.3	−26.6	−34.4	−35.9
G. Britain, nos.	−372.0	−1,101.0	−591.0	−2,063.0	−224.0
G. Britain, %	−32.9	−33.0	−22.3	−29.0	−31.5

(*Sources*: Estimates rounded to nearest thousand from *Employment Gazette* (1988, May, Table 1.5; 1987 Historical Supplement, pp. 9, 34–9) based on *Censuses of Employment* of 1978, 1981 and 1984.)

Table 1.3   Change in type of labour force across the 'north-south' divide, 1979–87 (June) (thousands)

Area	Employees				Self-employed	Total
	Male	Female full time	Female part time	Total employees		
'South', nos.	−344.0	+162.0	+217.0	+35.0	+634.0	+669.0
'South', %	−5.3	+5.7	+11.1	+0.3	+63.9	+5.4
'North', nos.	−1,219.0	−330.0	+192.0	−1,357.0	+324.0	−1,033.0
'North', %	−18.4	−11.9	+10.1	−12.0	+38.1	−8.5
G. Britain, nos.	−1,563.0	−168.0	+408.0	−1,321.0	+959.0	−364.0
G. Britain, %	−11.9	−3.0	+10.5	−5.8	+52.1	−1.5

(*Sources*: Estimates rounded to nearest thousand from *Employment Gazette* (1988, March, p. 162; May, Table 1.5; 1987, Historical Supplement no. 1, pp. 28–40.)

Note
The *Employment Gazette* 1988, November, Table 1.5 shows increases of total employees 1987–1988, (June) of +194.0 (1.7%) in the 'South' and +88.0

relative shift of employment out of public industries and services). The effect of this has been especially marked in net job losses for full-time, male employees – with a reduction of 1.6 million across the country (Table 1.3) – which have not been matched in the north by sufficient growth in part-time, female employment or self-employment.

Poorer employment trends in the north were not just a feature of the early 1980s but have continued to the present. Since the lowest level of national employment was reached just before the 1983 General Election, the number of employees had grown by 745,000 (3.6 per cent) and those in self-employment by 641,000 (29.7 per cent) by 1987. Much of this has been associated with a continued expansion of service employees, amounting to 1,331,000 (10.1 per cent) over the four years – nearly one quarter of which was in the group of banking, financial, insurance and business services. Unlike public services, such as health and education, which are relatively evenly distributed across the country, these sorts of private service are concentrated in the south (which had 63.7 per cent of financial and producer-service employment in 1986), though Leyshon and Thrift (Chapter 5) show that some of this expansion is taking place in the leading provincial centres too.

During these years of rapid economic growth and employment recovery, the continuing structural disadvantage of the industrial north has often been overlooked. From 1983 to 1987, national manufacturing employment fell by a further 6.9 per cent to reach 5,040,000 (and since then had declined below five million in the spring of 1988). Employment levels remained stable in the non-metal-using sectors (especially textiles, timber, plastics, paper and chemicals) but the metal-using industries showed signs of continuing difficulties. These were most marked in the capital-goods sectors, where electronics recorded no employment increase, mechanical engineering had continued job losses and transport equipment lost another 125,000 employees (20.4 per cent). The latter was due in almost equal measure to net losses in the motor-vehicle industry and extensive cuts in shipbuilding, naval dockyards and railway workshops. These all had a disproportionate effect on the north, as did government policy on another of the nationalized industries: coal. Since the miners' strike of 1984–5, employment by British Coal was reduced from 191,000 to 125,000 in three years.

These industrial trends meant that the rate of redundancies fell more slowly in the north than in the south, at a time when the growth of service-sector employment was faster in the south. Hence the net job gain between 1983 and 1987 was 94,000 (1.0 per cent) in the north, compared to 652,000 (6.1 per cent) in the south.

Even with the gathering speed of improvements in employment conditions in 1987–8, this division remains apparent. During the twelve-months ending June, 1988 (the latest available at the time of writing), the increase in employees in employment in the south was at twice the rate of the north. This is not always the impression given by government when presenting another of their official series – the unemployment statistics – and it is important to appreciate how an apparently contradictory set of indicators can be produced from the same basic data.

The level of coverage of official unemployment statistics is itself a subject of some debate (e.g. Employment Institute, 1988), but there is no particular suggestion of any marked geographical bias in their recording. Thus the main series – claimants of Unemployment Benefit – can be used to study changes in regional rates over time. Table 1.4 gives a consistent series from 1979 to 1988 and shows that, even on this 'low' definition of rates of unemployment, the south has consistently been below the north.

Table 1.4 Alternative measures of unemployment across the 'north-south' divide, 1979–88 (June)

	1979		1986		1988	
	Nos. (000)	%	Nos. (000)	%	Nos. (000)	%
Percentage rates:						
'South'	392.7	3.0	1,261.9	8.9	858.6	6.0
'North'	739.3	5.4	1,947.3	14.0	1,516.8	10.9
UK	1,132.0	4.3	3,209.2	11.5	2,375.4	8.4

	1979–86 %	1986–8 %	1979–88 %
Percentage change:			
'South'	+ 221.3	− 32.0	+ 118.6
'North'	+ 163.4	− 22.1	+ 105.2
UK	+ 183.5	− 26.0	+ 109.8
'Percentage-point difference':			
'South'	+ 5.9	− 3.0	+ 2.9
'North'	+ 8.7	− 3.1	+ 5.6
UK	+ 7.2	− 3.0	+ 4.2

Note: Continuous time series consistent with coverage of claimants statistics, June, 1988; rates calculated by expressing the number of unemployed as a percentage of the 'total workforce' (including participants on work-related government training programmes), series established from June 1988.

(*Source:* National Online Manpower Information System, (NOMIS), University of Durham.)

The table also allows the separation of changes in the most recent period from June 1986 to June 1988, when seasonally-adjusted unemployment declined in 23 of the 24 months. In order to describe the pattern of unemployment change during this period of reduction, the actual number of claimants can be expressed as a percentage of the number at the start of the period. On this basis, the percentage change in these two years has clearly been higher in the south, with a fall of 32.0 per cent, than in the north (22.1 per cent). Figure 1.1 presents a similar picture, using the percentage change in unemployment in relation to the national trend for the standard regions. Even if we turn to the same data at the level of travel-to-work areas (Figure 1.2), there is a remarkable belt of faster improvement covering most of the South East and adjoining areas (though excluding London itself).

This pattern of recovery from the levels of unemployment of the mid-1980s underlines the extent of regional division in employment conditions that has emerged, but it is not widely appreciated. The prevailing view comes from ministerial pronouncements that improvements in unemployment are recently greatest in, for example, the North West or Wales; a claim that can be supported

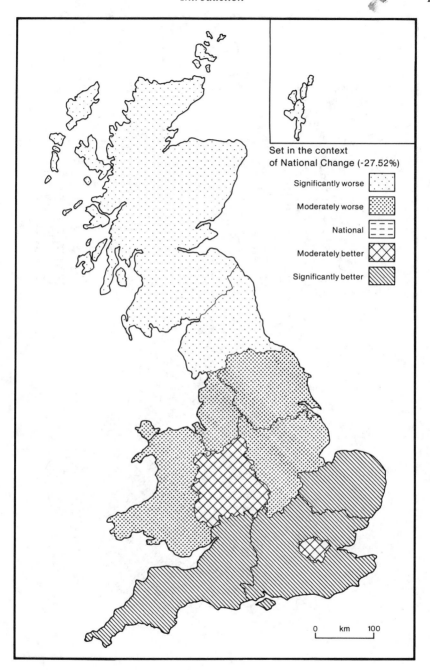

Figure 1.1 *Percentage change in unemployment, June 1986 to June 1988; significant variation from national average (standard regions)*

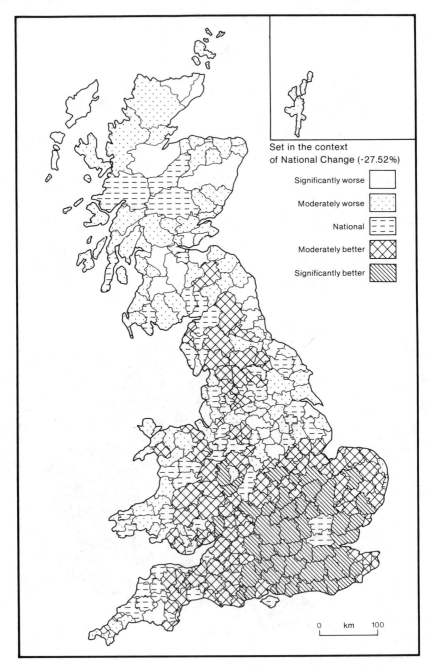

Figure 1.2 Percentage change in unemployment, June 1986 to June 1988; significant variation from national average (travel-to-work areas)

by using a different indicator – 'percentage-point difference'. By expressing the reduction in the number of claimants as a percentage of the total workforce, the percentage-point difference method gives a much more uniform impression of recent improvements in unemployment across the north-south divide. This is the method used for calculating change in unemployment rates in the 'Change Index' of Champion and Green (Chapter 3) and they, too, found a relatively-even scatter of local-labour markets with significant improvements between north and south. For the period 1986–8, this calculation of the fall in unemployment in the north (3.1 per cent) and south (3.0 per cent) suggests a marginally better performance in the north (Table 1.4). This is partly a reflection of the pattern of greater initial deterioration in employment levels in the north, especially in 1980–1 (Martin, 1982; Townsend, 1983), which has meant that there were simply larger numbers of claimants there by the start of the recovery.

The choice of these different measures – or, indeed, others such as difference from the national average, as used by Martin (Chapter 2) – is not purely a technical one. Any attempt to compare regional unemployment rates is influenced by the presence of regionally-differentiated unemployment cycles. Crouch (1982, 1989) has sought ways of addressing this problem and concluded that the percentage-point change method gives the most reasonable results during an economic downturn – such as 1979–86. However, during that period, official sources argued against the view that increasing unemployment was particularly a problem of the north by quoting percentage-change figures: northern unemployment up by 163 per cent, southern up by 221 per cent. In the late 1980s upturn, the preferred method has been changed and more-rapid improvements in unemployment in the north are claimed on the basis of the sorts of percentage-point diffferences noted above.

Yet the use of either method consistently reveals the different scales of the unemployment problem that still confronts the north and the south. For the whole of the period 1979–88, the percentage-point difference method shows a greater increase in unemployment in the north (5.6 per cent, compared with 2.9 per cent in the south), with a recent rate of reduction that is marginally above the national average (Table 1.4). The percentage-change method indicates a higher rate of increase in unemployment in the south (118.6 per cent, compared with 105.2 per cent) over 1979–88 but also a higher rate of reduction in the latest two years. Either way, the south as a whole is currently heading for 'zero unemployment' at an earlier date than the north. A similar conclusion was reached by Cambridge Econometrics and the Northern Ireland Economic Research Centre (1987), using more sophisticated employment forecasts to the year 2000. Their prediction for 1986–2000 was for a small net decline in employment (0.8 per cent) in the north but an employment increase of 12.0 per cent in the south (in this case including the West Midlands). As they put it, 'what this amounts to is a strengthening of the North-South divide which has become increasingly evident since the end of the long postwar boom in the mid-1970s' (p.6).

The differing economic and social fortunes of the north and south are also evident through non-employment data. Output, measured in terms of GDP per capita, has not only remained higher in the south from 1979 to 1986 but has also increased more rapidly. As Table 1.5 shows, the southern average of £6,197 per capita was

Table 1.5 Measures of per-capita production, income and expenditure for north and south

	GDP per capita				Personal disposable income, per capita			
	1979 £	1979 Relative	1986 £	1986 Relative	1979 £	1979 Relative	1986 £	1986 Relative
'South'	3,114	103.6	6,197	109.8	2,604	105.7	4,884	106.9
'North'	2,888	96.2	5,143	91.1	2,328	94.5	4,247	93.0
G. Britain	3,003	100.0	5,646	100.0	2,464	100.0	4,567	100.0

	Consumer expenditure, per capita				Consumer expenditure on housing and fuel, per capita			
	1979 £	1979 Relative	1986 £	1986 Relative	1979 £	1979 Relative	1986 £	1986 Relative
'South'	2,223	106.0	4,564	110.4	443.2	111.9	929.6	113.7
'North'	1,975	94.2	3,700	89.5	350.4	88.5	704.4	86.2
G. Britain	2,097	100.0	4,134	100.0	396.0	100.0	817.5	100.0

(*Sources: Regional Statistics*, 1981, 1982; *Regional Trends*, 1988; HMSO, London.)

9.8 per cent above the national figure in 1986, while northern output at £5,143 had fallen to 8.9 per cent below. Income levels have displayed similar, but less marked trends. Personal income per capita rose nationally from £2,464 to £4,567 between 1979 and 1986, with that in the north staying about 6 per cent below these levels, and income in the south growing from 5.7 per cent above to 6.9 per cent above.

The gap in terms of average consumer expenditure has increased more sharply: in 1979 expenditure per capita in the south was only 12.5 per cent higher than in the north, by 1986 it was 23.4 per cent higher (Table 1.5). This difference is often explained in terms of the higher and more rapidly-rising private house prices in the south during this period (as shown by Hamnett in Chapter 4). However, no more than £222 of the 1986 expenditure gap of £864 is directly attributable to housing costs and the proportions of expenditure devoted to housing and fuel are virtually the same (19.0 and 20.4 per cent) in the two parts of the country. This is not to deny the very real problems faced by house purchasers having to borrow sufficient to meet southern prices, or council tenants having to cope with rising London rents, but it does suggest that consumer expenditure is higher on a broader range of goods and services (such as private health insurance, pp. 187-9 and private schooling, pp. 194-212).

Data on different consumption levels by region are not really detailed enough to investigate these expenditure trends further. Certainly, in terms of modern consumer durables, the proportion of households owning deep freezers or colour televisions - 63.1 per cent and 84.8 per cent respectively in 1984-5 - was not greatly different in north and south (Table 1.6). Indeed, over the years considered here, northern ownership of deep freezers rose more rapidly (from 37.2 per cent of households in 1979-80 to 57.1 per cent in 1984-5) than the increase in ownership in the south. At the same time, the proportion of southern households owning colour televisions grew faster (68.0 per cent to 84.8 per cent) and converged on the northern level. What is not available from these sources is information on the quality of goods or on multiple ownership - aspects in which regional differences may be more apparent.

The same difficulty arises in studying purchases of holidays and new cars in relation to the two regions' shares of the national population in Table 1.7. It is clear that people in the south bought more than half the new cars registered each year in 1986 as in 1979; they also accounted for 53 per cent of foreign holidays in both years. However, we cannot tell if the cars were Porsches or Polos, nor if the holidays were taken in Benidorm or the Bahamas. The only one of these indicators that shows any obvious movement is for those who take no holiday: such people are increasingly likely to be from the north (although the actual numbers of people concerned could still be falling).

Taken together, the measures considered here show that average living conditions in the north and the south of Britain have diverged during the 1980s. Be it in employment opportunities or consumer expenditure, wherever there is a clear trend over the whole period, it is towards greater imbalance. Some reduction may be occurring in the late 1980s, as unemployment falls, employment mobility increases and southern house prices stabilize, but there are now significant gaps to be overcome.

Table 1.6 Ownership of consumer durables

	1979–80 Households owning:				1984–5 Households owning:			
	Deep freezers	%	Colour TV	%	Deep freezers	%	Colour TV	%
'South'	5,585	49.1	7,724	68.0	6,732	69.4	8,230	84.8
'North'	4,401	37.2	8,188	69.1	5,750	57.1	8,546	84.9
G. Britain	9,986	43.0	15,911	68.6	12,482	63.1	16,776	84.8

Table 1.7 Purchase of holidays and new cars (%)

	1979	Holidays			1986	Holidays		
	Population	No holiday	Abroad	New car	Population	No holiday	Abroad	New car
'South'	49	48	53	54	50	45	53	54
'North'	51	52	47	46	50	54	47	46
G. Britain	100	100	100	100	100	100	100	100

(*Sources: Regional Statistics*, 1982; *Regional Trends*, 1988; HMSO, London.)

As the contributions that follow show, the causes of these trends – and other important ones in political life – are many and varied. Few relate solely to real geographical differences between the north and the south, and most require explanations that involve an understanding of both international and local processes (Cooke, 1989). Nor are solutions to the problems that they have created necessarily best provided by a revitalized spatial policy alone. However, until Britain moves decisively towards a more-equal society again, its inequalities will continue to express themselves as a north-south divide.

2

THE POLITICAL ECONOMY OF BRITAIN'S NORTH-SOUTH DIVIDE

Ron Martin

Introduction: the debate

The political debate is now about the Two Nations ... . We are not two nations. We are one. The idea of Two Nations arises from the Industrial Revolution of the last century. This was almost entirely beneficial in its economic effects but many of the social results were catastrophic. There have always been two attitudes towards this evil – for evil it was, and if it still exists, evil it still is.

The society of the Two Nations was diagnosed and criticised by both Marx and Disraeli; but their prescriptions were totally different. Marx taught that it was historically inevitable that capitalism should be superceded by a new order in which all the means of production and distribution would be state owned. Disraeli taught that it was morally just that capitalism should be disciplined by the values and traditions of the old order – service and obligation. In the circumstances of the second industrial revolution through which we are now living, this fundamental difference and debate still persists ... .

It is a great disservice to the nation to pretend for electoral reasons that the north of England and Scotland are either in despair or are weak ... .

The nation is one. And surely the proof that we are in fact 'One Nation' is that only in conditions of economic expansion can the needs of the problem areas be fully met.

(Macleod, 1952, p. 1)

Over the past two years a major debate has broken out within the British public and political arena as to whether during the course of the 1980s the country has become a 'divided nation'. This means a society split between the rich and the poor, between the unemployed and the employed, between those communities entrapped in impoverished inner-city areas and those living in comfortable suburbia and ex-urbia, between one nation residing in a depressed 'north' and another in a much more prosperous 'south'.[1] Indeed, one of the central elements of this controversy is the charge that since 1979 the economic policies pursued by Mrs Thatcher have created a major 'north-south divide'. Much of the case for such an argument has derived from evidence produced by Mrs Thatcher's own government departments. First there was the government's submission in 1986 of its regional development programme to the European Regional Development Fund

(Department of Trade and Industry, 1986). This report highlighted the serious economic plight and poor future prospects of much of Britain's 'north'. As such the study proved embarrassing to the government; while the catalogue of economic decay it portrayed may well have strengthened Britain's case for assistance from the Fund, at the same time it reflected badly on the government's economic record: Then, in early 1987, new estimates of national and regional employment trends, based on the much-delayed publication of the 1984 *Census of Employment*, confirmed the existence of a marked 'jobs gap' between the 'north' and 'south' of the country (Department of Employment, 1987; HM Government, 1987). Not surprisingly, both the Labour Party and the SDP-Liberal Alliance (now the Social and Liberal Democratic Party) have seized upon this regional inequality as a key issue in their political manifestos.[2]

For her part, Mrs Thatcher has persistently dismissed the idea of any serious 'two-nation' problem, claiming that the scale of relative disparity between southern and northern regions of Britain is far less than many have suggested, that the issue is grossly oversimplified: 'Everything that once made the north a prosperous part of our country is still there. Our task is to bring that enterprise out'; and, furthermore, that the difficulties in inner-cities such as London are as great as in the north (Mrs Thatcher, quoted in *The Financial Times*, 1987, p. 6). However, Edward Heath, the former leader of the Conservative Party, has taken a somewhat different view. Speaking in 1985, and thus anticipating the current debate, he argued that 'the North is getting larger as massive unemployment has crept Southward through the Midlands and Eastward from Wales to engulf much of England. And the South is little more than a small patch in London, the South East and South of England' (p. 2). In his opinion, the 'north-south problem' has become sufficiently acute and politically disturbing to warrant concerted remedial intervention by the government. But speaking more recently in London, Lord Young, the Secretary of State for Trade and Industry and the member of Cabinet in charge of regional policy, flatly rejected the need for such interventionist sentiments with a simple and unapologetic appeal to the justice of history:

> There was more industrialisation in the North, originally, therefore there now has to be more de-industrialisation. Until 70 years ago the North was always the richest part of the country. The two present growth industries – the City and tourism – are concentrated in the South. I try to encourage people to go North; that is where all the great country houses are because that's where the wealth was. Now some of it is in the South. Its our turn, that's all.
>
> (Quoted in *Business*, 1987, p. 48)

He goes further. He suggests that the north-south debate is a political contrivance foistered on the electorate by Labour: 'I don't think it's North-South at all. I don't think there is anything deprived about, say, Chester, and if you go a few miles from Whitehall there are five areas with unemployment as high as anywhere in England' (*ibid.*).

This idea that the 'north-south divide' is a myth is no less provocative than the accusation that the divide is the direct result of ten years of 'Thatcherism'. Of course, no one would deny that London contains some of the country's most serious inner-city problems; nor that pockets of high unemployment and economic decline can be found at several locations in the 'south', just as it is possible to point to numerous examples of economic prosperity and low unemployment in the 'north'. However, such intra-regional disparities are not new. For example, marked local variations in unemployment occurred in the 1930s, with both high and low rates observable, then as now, across all of the major regions of the country (Beveridge, 1944; Fogarty, 1945; compare Armstrong, 1987). And as is well known, the degree of spatial inequality in the socio-economy is scale-dependent; measured differences tend to increase as the geographical coverage of the areal divisions employed decreases. The debate is not just over the existence or significance of local disparities, which can be found everywhere: the issue is also that these local disparities map out and form part of a broader 'north-south' geography of socio-economic inequality, and that this regional divide has become an increasingly prominent feature of British society. The aim of this chapter, therefore, is basically twofold: first, to trace the origins, evolution and contemporary scale of the divide; and, second, to explore its political implications, particularly with respect to the concept of 'one-nation politics' that has long been a recurring theme in British political culture.[3]

Britain's regional problem: prior history and inter-war origins

Lord Young's claim that until about seventy years ago the 'north' of Britain was richer than the 'south', and that thereafter this pattern was reversed, accords closely with what has become the 'conventional wisdom' concerning the impact of the inter-war economic upheaval on the geography of the country. According to many economic historians and geographers, a major turnaround in the regional configuration of uneven development occurred in the 1920s and 1930s. Two leading adherents of this view are cited by Southall (1988) in his re-appraisal of the origins of the inter-war regional problem. The first is the economic historian von Tunzelman, who is emphatic that 'The familiar division between Inner [London and the Midlands] and Outer Britain [the 'north'] dated only from the First World War ... . The very abruptness of the turnaround ... , coupled with its intensity, helps to account for the length of the shadow cast over inter war Britain' (1981, pp. 247-8). The second is the geographer, Peter Hall, according to whom 'Within Britain the northernmost part of England ... has presented economic problems ever since the interwar period. The former basic industries of coalmining, shipbuilding and heavy engineering have declined: heavy unemployment and low income were the result in the 1930s' (1975, p. 81). Similarly, in Doreen Massey's various analyses of the changing spatial divisions of labour in Britain (1979, 1984, 1986), the inter-war years stand out as marking a historic transformation of the 'regional problem'. Her version of the story runs something as follows.

During the 19th century and up to about 1914, the 'north' was the dynamic and prosperous part of Britain, a spatial structure forged by the Industrial Revolution of the late 18th century, centred on cotton in Lancashire, and later reinforced by the growth of key export-based industries (such as shipbuilding, engineering, coal-mining and textiles) associated with the expansion of Empire and international dominance. Unemployment was primarily a problem of the 'south', with its difficulties of agricultural depression, and of the decline of old handicraft industries as in London. Immediately following the First World War, however, adverse shifts in Britain's world trade position imposed severe shocks on the industrial 'north'. These were associated with the decline of Empire and the rise of new international competition, combined with restrictive domestic economic policies and recurrent recession in the 1920s and 1930s. They resulted in rapid structural decline and the emergence of acutely high unemployment. Meanwhile, the new 'growth' industries of the period, based on light engineering and electrical and consumer-goods sectors, became clustered in the south and east of the country and in the Midlands. Hence 'In terms of many of the basic measures of social inequality, the geography of the country had to a large extent been reversed' (Massey, 1986, p. 31), producing in the process the modern 'regional problem' of a depressed 'industrial periphery' versus a prosperous south and Midlands.

While some aspects of this history are correct and well documented, there is also evidence that suggests that some important qualifications and modifications are called for. In the first place, although the bulk of industrial employment in the 19th century was to be found in the north and west of Britain, there was also a clear distinction between what might be called the 'manufacturing heartland', comprising the West Midlands, North West and Yorkshire & Humberside regions, and the 'industrial periphery', made up of Wales, Scotland and the Northern region. The employment base of the latter three regions was highly specialized in coal-mining. In 1841 coal-mining accounted for 8 per cent of British industrial employment, and the 'industrial periphery' in turn accounted for 45 per cent of the national sectoral total. Between 1841 and 1921 national employment in coal-mining grew at an average annual rate of 6.3 per cent, whereas in the 'industrial periphery' it grew by 7.0 per cent, so that by 1921 this broad division of the country had increased its share of the total to 50 per cent. But within manufacturing the situation was somewhat different. Although all parts of the country experienced a sustained growth in manufacturing employment during the 19th century, the fastest expansion occurred in the 'manufacturing heartland', at a rate of 3 per cent per annum, with the result that this area of Britain progressively increased its share of national manufacturing employment (see Figure 2.1). The 'industrial periphery', however, experienced a much slower rate of growth, 1.9 per cent per annum, and its share of national manufacturing employment actually declined between the 1840s and the 1920s (Lee, 1979, 1980; Marshall, 1987). In other words, as far as the manufacturing sector is concerned, the industrial periphery was undergoing *relative* decline long before the inter-war depression. And while much of the 'south and east' (the South East, East Anglia, South West and East Midlands) was predominantly agricultural, even here manufacturing employment had been growing faster (2.1 per cent per annum) than in the three peripheral regions. Moreover, the South East region itself ranked alongside the North West as a major spatial concentration of manufacturing activity; in fact London was the single largest centre of manufacturing in the country. In addition, even by the early 19th century London and the South East had become firmly established as the country's

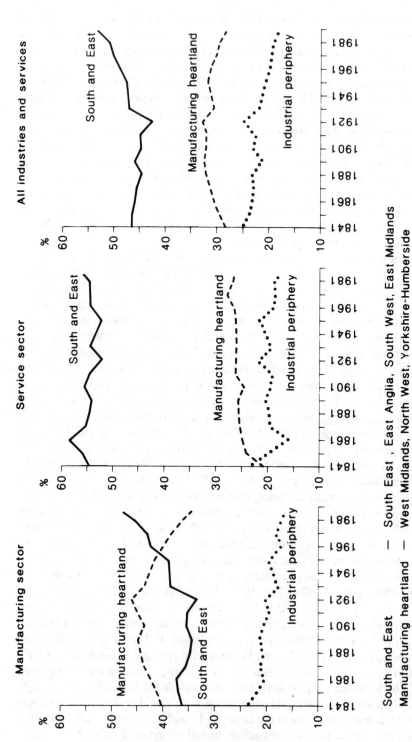

Figure 2.1 *Distribution of national employment by major geographical division, 1841–1988 (GB = 100%) (Sources: Lee, 1979; DE, 1987)*

South and East   — South East , East Anglia, South West, East Midlands
Manufacturing heartland — West Midlands, North West, Yorkshire-Humberside
Industrial Periphery   — North, Wales, Scotland

leading centre of commerce and finance, and of service employment in general (Lee, 1984).

Second, recent research on the geography of unemployment in Victorian and Edwardian Britain has cast serious doubt on the view that prior to the inter-war years unemployment was higher in the 'south' of the country. To the contrary, using trade-union records, Southall (1983, 1988) found that in a number of occupations high rates of unemployment were primarily a feature of the industrial areas of northern Britain, and that the lowest rates were in southern and eastern England. Furthermore, within all regions the rural hinterlands exhibited lower rates than did the urban cores. Thus whereas the high unemployment problem of the industrial north and periphery in the inter-war period is usually attributed to the decline of the previously-prosperous Victorian staple industries in these areas, these industries also created widespread unemployment in these same regions during the 19th century, this time as part of their normal functioning (that is as a consequence of their inherent sensitivity to the trade cycle). As Southall (1983, p. 400) puts it:

> much of Victorian Britain was enmeshed in a pattern of development which created intrinsically unstable regional economies, the benefits of growth being denied to much of the population of such areas by repeated and prolonged episodes of unemployment ... . This burden was ... part of the price Britain paid for an apparently prosperous industrial system based on exports rather than indigenous demand, and it seems that the burden fell most heavily, both then and subsequently, on those regions which created her prosperity.

Hence, as far as employment and unemployment are concerned, there would appear to be sufficient grounds for arguing that the inter-war period witnessed not so much a 'reversal' of the geography of inequality in Britain as an intensification of a pre-existing imbalance between the 'industrial periphery' and certain parts of the north on the one hand, and the 'south and east' on the other.

Third, the evidence on wages and wealth also suggests that the geography of inequality in Victorian Britain was not a simple one of a prosperous 'north' and a less prosperous 'south'. In his study of regional wage variations in the second half of the 19th century, Hunt (1973) identified two, main, high-wage areas. The first consisted of a band of industrial counties stretching from Northumberland and Durham in the north east, to the West Riding and Lancashire in the north west, and to Staffordshire, Derbyshire and Nottingham in the Midlands. Wages in this area were above the national average throughout the period. But the highest-wage region was that of London and the surrounding 'home counties'; for several occupations, in fact, wages were higher in London than in any of the major provincial cities. The rest of the rural south and east, and especially East Anglia and the South West regions, were certainly low-wage areas, but equally so were Wales, Scotland and much of Yorkshire & Humberside. Only towards the turn of the century did the industrial peripheral regions of south Wales and central Scotland join the group of high-wage areas. Similarly, the spatial distribution of middle- and upper-class wealth in the 19th century was not concentrated in the industrial towns of the 'north', as Lord Young argues, but rather was focused on London. The importance of northern regional trading centres such as Liverpool, Manchester, Leeds and Glasgow notwithstanding, more than 50 per cent of middle-class income in Victorian times was accounted for by London. This was due not just to its larger middle-class population but also to its higher middle-class per-capita income (Rubenstein, 1977).

In fact, estimates of regional average per-capita incomes indicate that the relative affluence of the South East during the 19th century is beyond question (see Table 2.1). Not only was the gap between the South East and almost all other regions

Table 2.1   Regional disparities in per-capita income in the second half of the 19th century (North West = 100)

	1859–69	1879–80	1911–12
South East	122	147	331
East Anglia	109	104	97
South West	94	93	138
East Midlands	114	108	78
West Midlands	89	87	94
Yorks. & Humberside	82	90	78
North West	100	100	100
North	93	84	81
Wales	68	70	87
Scotland	80	96	88

(*Source:* Lee, 1986, p. 131.)

substantial, but from the 1850s onwards the gap appears to have grown wider. Conversely, much of the industrial 'north' fared poorly in comparison with the national average, and especially against the South East; and some parts of the 'north' – specifically the Northern region itself together with Yorkshire & Humberside – probably witnessed a deterioration in relative per-capita incomes over the period. There is no convincing evidence to suggest that the pre-eminent position of the South East was due to large transfers from the industrial 'north'. The means by which the South East acquired its wealth therefore represent an important enquiry in the context of British economic growth and the history of the 'regional problem'. The economic structure of this region was much different from that of the industrial regions primarily because of the very high concentration there of service employment (see Figure 2.1). This was particularly true of those service sectors (like banking and financial services) that were closely related to wealth (Rubenstein, 1981; Lee, 1984). The key feature of the metropolitan economy lay in international trade, a role that pre-dated the Industrial Revolution. By the 18th century, profits made from overseas trade formed the basis of established City fortunes; and increasingly this wealth itself promoted, and in turn was augmented by, the growth of London as a financial centre, which developed from national leadership to international pre-eminence between 1700 and 1914 (Lee, 1986). And as the government was based in the capital, so the network of financial and banking institutions needed to service it naturally developed there. Furthermore, the scale and established expertise of this London-based financial system, together with its international connections, enabled it to dominate the immense increase in demand for investment that was associated with the rapid expansion of the international economy during the second half of the 19th century. This financial, international and governmental role of the South East, and its associations with the landed wealth of the surrounding shires, were far more important and profitable than its links with the industrial regions. It was, in addition, a base of wealth that extended to consumer goods manufacture, construction and a host of service activities.

This excursion into economic history is not meant to refute the conventional interpretation of regional development during the 19th century, nor to imply that London did not have its well-documented problems of poverty and deprivation. But it is meant to suggest that the alleged economic advantages of the 'north' over the 'south' during the 19th century can be exaggerated. For much of the working population of the industrial 'north', socio-economic misery was a prevalent condition. Indeed, the plight of the urban-industrial working classes, throughout the Midlands and the 'north' as well as in London, was an important element in the popular and political awareness of 'two nations' that emerged in the second half of the century.[4] Neither is it meant to imply that the inter-war depression was unimportant in shaping the geography of inequality: to the contrary. The basic point is that 19th-century economic prosperity and dynamism were not a uniform feature of the industrial 'north', and by no means concentrated in that particular area of the country. There was a substantial dualism in 19th-century Britain: between a 'north' based primarily on industrial growth and exports, and the metropolitan South East specialized in commerce, banking, finance and government. In terms of wealth, the South East was clearly the leading region. As Rubenstein (1977, 1981) has demonstrated, Victorian Britain in effect contained two middle classes: by far the largest and wealthiest based on commerce and finance in London and the surrounding 'home counties'; and the other on industry and manufacturing in the 'north'. This was a spatial and economic dualism that translated into social and political divisions. For example, the London middle class returned Conservative MPs earlier and with greater consistency than its more Liberal-orientated counterpart in the northern industrial regions.

The relatively advantageous position of the South-East economy and the inherent weakness and instability of the industrial 'north' were, therefore, established features of the British space economy well before the inter-war period. The effect of the economic climacteric of the 1920s and 1930s was to consolidate this dichotomy. Its impact was basically threefold. In the 'industrial periphery' the structural collapse of the coal-mining and associated heavy-engineering sectors was superimposed on that area's long-standing slower growth in manufacturing. In many ways, however, the real regional 'turnaround' occurred in the 'manufacturing heartland': the heartland's share of national manufacturing employment reached a peak in the 1920s and thereafter started to decline, as a result of a relative deceleration in industrial growth in the North West and in Yorkshire & Humberside. The share of the 'south and east', in contrast, began to rise sharply (Figure 2.1), as this area began to benefit from the development of the new engineering and consumer-goods sectors that in turn the older regions of the industrial 'north' proved unable to attract or generate on any significant scale sufficient to redress the decline of the 19th-century staple industries. The South East's pre-existing monopoly position as a financial and banking centre remained intact. As reflected in unemployment, the rates in the regions of the 'industrial periphery' – what became officially designated as the 'special' or 'depressed' areas – had become by the early 1930s structurally fixed at double those in the 'south and east'.

The post-war evolution of the divide

Since the Second World War, the pattern of regional development has had two dominant characteristics: a progressive concentration of economic activity and employment in the 'south and east'; and a progressive growth and extension southwards of a relatively depressed 'north'. There have been two stages to this historical evolution. During the first phase, the long 'post-war boom' from 1945 to the late 1960s, it was possible to think of the 'north-south' regional problem as a marginal one in an otherwise buoyant economy. Although the unemployment rate in the 'industrial periphery' remained twice that of the 'south and east', unemployment everywhere was at an unprecedently low level. Nevertheless, there were important shifts in the regional distribution of employment in this period. Following its recovery from the 1930s depression, manufacturing employment grew to its historical peak (of 8.4 million) in 1966. The bulk of this growth, however, occurred in the South East region, outside London, followed by the West Midlands (Figure 2.2). Much smaller increases were registered in the other regions of the country, and in the case of Scotland and the North West the growth that took place was not sufficient to restore manufacturing employment back to its pre-1930 levels. Reduced to broad fundamentals, the quarter-century after 1945 saw a further decline in the share of national manufacturing employment accounted for by the 'industrial periphery' and a marked fall in the share of the 'manufacturing heartland', where the rapid expansion of the West Midlands was outweighed by the sluggish growth of the North West and Yorkshire & Humberside regions. By the mid-1960s, the 'south and east' of Britain had emerged as the country's major geographical concentration of manufacturing (Figure 2.1).

The second phase, from the mid-1960s to the present, has been one of quite different economic conditions: the end of the long boom, followed by 'stagflation' during the 1970s, deep recession in the early 1980s and partial recovery since. It is now widely agreed that over this period Britain, in common with other industrial western nations, has been undergoing a fundamental process of socio-economic reorganization. What has been underway for the past decade and a half is not some mere inflexion or disturbance of the 'post-war norm', nor simply a major recessionary crisis, albeit a particularly prolonged one, but arguably a transition to a new phase of economic development. Opinions differ as to the precise nature of this new configuration. Some view it as the advent of a new information technology based society; some see it as marking the end of 'organized capitalism' and the emergence of a more 'disorganized' phase of development (Lash and Urry, 1987); others interpret the current upheaval as representing a shift from Fordist to post-Fordist or 'flexible accumulation' (Harvey, 1987); yet others have suggested that we are witnessing a switch from 'modernism' to 'post-modernism' (Cooke, 1987). But whatever the perspective, one thing is clear: several processes are in

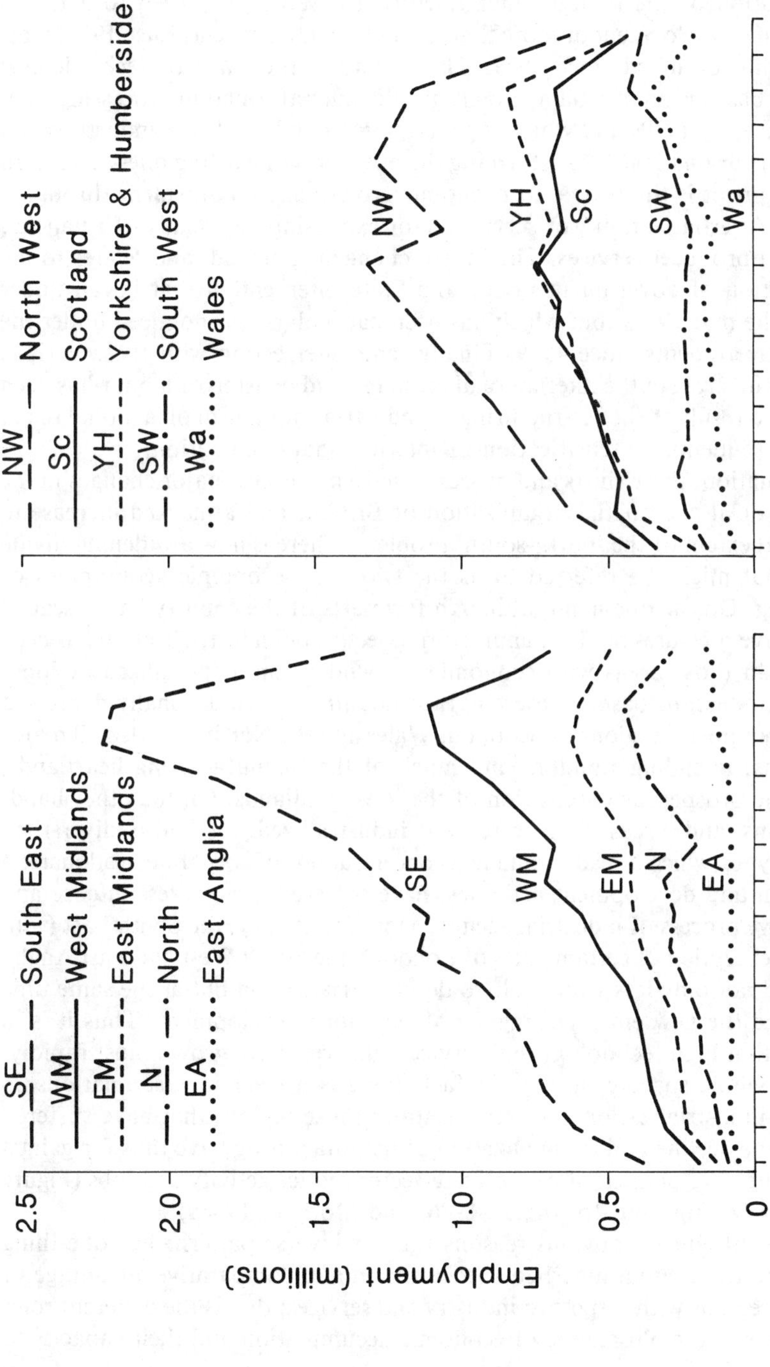

Figure 2.2 Manufacturing employment by region, 1841–1986

motion that have had pronounced effects on the geography of inequality in the country.

The first and most apparent of these is the rapid and sustained de-industrialization of the nation's manufacturing base. This has led to a fall in manufacturing employment of more than 2.8 million (36 per cent) since 1971, most of this having occurred since 1979. The second is the wave of technological innovation, based primarily on micro-electronics and information processing, that began in the early 1970s and which is generating a number of new industries and services while dramatically transforming the operation of existing ones. The third new development is the revival of economic growth and employment through a new wave of 'tertiarization', or service-sector expansion, especially of financial, banking and producer services. The fourth change is political, and relates to the reconfiguration of government policy and State intervention that began under Labour in the mid-1970s, but which has been particularly pronounced under the Thatcher governments since 1979. Finally, and intersecting with these various forces, Britain's role in the international economy and division of labour has been changing as a result of the restructuring of industrial capitalism on a global scale, and the consequential intensification of international competition.

In combination, these shifts and processes have promoted major changes in the economic, social and spatial organization of Britain, and a marked increase in the scale and extent of the 'north-south' problem. There is now a widening divide between what might be referred to as the two socio-economic geographies of restructuring. On the one hand, although few parts of the country have escaped the cumulative pressures on the manufacturing sector, de-industrialization has been most acute in those areas with economies dependent on a specialized or long-established industrial base. These embrace not just the traditionally-depressed 'industrial periphery' regions of Scotland, Wales and the North, but also all major conurbations, including London, and much of the 'manufacturing heartland', including the prosperous core region of the West Midlands. On the other hand, those regions and areas that were less industrialized, or more diversified economically, or which already contained concentrations of corporate headquarters and research and development activities, have suffered a much less intense and less disruptive process of industrial decline. More specifically, the South East (with the notable exception of certain parts of London), the South West and East Anglia have proved not only less vulnerable to de-industrialization but at the same time have also led the new emergent regime of economic development. Thus it is in these areas that high technology and service industries have grown most rapidly. Across the whole space economy, in fact, there is a clear inverse relationship between de-industrialization and tertiarization: those regions that have suffered most from the decline and rationalization of manufacturing have thus far gained least from the development of new private-sector service activity and jobs (Figure 2.3; see also Martin and Rowthorn, 1986, and Morgan, 1986a).

There are, of course, obvious reasons for this inverse pattern. For one thing it reflects the differential inherited specialization and comparative advantage of the various regions with respect to industry and services; that is the different roles of the regions in the old regime of economic accumulation and their capacity to adapt to the newly-emerging regime. Second, the depth of contraction of the industrial employment base in many areas of the 'industrial periphery' and 'manufacturing heartland' has been such as to prove inimical to compensating service-sector growth: not only have those services that are dependent on manufacturing suffered, but also a debilitated and derelict local economy with high unemployment and low incomes has hardly offered the most conducive market conditions for new consumer or producer service activities and jobs. What has happened as a result, therefore, during the past decade and a half, is a systematic widening of regional unemployment differentials. As Figure 2.4 shows, regional unemployment disparities as measured by percentage-point differentials – and these rather than relativities are the appropriate indicator of inequalities – have varied pro-cyclically, widening during recessions and narrowing during periods of economic boom: compare, for example, the downturn of 1970-2 with the recovery of 1972-4. But as Figure 2.4 reveals only too clearly, there has also been an underlying secular growth in regional disparities: contrary to Keeble's (1977) claim that spatial convergence occurred between 1965 and 1975, a process of slow divergence in regional unemployment was already underway in the late 1960s, and this accelerated sharply after the mid-1970s so that by 1985 regional differentials had reached their widest since the 1930s. Associated with this trend there has been a progressive spatial extension of the areas of high unemployment. Up to the early 1970s, the three regions of the industrial periphery were the high-unemployment areas. By the late 1970s, these three regions had been joined by the North West. Since the late 1970s, the West Midlands and Yorkshire & Humberside have also become high-unemployment regions (Figure 2.4). Thus as Edward Heath observed, the depressed 'north' has spread southwards and eastwards to encompass all of Britain save the four southern regions (South East, East Anglia, South West and East Midlands, referred to below as the 'south').

The contemporary north-south geography of inequality

There can be little doubt that there is now a serious 'jobs gap' between these 'two Britains'. Between mid-1979 and mid-1987 the number of employees in employment in Great Britain declined by 1,321,000. The geography of this decline has been particularly uneven: the number of employees in employment in the 'north' (defined as the 'industrial periphery' plus the 'manufacturing heartland') fell by 1,357,000, whereas in the 'south' the numbers actually increased slightly (by 35,000) (Table 2.2). Two-thirds of the net 2,063,000 employee jobs lost through de-industrialization over this period have been in the 'north', where 44 per cent of the national labour force lives, while the 'south', which houses 56 per cent of the national labour force, has generated three-quarters of the 1,243,000 new jobs in services (Martin, 1986a). When allowance is made for the estimated increase in self-employment this geographical imbalance is sharpened yet further: between mid-1979 and mid-1987 (at the time of writing the most recent year for which estimates of self-employment by region are available), the fall in total employment nationally of 364,000 was made up of a decline of 1,033,000 (9 per cent) in the

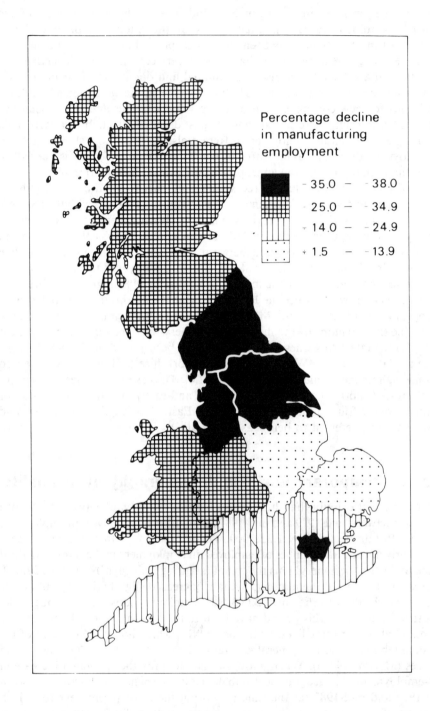

Figure 2.3 (a) Industrial employment decline, 1976–86 (source: DE, 1987)

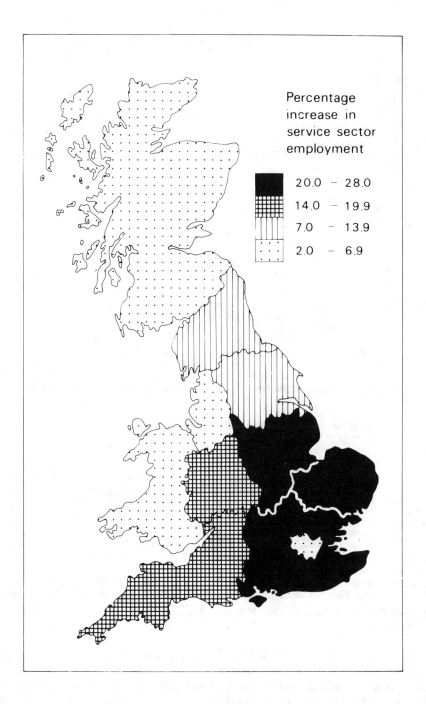

Figure 2.3 (b) Service employment growth, 1976–86 (source: DE, 1987)

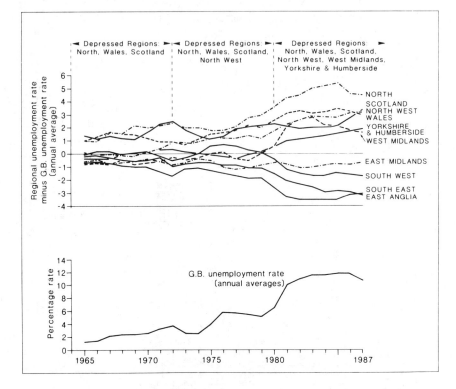

Figure 2.4   Regional unemployment disparities in Great Britain, 1965–87

Table 2.2   The 'north-south' jobs divide, 1979–87

Area[2]	Absolute change (thousands) 1979–87			
	Total employees	Manufacturing employees	Service employees	Total employed labour force[1]
'South'[2]	35	− 698	922	669
'North'[2]	− 1,357	− 1,374	321	− 1,033
G. Britain	− 1,321	− 2,063	1,243	− 364

Notes
1. Including self-employed.
2. 'South': includes South East, East Anglia, South West, East Midlands.
'North': includes West Midlands, Yorks. & Humberside, North West, North, Wales, Scotland.

(*Sources: Employment Gazette*, 1988, March, p. 162; May, Table 1.5, Historical Supplement no. 1, pp. 28–40.)

'north' but an increase of 0.669 million (5 per cent) in the 'south' (Table 2.2). It is not surprising, therefore, that by the mid-1980s a 7–10 'percentage-point differential' in unemployment rates had emerged between northern and southern Britain, or that the vacancy rate in the 'south' averaged twice that in the 'north' (Figure 2.5).

While the 'jobs gap' is the most prominent dimension of the contemporary geography of inequality, there is, however, much more to the 'north-south' issue than differential employment opportunities (Massey, 1985). The problem is also one of a distinct geographical cleavage in the type of employment available, in socio-economic class, in income, wealth and social welfare, and in political alignment. With 27 per cent and 39 per cent of national manufacturing and service employment respectively, the South East region alone contains some 41 per cent of jobs identified with advanced- and high-technology engineering, and 55 per cent of research and development employment (Table 2.3). It is in southern England, and especially the 'sunbelt' corridor stretching from Cambridge through Berkshire to Bristol, that Britain's high-technology industries and services, and more importantly the core functions of these activities, are concentrating (Morgan, 1986b; Sayer and Morgan, 1986; Hall *et al.*, 1987). Indeed, of the 23 (out of 66) British counties with above-average concentrations of high-technology employment, all but two (Lancashire and Warwickshire) are in the 'south' (Keeble, 1987). The South East region itself accounts for 53 per cent of national employment in electronics – no other region has more than 10 per cent – and for some 43 per cent of corporate research and development units, 77 per cent of other private-sector research and development companies, and 54 per cent of government research and development establishments (Rothwell, 1982).

Table 2.3   The regional distribution of some leading industries and services, 1984

Region	Percentage share of GB employment		
	High-technology manufacturing sectors[1]	Producer services[2]	Research and development
South East	41.1	49.3	54.9
East Anglia	2.5	2.7	7.1
South West	9.3	7.0	7.2
East Midlands	5.8	4.3	4.3
West Midlands	10.7	7.6	4.6
Yorks. & Humberside	2.8	5.9	2.2
North West	11.8	9.2	7.0
North	2.7	3.4	3.0
Wales	3.8	2.8	1.7
Scotland	7.7	7.3	7.2

Notes
1. Office machinery, data-processing equipment, electrical and electronic engineering, aerospace equipment, instrument engineering.
2. Banking, finance, insurance and business services.

(*Source:* DE, 1987.)

In addition, the spatial distribution of 'producer service' employment is also dominated by the South East region, which accounts for 50 per cent of the national total (Table 2.3 and Figure 2.6). And with the dramatic growth of international finance over the past decade and a half, the establishment of the Eurodollar market, the influx of foreign banks and the 1986 deregulation of the Stock Exchange,

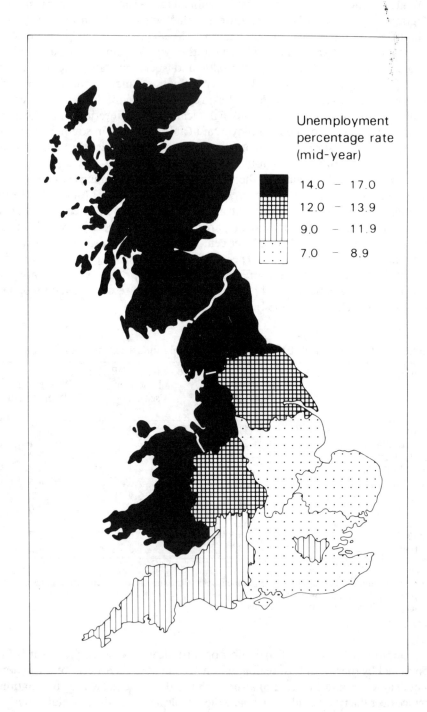

Figure 2.5   Mapping the jobs divide: (a) Unemployment, 1986 (source: DE, 1987)

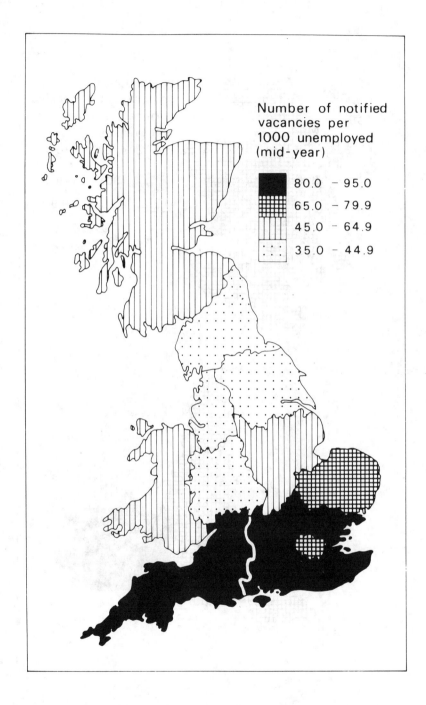

Figure 2.5   Mapping the jobs divide: (b) Job vacancies, 1986 (source: DE, 1987)

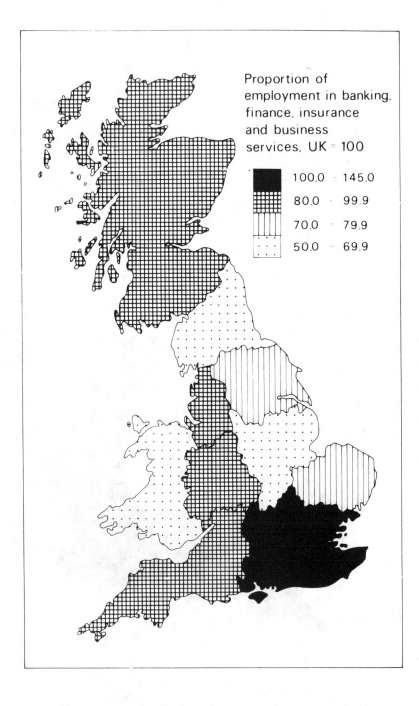

Figure 2.6   Financial and producer service employment, 1986 (source: DE, 1987)

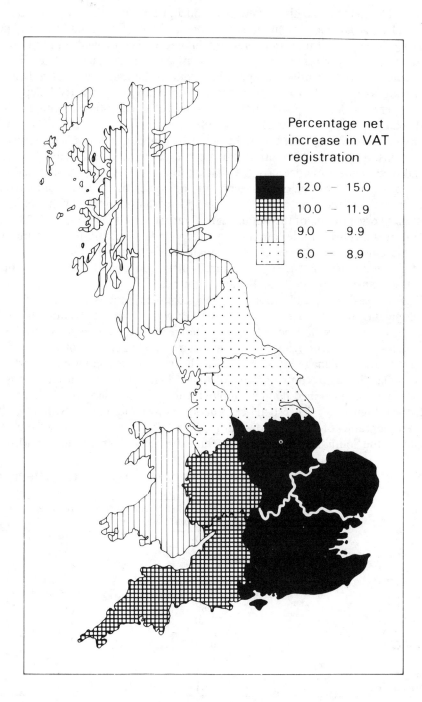

Figure 2.7   Small-business creation, 1980–5 (source: DE, 1987)

London has increased its historically pre-eminent position as the country's leading financial centre and money market (see Chapter 5). One effect of this is that because banking, investment funds and venture capital are all controlled primarily from London, in many instances this tends to impart a regional imbalance in the financing of new innovative enterprise in favour of the southern areas of Britain, which are viewed as 'low risk' in comparison with the 'high-risk' depressed industrial north. Another factor in the spatial bias of London-based venture capital is the high London overheads – themselves a product of London's national monopoly and leading international role – which make such funds expensive in the regions. At present the South East region alone attracts more than 50 per cent of national venture finance, a share that undoubtedly reflects the high level of demand generated by the greater economic buoyancy of the area compared to northern parts of the country, but a demand partly shaped in turn by the spatially-centralized organization of the venture-capital industry itself (Mason, 1987; Martin, 1988a). It is this favourable conjunction of economic and institutional conditions that explains why the rate of new small-business creation – the Thatcher government's index of 'enterprise culture' – has been much higher in the south and east than in other parts of Britain (Figure 2.7).

This increasing specialization in high-technology industry, research and development, and producer services, together with the more dynamic business climate, helps to account both for the better relative economic performance of the 'south' over recent years and the associated agglomeration of high-earning professional and managerial occupational classes there as compared to northern regions. The latter, in contrast, have distinctly higher relative concentrations of unskilled and semi-skilled manual employment, unionized labour and industrial militancy (Figure 2.8). This social-class divide corresponds closely with a parallel uneven geography of income and wealth (Table 2.4). Average personal disposable income in the South East region is more than 20 per cent higher than in Yorkshire

Table 2.4   The gap in regional wealth generation: Gross Domestic Output per capita, 1975–86

Region	GDP per head relative to UK average	
	1975	1986
South East	112.9	117.5
Greater London	125.8	124.6
Rest of S.E.	103.6	112.6
East Anglia	92.8	100.8
South West	90.3	96.1
East Midlands	96.7	96.1
West Midlands	100.0	90.6
Yorks. & Humberside	94.1	93.2
North West	96.2	93.5
North	93.6	91.9
Wales	88.7	85.7
Scotland	97.1	93.5

(*Source: Economic Trends,* 1977, 1988.)

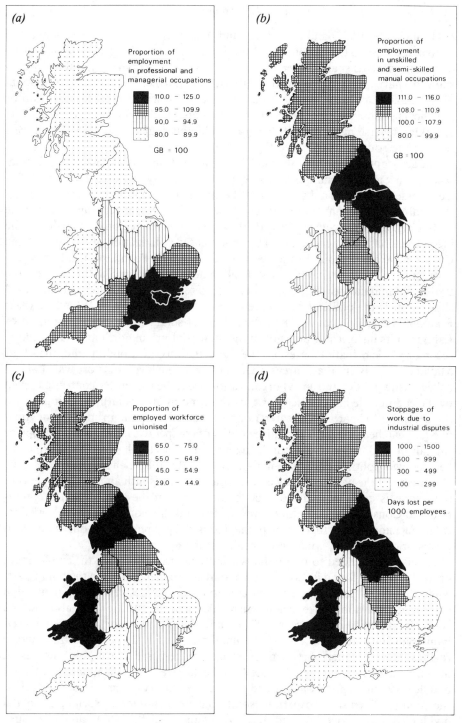

Figure 2.8   Mapping the social divide: (a) The professional and managerial classes, 1981 (source: Census of Population, 1981, HMSO, London); (b) The unskilled and semi-skilled manual classes, 1981 (source: Census of Population, 1981, HMSO, London); (c) Degree of unionization, 1985 (source: DE, 1987); (d) Industrial militancy, 1980–4 (source: DE, 1987)

& Humberside, Wales and the North, and outside the 'south' only Scotland has an average close to the national level (Figure 2.9). Other correlates and indicators of wealth, such as share ownership – Mrs Thatcher's 'popular capitalism' – also show a sharp gradient between southern and northern Britain. The regional distribution of poverty, on the other hand, as represented by the proportion of low-income households or by dependence on State supplementary benefits, exhibits a striking reverse pattern, both being considerably higher in the north and west than in the south and east (see Figure 2.9).

The geography of the 'two Britains' is thus a divide in which economic and social factors show a highly-consistent pattern and are mutually reinforcing in their effects (see Massey, 1987, for a discussion of the cumulative multiplier forces involved). But it also a divide that finds further expression in political geography. Since the mid-1970s, and particularly since 1979, the widening of regional socio-economic inequalities has been accompanied by an increased polarization of support for the Conservative and Labour Parties (see Chapter 9). While de-industrialization, social restructuring, and arguably class de-alignment have reduced the size of the traditional manual working-class vote, and thereby helped to underpin a national shift towards the political right (Crewe, Sarlvik and Alt, 1977; Whiteley, 1982; Franklin, 1985; Dunleavy, 1987), the net effect spatially has been the retreat of Labour to its historical heartlands in the industrial-urban north and its shrinking secondary socio-spatial bases in the conurbations of London and the West Midlands.[5] It is in these areas that the main enclaves of post-war Labour collectivistic politics and social organization are to be found. By contrast, fuelled by its leading role in the emergent growth economy, the 'south' of Britain, with the exception of parts of Greater London, has become the primary stronghold of Mrs Thatcher's New Conservative politics of competitive individualism, 'popular capitalism' and 'enterprise culture'. In terms of its electoral geography Britain has become two political nations (Figure 2.10). At the 1987 General Election, some 88 per cent of the parliamentary constituencies in the 'south and east' (96 per cent if London is excluded), and 67 per cent of those in the two Midlands regions returned Conservative MPs; in the rest of Britain, the North West and Yorkshire & Humberside regions together with the 'industrial periphery', Labour maintained its historical position, winning 63 per cent of the seats.

This is not intended to imply that virtually all economic growth, employment or wealth is to be found in Conservative southern England, or even the South East, while the remainder of the country is a zone of relentless economic depression and social deprivation. Like regional disparities, local inequalities have also widened considerably over recent years. There are sharp distinctions between newly-industrializing rural areas on the one hand and heavily de-industrialized mature regions on the other; between buoyant service-based towns and depressed manufacturing communities; and between the deprived inner-cities and the affluent middle-class suburbs. As was stressed earlier, these local dualisms occur right across the country. Even the prosperous 'south' has its own internal social and spatial divides (Boddy, Lovering and Bassett, 1986; SEEDS, 1987): and of course throughout the 'north' one can find business 'success stories' to match any of those found in the 'south' (see *Business*, 1987). But there *is* a broad and consistent

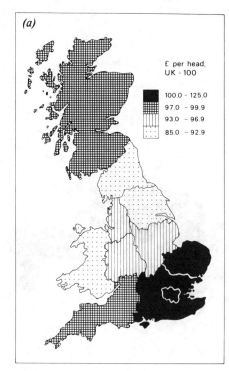

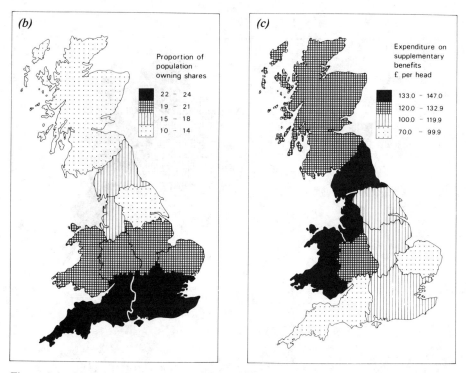

Figure 2.9   Mapping the wealth divide: (a) Personal disposable income, 1985 (source: CSO, 1987); (b) Share ownership, 1986 (source: Business, 1987); (c) Supplementary benefits, 1984–5 (source: DHSS, 1987)

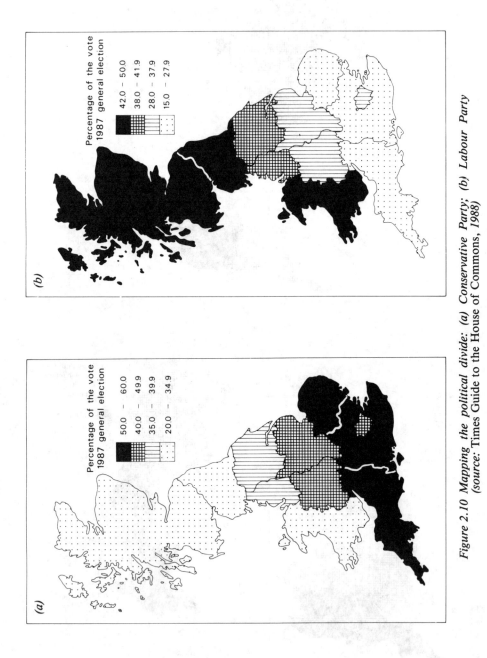

Figure 2.10 Mapping the political divide: (a) Conservative Party; (b) Labour Party
(source: Times Guide to the House of Commons, 1988)

geography of socio-economic inequality between 'north' and 'south': without doubt the *concentration* of relative individual social and economic disadvantage is significantly greater in northern regions than in the more prosperous south. Thus in their recent study of local variations in economic prosperity, Champion and Green (Chapter 3) show that despite the existence of considerable differences in performance between local labour markets within all of the major regions, the 'north-south divide' emerges as the primary dimension in inequalities in economic health across Britain, and that this divide has sharpened during the 1980s. According to their index of prosperity, over three-quarters of the local labour markets in the South East and half of those in East Anglia have scores higher than any in Wales and Scotland.

The obvious question that immediately arises is: does this geography of inequality, and the political divide that is associated with it, really matter? There are, in this author's belief, several reasons why it does. As a problem whose origins span back at least seventy years, and in some respects much further back than that, it must surely be disturbing that now in the late 1980s the 'north-south divide' not only still persists but, in terms of many social and economic indicators, has also actually widened. The history of the 'north-south' regional problem is in large part the history of an evolving divide between old and new industry. As successive waves of economic development and international competition have rendered previous growth industries mature or even obsolete, and thus the focus of defensive rationalization and restructuring; so the boundaries of the depressed 'north' have moved successively southwards. At the same time new growth industries and expanding sectors have agglomerated increasingly in the south and east of the country. This process, although shaped in a major way by international pressures, has unquestionably been reinforced by, and in its turn has intensified, the unequal territoriality of the country's leading corporate, institutional, commercial and political structures. These are overwhelmingly concentrated in the 'south' and so tend to bias the operation of the 'market' in favour of this part of Britain as against the 'north'. In a very real sense the 'north-south' issue is not simply a 'regional' problem but a national one. On the one hand, the emergence and growth of the divide reflect the long-term deterioration, from the 1870s onwards, of Britain's national position in the international economy, a decline that still continues. On the other, the divide cannot be separated from the historical loss of economic and political power from the regions to London and its environs, a spatial polarization that serves to reproduce and perpetuate the national pattern of regional imbalance.

Moreover, the divide has important implications for the performance and management of the national economy. Given their somewhat disparate economic structures, the northern and southern sections of the country contribute differentially to national output, exports and inflation, and similarly respond differentially to government policies and international economic conditions. For some years now Britain's balance of trade in manufactures has been deteriorating (one measure, of course, of the de-industrialization problem), while that in non-manufacturing (services and other invisibles) has been steadily improving (see Rowthorn, 1986; Rowthorn and Wells, 1987). Although no specific regional trade data exist (see Rhodes, 1986, for some rough estimates), it can be confidently postulated that this shifting structure in the balance of trade has an 'internal geography' that accords in many respects with the 'north-south divide': that is, with the erosion and inferior competitiveness of manufacturing in the 'industrial periphery' and 'manufacturing heartland' regions, and the growth of international banking, financial and related services in the South East. Therefore, to the extent that the weakness of the visible manufacturing (non-oil) trade balance is considered to have serious consequences for the vitality of the national economy (Department of Trade and Industry, 1985; House of Lords, 1985), this translates into a need to regenerate – some might say 're-industrialize' – the manufacturing base of much of Britain's 'north'. But equally, the increasing divergence between the economic structures of the 'north' and 'south' means that central government policies are likely to impact in quite different ways on the two areas, particularly if those policies are geared primarily towards the monetary rather than the 'real' side of the economy. This has definitely been the case since 1979: thus the net effect of the restrictive monetary policies pursued by the Thatcher governments during the 1980s has been to squeeze financially the manufacturing regions but to stimulate the financial and banking sectors based in the 'south'.

Intersecting with these economic issues is the crucial and highly-political question of regional social equity. Fundamental to the Conservative government's view is the belief that increased equity is necessarily purchased at the expense of economic efficiency or growth, and that the pursuit of the latter must be given priority over that of the former. But surely the contemporary socio-economic divide between the 'two Britains' is both socially inequitable *and* economically inefficient. It is grossly inefficient because, since 1979, on average some 12 per cent of the labour force in the 'north' have been unemployed and unproductive, twice the average rate in the four southern regions. In addition to the lost output that this implies, it has cost dear in social-security spending. It is socially inequitable both because of the disproportionately higher unemployment and lower per-capita incomes in much of the 'north', and because these forms of relative disadvantage themselves feed back to exacerbate problems of poverty, poor housing, lack of skills and other aspects of social deprivation. All of these in turn lower economic efficiency, in the sense of lowering the quality of the human resources required to assist economic growth. Of course, to argue for equality of outcome across different social groups and geographical areas of the country would be wholly unrealistic; but the current inequality of opportunity across the 'divide' can hardly be said to be efficient, whereas it does offend basic moral principles of social justice and national unity. It is this latter issue, of the significance of the 'north-south' divide in relation to the politics of national unity, that occupies the remainder of this chapter.

'One-nation politics': rhetoric and reality

The notion of 'one-nation politics' goes back to Benjamin Disraeli. It was Disraeli who, in 1845, said Britain was two nations – one rich, one poor; one privileged and one under-privileged. It was his aim to reconcile the two classes, to improve the economic and social conditions of the industrial and urban working population, and to secure thereby the political support necessary to enable the Conservative

Party to claim itself the party of national unity.6 As Gilmour (1977, p.86) observed:

> Disraeli believed profoundly that England should be one nation not two. He thought that this aim would only be achieved if the Tory Party were true to its traditions, avoided oligarchy and became a truly national party ... . The Tory Party could properly defend the national institutions and enlist in their support the bulk of the nation. The nation would then support the national party, and the national party would then represent the nation.

For Disraeli, the route to 'one nation' lay in fostering the paternalistic responsiveness of an otherwise liberal capitalism to social needs, medicated if need be by limited State action to allay the most pressing manifestations of poverty and deprivation. The main functions of the Conservative State were to protect the nation, to enforce the rule of law and to foster a sense of national identity and unity (Norton and Aughey, 1981). He bequeathed to the Conservatives a set of principles for electoral success in an urbanized and industrialized Britain: one nation at home and imperial strength abroad were the twin Disraelian maxims, which have exercised a powerful influence on Conservative Party discourse ever since. Historically, Disraeli's 'one-nation politics' has been invoked on a number of occasions to justify the adaptation of the Conservative Party and its policies to changed socio-economic conditions, and simultaneously to legitimize such adaptations in terms of a proclaimed continuity of, or return to, traditional party principles.

There was evidence of this, for example, in the inter-war years. By the mid-1930s, the disintegration of Empire, the loss of working-class support to the expanding Labour Party, and the social and regional problems caused by the economic crises of the early 1920s and early 1930s, had all combined to stimulate a reassessment of Conservative principles and policies. Conscious that the Conservative Party would not recover its working-class support unless it addressed itself to the social conditions of the depressed industrial areas, a younger generation of MPs, including Anthony Eden, Harold Macmillan and Robert Boothby, sought a revival of the 'one-nation politics' that Disraeli had campaigned for in his day, but this time based upon government intervention and planning in the economy (Macmillan, 1938, 1966; Pugh, 1985). Indeed during the 1930s, Macmillan alluded on more than one occasion to the 'north-south divide', to the unacceptability of high unemployment in the northern regions of Britain and the need for positive remedial government action, a theme and plea he was to return to fifty years later (in 1984) as part of his maiden speech in the House of Lords.[7] But it was Labour's landslide election victory in 1945 that finally convinced the Conservatives of the need to shed their image as the party of unemployment and negative economic liberalism – an image that Labour had worked sedulously and successfully to cultivate – and to accommodate themselves to the changed circumstances of post-war Britain. This accommodation was achieved by dropping the earlier *laissez-faire* philosophy in favour of the Keynes–Beveridge social-democratic collectivism already embraced by the Labour Party. This shift – itself a prudent recognition of necessity and circumstance – was legitimized as a re-affirmation of the party's Disraelian tradition. This had again become relevant to the needs of the day, although it was now the State that ensured the welfare of the people, and the State that ensured that capital and private property recognized its social responsibilities (Norton and Aughey, 1981). If it was a myth that Disraeli had something of practical significance to say to post-war Britain, it was nevertheless – in this revised mould – an effective myth, for it clearly established the Conservative Party's credentials to manage the new 'mixed' economy.

Thus, for three decades up to the mid-1970s, both Labour and Conservative governments were at least united by a broad common commitment to a policy settlement geared to the maintenance of full employment and the provision of an extensive Welfare State, two imperatives regarded by each party as emblematic of 'one-nation politics'. Beneath this apparent consensus, however, the two main parties maintained their own rather different visions of 'one nation': 'the main division between the Parties in the field of economics was between prosperity and fair shares. Neither side denied the other's assumptions. Socialists said prosperity is not being fairly shared, while Conservatives just said that people were better off and left it at that' (Ramsden, 1980, p. 116). For Labour, the party of the working class and under-privileged, the concept of 'one nation' meant 'equality', 'fair shares' and a 'classless society'. Stemming from this political ideology the stated aim was to eliminate social and spatial inequalities through the redistribution of wealth and economic opportunity. The task required 'positive' government, that is extensive, central State intervention and planning to regulate or replace the market – viewed as the primary source of inequality – and appropriately-structured systems of progressive taxation and social benefit. However, although the Labour government's welfare and nationalization policies between 1945 and 1951, and its attempts at national economic planning between 1964 and 1970, can be seen as consistent with this objective, when in office the party has never undertaken the degree of *dirigisme* implied by its underlying political ideology as laid down in its constitution (Labour Party, 1918, 1935).

For the Conservatives, the concept of 'one nation' was that of a 'property-owning democracy' (the phrase was Churchill's), to be achieved by spreading wealth creation rather than by redistributing wealth. This approach was most clearly expressed in the statements of the 'One Nation Group' of Conservative MPs in the early 1950s, namely: 'to promote a unified prosperous democracy, with management and men working together for an ever improving standard of living and a financial surplus to provide generous help for all those who needed it', to create 'One Nation' by 'strengthening the weak without weakening the strong' (One Nation Group of MPs, 1976; see also Macleod and Maude, 1950, and Macleod, 1952).[8] The underpinning philosophy was that if the economic cake was constantly increasing, the Conservatives could be sure that the shares of the cake would be relatively safe from questioning: if Britain was not becoming a more egalitarian society, it was becoming a generally wealthier one.

This was certainly the thrust of Harold Macmillan's 'progressive Toryism' between 1957 and 1963. His vision of 'one-nation politics' was to try to create an *embourgeoisé* society by choosing the priority of economic growth, even at the expense of higher inflation, in order to produce the widest possible spread of consumer affluence (the years of 'You've never had it so good'), a strategy that soon degenerated into a policy of alternating 'stop-go' regulation rather than continuous expansion. Essentially the same emphasis on growth rather than redistribution characterized Edward Heath's Conservative government from 1970 to 1974. In Heath's view the politics of planned modernization and redistribution implemented by the Labour government between 1964 and 1970 were socially divisive (Heath, 1965). The centre-piece of Heath's own approach was to unite the nation around a 'quiet revolution' of improved economic efficiency, competitiveness and modernization based upon a greater reliance on market forces. As such this policy marked a distinct break from previous post-war Conservatism. But it was to prove anything but quiet: it led to some of the worst industrial disputes of the post-war period, and ended in a series of policy 'U-turns', and finally an overall issue of class confrontation with dockers and miners that undermined any rhetoric, let alone reality, of 'one-nation politics' of the sort that Heath himself had long subscribed to as a founder-member of the One Nation Group.

These different political visions of, and approaches to, 'one nation' adopted by the two major parties also emerge in their respective commitments and attitudes towards regional policies, designed to reduce the geographical inequality between the 'north' and 'south' of the country. Given Labour's egalitarian ideology and its historical electoral base in the industrial 'north', we would expect the party to be more disposed than the Conservatives towards redistributive regional assistance. To a certain extent this appears to have been the case. Under the Labour governments of 1945–51 and 1964–70, regional policies were operated vigorously and considerably strengthened by new policy instruments. The first period saw the setting up of the basic policy machinery that, until recently, formed the accepted framework for regional aid in post-war Britain. In the second, Labour established regional planning bodies, extended the coverage of the Assisted Areas to some 40 per cent of the working population, and increased spending on regional aid tenfold (Parsons, 1986). This was in contrast to the situation under the Conservatives in the intervening years, 1951–63, a period usually viewed as characterized by more 'passive' regional policy; this was justified by the government of the day in terms of the generally-low level of unemployment, and hence low visibility of the 'regional problem', and the Conservative Party's policy preference for national prosperity rather than social and spatial redistribution.

Although important, these cross-party differences should not be exaggerated. After all, regional policy in Britain was not a Labour creation, but was inaugurated by its political opponents, the Conservatives, in their setting up of the Industrial Transference Board in 1928 and the national government in its Special Areas Act 1934. Similarly, the concept of regional plans was not a Labour innovation but was first promulgated by the Conservatives in 1963, when Edward Heath was made Secretary of State for Industry, Trade *and* Regional Development. But it *was* a Labour government that, between 1975 and 1979, imposed the largest post-war cut in real spending on regional aid, a reduction in real terms of some 50 per cent (about £700 million), from 0.7 to 0.3 per cent of GDP. Moreover, Labour's professed commitment to redressing regional inequalities has not been reflected in the actual fortunes of the depressed 'north'. Much has been claimed for the impact of regional policy in the assisted areas, especially up to the mid-1970s (see, for example, Keeble, 1976; Moore, Rhodes and Tyler, 1986). Yet the fact is that even under the generally-favourable growth and policy conditions that obtained during the quarter-century after 1945, regional policy did little to reduce or eliminate the unemployment differential between the 'industrial periphery' and the prosperous 'south and east'. Indeed, as we have seen, this differential actually began to widen after the mid-1960s, that is during Labour's operation of a 'strong' regional policy. And regional inequalities worsened yet further under the last Labour government between 1974 and 1979. Although this was largely due to the reversal of the post-war boom and the onset of stagflation and accelerating de-industrialization, Labour's own policies also contributed to the problem. It was the last Labour government that began the abandonment of Keynesian full-employment economics in favour of a more monetarist-deflationist policy stance and that, as part of this process, began the reversal in regional assistance referred to above, at the very time that the unemployment gap between 'north' and 'south' was widening rapidly.

Thus, well prior to the election of Mrs Thatcher's government in 1979, Labour's record in improving the degree of regional equity had not been significantly better than that of the Conservatives. In Sharpe's (1982) view this failure on the part of Labour to reduce the 'north-south divide' stemmed from a reluctance to make its elimination a central plank in the party's political programme. This is puzzling in itself, given that the party espouses 'equality' and is supposedly the champion of the working population in the industrial 'north'. Yet its actual policies when in power have not matched its party rhetoric of 'one-nation' politics. Sharpe ascribes this disjunction in part to the overly centralist nature of the Labour Party, and to the consequential tendency for national goals and policies to displace questions of regional socio-economic equity. Historically, Labour has regarded the centralization of power as the first step towards redressing inequalities, which are viewed in terms of nationwide social-class differences rather than specifically regional or territorial differences. These social inequalities would then be tackled by action from above and from the centre. This approach obviously assumes that equality is solely related to personal attributes, and that there exists a spatially-undifferentiated value-system in which a given form of State intervention will be of equal value regardless of location. But whatever the precise extent of Labour's redistributive intentions, the central motive does not seem to have been so much to change the geography of inequality, as to stop it getting worse, and even in this task it can be argued that they failed.

This failure is all the more puzzling, Sharpe suggests, 'when viewed in relation to the growth of the Party's support in the periphery' (*ibid*. p. 139). It would be more accurate, however, to say that it has been the long-term erosion of support in the 'south and east' and in the Midlands that has increasingly left Labour confined to the 'north' (see Figure 2.11). As a consequence, Labour's failure to revive its historical heartland represents not only a puzzle, but also a dilemma. On the one hand, it can be argued that because of its geographical base in the 'north', Labour should be firmly committed to policies designed to revitalize this part of the country and to close the 'north-south divide'. But on the other, in order

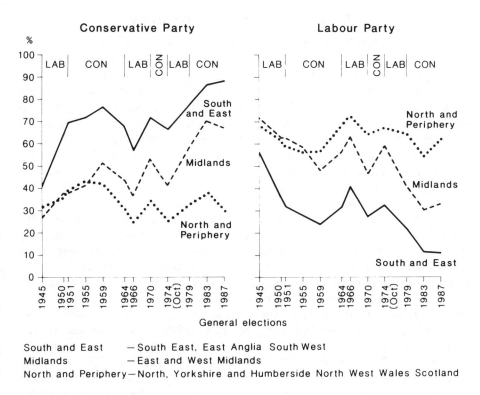

South and East   — South East, East Anglia South West
Midlands   — East and West Midlands
North and Periphery— North, Yorkshire and Humberside North West Wales Scotland

Figure 2.11 Parliamentary seats won by Conservative and Labour Parties, 1945–87

to be elected into government the party needs to win back support in the 'south', and this is unlikely if it proposes redistributive policies that threaten to curb or reverse the relative economic gains made over recent years in the southern regions. In other words, for Labour the growth of a 'north-south divide' – socio-economic and political – itself may now pose an obstacle to the formulation of a 'one-nation politics' acceptable to the electorate in the 'south' as well as the 'north'. (See Chapter 9 and Hattersley, 1987, pp. 14–19, for a discussion of the implications of the changed social, economic and political map of contemporary Britain for the electoral prospects of the Labour Party.) The Conservatives, in contrast, seem to be much more favourably placed: the pressure on the Conservative governments since 1979 to change their policies specifically to woo the industrial 'north' has been far less than that on the Labour opposition to adjust its political manifesto in order to win support to the 'south'.[9] The Conservative electoral base in the 'south and east' and the Midlands – which together contain 60 per cent of British parliamentary constituencies – is large enough to assure the party political success. It is also prosperous enough to enable the government to claim that its policies to encourage wealth creation have worked for this part of the country and therefore provide the best route to the recovery of the 'north'. In practice, however, if not by intent, these policies have widened rather than narrowed the north-south gap.

The new politics of inequality

In its ambitions Mrs Thatcher's 'new Conservatism' sought to create a new 'one-nation politics': 'The Conservative government's first job will be to rebuild our economy and unite a divided and disillusioned people' (Conservative Party, 1979, p. 1). The problem faced by the Conservatives in the late 1970s was that the old formula of 'one-nation politics' on which they had relied was fast disappearing: the party had suffered serious electoral reverses under Edward Heath; its reputation for competence in government had been seriously impaired; and the post-war Keynesian welfare-policy consensus was itself crumbling. To rebuild support the Conservatives needed to find a new national appeal. The focus of that appeal was to be the reversal of Britain's long and accelerating economic decline. This programme was to proceed on two main fronts. The first and most urgent was to purge the economy of the inflation that had become endemic during the 1970s and to revive the regenerative powers of efficient private capitalism, by controlling the money supply, limiting State spending, and fostering free-market competition and a climate of entrepreneurial innovation. The second objective has been to forge a new social and ideological consensus, a new *Weltanschauung*, consistent with this free-enterprise economy; a 'cultural revolution' based on the virtues of individualism, self-help, private property and respect for law and order. If the primary targets of the first Thatcher government (1979–83) were the reduction of inflation and the promotion of a much-needed economic restructuring, during the second (1983–7) and the third (1987 onwards) the focus has widened to include both the reversal of the post-war trend towards social-democratic collectivism and the 'eradication of socialism', tasks seen as crucial for the recovery of wealth generation.

Some aspects of these policies are not new, of course: the last Labour government initiated the shift towards monetarism; and the political prioritization of the market, of competition and efficiency were key elements of Heath's unsuccessful Conservatism of the early 1970s. What has distinguished Mrs Thatcher's governments is the dedication with which the rejection of Keynesianism and the liberalization of the economy have been pursued. According to the government 'there is no alternative' way by which growth, prosperity and affluence, of the sort enjoyed in the early 1960s, can be re-established. Though the process would require some painful deflationary and efficiency-improving rationalization in the early stages, these short-term costs would be outweighed by the consequential long-term renewal of wealth creation. This, combined with lower taxes, less government regulation and the spread of private property, should benefit all, and thus unite the nation. For given that a competitive-market society is viewed by the New Conservatives as guaranteeing maximum individual liberty, theirs, they argue, is a project in which all can participate. Private-wealth creation is thus at the base of Thatcherite 'one-nation politics': more than under any previous post-war Conservative government, Tory populism has been linked directly to the *embourgoisement* of the electorate.

In practice, however, such a programme for restructuring Britain was almost certain to have socially and regionally divisive effects. There is little doubt that the recession of 1979–82 would have occurred even in the absence of the Thatcher government; but equally there is also considerable evidence to suggest that the severity of the downturn, and the resultant widening of the gap between the 'two Britains' – social and geographical – over the 1980s, can be attributed to the cumulative impact of the government's policies (Buiter and Miller, 1983; Martin, 1986b; Solow, 1987). The Thatcherite strategy both required and stimulated an intense rationalization of much of the manufacturing base of the 'north', and of its workforces and communities. The restrictive and deflationary monetary policies of the early 1980s, together with the streamlining of the major nationalized industries (coal, steel and shipbuilding), all measures intended to induce economic efficiency and modernization, have inevitably impacted most severely on the older manufacturing regions. And as de-industrialization continued apace, so the government progressively abandoned manufacturing and increasingly aligned itself with and directed support to other sectors, identified as holding out the main prospects for growth and re-establishing Britain's position in the international economy, namely high technology, the financial sector and internationally-tradable business services, all of which were already concentrated in the 'south'.

Thus, the prosecution of policies to secure a new 'one-nation politics' based on economic revival has instead undermined the basis for achieving that consensus. Rather, what has emerged, as several observers have noted, is a form of 'two-nation politics' (Jessop *et al.*, 1984; Gamble, 1987), a politics of inequality wherein certain groups, such as unionized labour, unskilled and traditionally-skilled manual workers, public-sector employees, inner-urban residents and the working population in the industrial 'north', have been required to bear the main costs and destructive aspects of restructuring; while other groups, particularly the private-sector professional, managerial, technical, scientific and clerical classes, especially in the 'south', have been the chief beneficiaries of the government's economic programme. These divergent effects have rendered 'one-nation politics' less and less viable, both economically and electorally. The growth of the 'north-south divide' since 1979 has been closely tied to this new politics of inequality.

Few would probably disagree that the rationalization of the 'old' economy of the industrial 'north', with its problems of industrial maturity, overmanning, low productivity, union rigidities and sclerotic managerial and work practices was needed. And it can be argued that only a policy as committed as Mrs Thatcher's to exposing the industrial base to the rigours and discipline of market forces and international competition was capable of setting the long-overdue restructuring process in motion; that, in any case, a Labour government would have been compelled to adopt a similar, even if less strident, policy position. But what is disputable is the intensity with which such rationalization has been forced on the older manufacturing areas in the absence of explicit government measures to assist their compensating regeneration and re-absorption in the growth of the 'new' economy. The decline in many of these areas has been such that a sort of 'economic hysteresis' effect has occurred, whereby the depth of contraction has retarded the process of economic recovery. Certainly throughout much of the 'north' the market-led revival hoped for by the government seems to be taking considerably longer than anticipated, and as yet this part of Britain has not experienced its fair share of the regenerative benefits that the process of 'creative destruction' was supposed to bring.

The solution to the problem, the government believes, is not to be found in increased public spending on industrial and financial subsidies to the depressed regions, but rather on expanded efforts to stimulate local industrial efficiency, indigenous innovative enterprise and greater labour-market flexibility. In other words, the position of the government towards the 'north-south divide' – to the extent that the latter is acknowledged to be a problem – is essentially the same as its interpretation of and response to the national economic predicament (Martin, 1988b). The best way to help the 'north' to regain its economic dynamism is to 'help the region to help itself', not by increased automatic regional aid, but by a combination of macro-economic and selective policies that create the conditions under which competition and enterprise can flourish. To this end, official regional policy has been progressively streamlined in its spatial and financial scope since 1979 (Martin, 1985), and has now been recast into a limited component of Lord Young's new 'enterprise initiative' (Department of Trade and Industry, 1988). What has been taking place is a shift away from regional assistance towards, on the one hand, various forms of 'central government localism' that are increasingly urban-focused (first Enterprise Zones, more recently Urban Development Corporations and the extension of aid to Urban Programme inner-city areas); and, on the other, a greater reliance on general economy-wide policies, such as tax reductions and a plethora of schemes to promote new, small businesses and self-employment, policies that, being national in coverage, obviously also benefit the 'non-assisted' areas such as the prosperous 'south' (Harrison and Mason, 1986; Storey and Johnson, 1987).

Probably the most contentious aspect of the government's approach, however, is its call for more flexible labour markets. A key element here is the argument that the existence and persistence of higher unemployment in areas of the 'north' is attributable, in part at least, to the rigidity of wages there in relation to the lower demand for labour, this rigidity in turn being ascribed to the higher rates of unionization in the 'north'. Because wages are too high and inflexible, unemployment is higher than it would otherwise be in a more competitive labour market, and substantial regional mobility of labour is deterred. The evidence is not altogether supportive of this perspective, however. Although both unemployment and the coverage of collective bargaining are higher in northern Britain, average wages show a reverse pattern and are higher in the 'south' where the degree of collective institutionalization of wage setting is lowest (Figure 2.12). In fact during the 1980s, as the comparative unemployment position of the 'north' has deteriorated so its wage position relative to the 'south' has also worsened, suggesting that wages in the 'north' may not be as inflexible with respect to labour demand conditions as the government seems to believe. In the 'south', by contrast, 'flexibility' has meant the onset of inflationary 'over-heating' through a mutually re-inforcing process of faster wage growth and rapidly-escalating house prices (Figure 2.13), the latter leading to a marked widening of the pre-existing housing divide between northern and southern regions (see Chapter 4). While the net drift of population is from north to south (Figure 2.13), it would appear that it is the

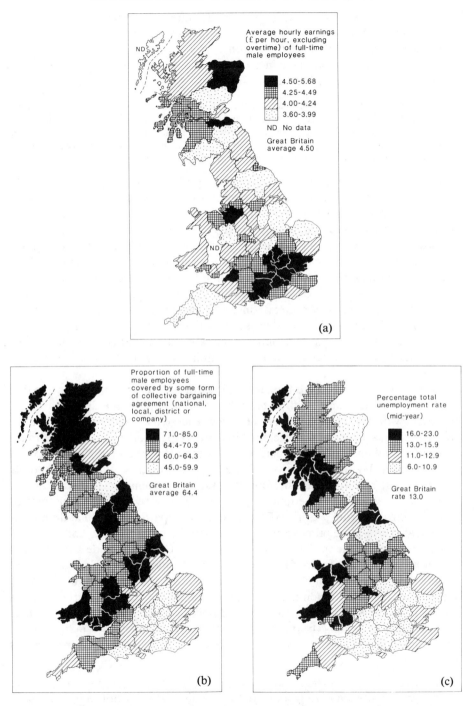

Figure 2.12 The labour-market divide:(a) Average hourly earnings, by county, 1985 (source: New Earnings Survey, 1985*); (b) Degree of collective bargaining coverage, by county, 1985 (source: unpublished* New Earnings Survey *data); (c) Unemployment rate, by county, 1985 (source: DE, 1987)*

much-higher house-price regime in southern Britain rather than the 'too-high' wage problem in northern areas that is the primary factor deterring the equilibrating movement of labour between the regions.

Yet Lord Young remains convinced that the success of the 'south' provides the key to the revival of the 'north':

> If you actually look at what is happening I believe you see that the market is actually beginning to work... . There is enormous pressure on house prices in the south of England, but there is evidence that the wave of price rises is spreading north... . The wave is moving north because the workings of the market mean that industrialists are forced further and further north to take business opportunities.   (quoted in *Business*, 1987, p.58)

The eventual extent of this 'northwards diffusion' of business activity remains to be seen, however. Furthermore, in both of the two previous major waves of house-price inflation since the late 1960s, the rate of inflation increased first in London and the South East region and then rippled progressively northwards in a catching-up process. Thus as a result, when averaged across the inflation cycles, regional house-price relativities as between northern and southern areas of the country have maintained a marked degree of long-term stability. The question is whether in the present cycle the ripple effect will follow the pattern of previous inflation waves, or whether, because of the greatly-increased north-south gap in employment, prosperity and incomes, its spread northwards this time will be much more limited. Even if the former outcome is ultimately the case, any catching-up in house prices in the 'north' could hardly be taken as an indication of that region's economic 'turnaround'.

There is in any case a more fundamental reason for questioning the notion that the revival of the 'north' will be brought about simply by the diffusion of the 'democracy of market forces' alleged to have generated the success of the 'south'. Markets do not operate in a vacuum, but are shaped and mediated by a range of institutional and political structures. As is argued here and in Chapters 5 and 6, in present-day Britain many of the key structures – such as corporate headquarters, research and development functions, commercial, financial and investment services, and government regulation – are overwhelmingly concentrated in and controlled from the South East, and London particularly. In addition, the whole pattern of State purchasing and procurement, both military and civil, and much of its infrastructural capital formation, all of which provide an important buffer *against* market forces for many firms, is channelled towards and serves to underwrite the economy of the 'south'. Thus not only is the prosperity of the 'south' built upon important 'non-market' forces and factors, but also the region's monopoly in crucial national economic and political structures means that it plays a leading role in shaping the operation of the 'market' across the remaining parts of the country. This is actually acknowledged by some leading Conservatives themselves:

> In a sense we are becoming a rather monopolistic political society. I don't say that in the narrow party sense. I say it in terms of the domination of Britain by the City of London, in terms of ownership and wealth. I say it in terms of the lack of obvious roots

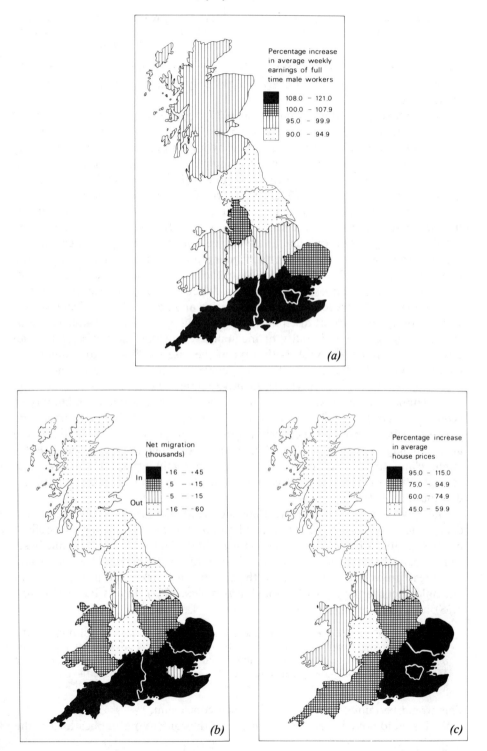

Figure 2.13 (a) Wage change 1979–86 (source: New Earnings Survey, *1980, 1987); (b) Migration, 1986 (source: OPCS, 1987); (c) House-price change 1979–86 (source: DoE, 1988), 1986*

of power outside the major political parties and the increasing location of the major corporate headquarters in London, the drift south of the public sector, of the military.
(Heseltine, 1987, p.17)

In view of this spatial monopoly, a reliance on a market-based approach to the regeneration of the 'north' is likely to have only limited success in reducing the 'north-south divide'.

The widening of the divide since 1979 highlights a central problem of contemporary Conservatism. On the one hand, Thatcherism presupposes a political community, one nation, a society united by a common goal – wealth creation. On the other, the neo-liberal free-market system, which the government vigorously supports as the basis of that wealth creation, both requires and generates socio-economic inequalities and differences. To the Conservative mind it is irrational to question social inequality and differentiation: inequalities are natural in the human condition and thus the society that gives sufficient scope for inequality, modified by a concern for acute disadvantage (the 'deserving poor'), encourages excellence and progress, dynamism and vigour (Joseph and Sumption, 1980; Norton and Aughey, 1981). The role of the State then is to conserve the natural order based upon the realities of capitalist production, and that means protecting inequalities and differences in the accumulation and possession of private wealth. It also argues for a social discipline that is nothing less than the acceptance of this naturalness and desirability of inequalities: and this social discipline is an essential element of legitimate authority, of the case for limited government. In reality, however, there may be no necessary correlation between an economic system based on free-market relations and a cohesive community. A possible contradiction of contemporary Conservatism then is that, while presupposing a community of economic interest and political belief, its disposition towards economic liberalism may well have dissevered the concept of 'one nation', or at least reduced it to the art of 'managing' social and spatial inequality. Although the Conservative Party might claim to be once more the national party in terms of the new class configuration of its support, it cannot claim this in terms of the geographical distribution of its supporters.

The government is optimistic that the de-industrialization and economic depression of the 'north' have bottomed out, and that a new breed of self-reliant business people is beginning to rebuild the region's industrial and economic base. Lord Young believes that 'in ten years time you will find that Newcastle and Gateshead are very thriving parts of the country, upmarket and profitable, with unemployment looking good' (quoted in *Business*, 1987). But as *Business (ibid.*, p.58) itself rejoined:

Perhaps the reason Young is so sanguine is that he has no choice. By insisting that the prosperity of the North depends not on the intervention of government but on the inventiveness, skill and hard work of individual Northerners he is putting the Prime Minister's philosophy to its greatest test. If this method fails to revive the North, it is a failure of Thatcherism.

This would certainly seem to be the logical conclusion.

Yet it should not be overlooked that one of the contentious implications of the government's philosophy is that if free-market forces do not revive the 'north', the government can then simply insist that this signifies the failure not of its chosen political approach, but rather of individual northerners themselves to respond sufficiently to the 'competitive challenge', their failures to be as 'enterprising' as their southern counterparts. However, as the government itself must recognize, it would be extremely difficult to argue that there are systematic differences in indigenous individual enterprise as between the 'north' and 'south' of the country. What does exist and has existed for some considerable time, as this chapter tries to demonstrate, is a growing structural and institutional divide that conditions in significant ways both the scope for and the success of that individual enterprise. Current policies, though quite different from those of previous post-war governments, seem no nearer to addressing these underlying causal factors. To the contrary, thus far a greater reliance on market forces appears to have increased the scale of Britain's 'north-south divide'.

Notes

1. See, for example: *The Financial Times* (1987), 'Jobs divide brought sharply into focus' (8 January), and Duffy (1987) 'Regional development in Britain: the gap widens' (20 January); Wilsher and Cassidy, (1987), 'Two nations - the false frontier'; *The Independent* (1987), 'Two nation jobs shock revealed' (9 January), and 'The north-south crisis: why the nation is divided' (3 June); *Business* (1987), 'Across the north-south divide' (September); Nationwide Building Society (1987), *House Prices: The North-South Divide* (August; Town and Country Planning Association (1987), *North-South Divide: A New Deal for Britain's Regions* (December).

2. *The Independent* (1987), 'Labour aims £6 billion jobs plan at the North' (9 January); SDP-Liberal Alliance (1987), *Turning the Tide of Decline in the Regions*, Alliance Work Search Report, London.

3. In what follows Northern Ireland is excluded from the discussion because of incomplete data comparable to those available for the other UK standard regions. Other related data indicate only too clearly, however, that in terms of many socio-economic characteristics Northern Ireland is the most depressed part of the UK, and is thus a major component of the 'northern' half of the divide.

4. Victorian novelists frequently drew attention to the distinctions between the grim, urban-industrial north and the more effete, prosperous and genteel south, for example: Charles Dickens' *Hard Times* (1854), Elizabeth Gaskell's *North and South* (1855) and Benjamin Disraeli's *Sybil: Or Two Nations* (1845).

5. This spatial retreat of the Labour vote in the 1970s and 1980s bears some striking parallels with the retreat of the Liberal vote to the Celtic fringes in the early part of the century (see Kinnear, 1981).

6. By the late 1870s Disraeli had succeeded in rehabilitating the Conservative Party in the eyes of the nation. He enabled the party to face in two directions at once. On the one hand, it could claim to be the party of property, stability and order, appealing to the interests of the landed gentry and the urban middle classes. On the other, by its image of a socially-reforming party with a concern for the rights of the working man, it could also claim to be the party of the people. The passing of the Reform Act 1867, which extended the franchise to most householders in borough (though not county) constituencies – in its own way a dramatic democratic gesture – was a crucial element in this rehabilitation: 'Disraeli's gamble of extending the franchise to the urban masses was, therefore, justified in the interests of his party: it won the victory of 1874, and in the longer term strengthened rather than weakened the electoral position of the Tories' (Feuchtwanger, 1968, p.10).

7. Macmillan had been the author of probably the most profound Conservative treatise in the inter-war years, advocating the 'middle way' in economic policy, between *laissez-faire* and State socialism (Macmillan, 1938; see also Macmillan, Boothby and Loder, 1927). Although it may have been a long-running joke in the corridors of Whitehall that his experience and memories of the inter-war depression years in Stockton on Tees became the yardstick of his approach to Conservative policy and politics, his sentiments were quite sincere. He was severely critical of the weak governmental response to the 'north-south' problem in the 1930s, and equally condemnatory of Mrs Thatcher's failure to tackle the problem in the 1980s.

8. The One Nation Group was set up by nine Conservative MPs in 1950, and continues to this day. The founding members included Edward Heath, Iain Macleod and Angus Maude. Subsequent members have included many who have held (or still hold) prominent positions in Mrs Thatcher's government, for example Sir Keith Joseph, John Biffen, Leon Brittan, Kenneth Baker, Kenneth Clarke, Sir Geoffrey Howe and Norman Fowler.

9. It is important to acknowledge, however, that the Conservatives were clearly shaken by the collapse of their Scottish vote to the Labour Party in the 1987 General Election, and were quick to undertake steps directed at rebuilding their image and appeal there (for example, the re-organization of the Scottish Conservative Party machinery, and public-relations visits by Mrs Thatcher). The underlying sources of local disaffection, such as being the first part of Britain to be subjected to the government's controversial proposed Community Charge, nevertheless remain.

3

LOCAL ECONOMIC DIFFERENTIALS AND THE 'NORTH-SOUTH' DIVIDE

Tony Champion and Anne Green

Introduction

The purpose of this chapter is to examine the latest available data relating to *local* economic fortunes. This is in order to discover whether the scale of inequality between places has been widening in the 1980s. If so, does this appear to be leading to a greater divergence between 'Two Nations' which are geographically separate in terms of the north-south divide, or to a widening of the range of prosperity between places *within* these broad regions? In recent years, particular attention has been given to the aggravation of the north-south dichotomy (Morgan, 1986a; Foley, 1987; Martin, 1987; TCPA, 1987; Veitch, 1987). However, others have argued against such a simplistic notion (Townsend, 1986; McLoughlin, 1987; Wilsher and Cassidy, 1987; Green, 1988).

Key questions raised by previous research and comment include, does the full range of indicators suggest an intensification of north-south differences or, alternatively, are there signs of the emergence of an *east-west* dimension as suggested by White (1985)? How far does the recent recovery in London's rate of population change (Champion, 1987) reflect improvements in the strength of its local economy? Has the maturing of the North Sea oil development programme, accelerated by the dramatic fall in oil prices in 1985, removed a significant source of economic optimism in the north, particularly north-east Scotland? Have the more rural and peripheral parts of Britain managed to maintain the momentum of rejuvenation they built up as a result of strong forces of 'counterurbanization' in the 1970s? Have the brighter spots in the north consolidated their position as bases on which the future prosperity of their wider regions can grow? With the continuing re-organization of manufacturing (Lloyd, 1987), are there sources of growth in the old industrial conurbations that allow these places to be seen in a more favourable light?

The impact of general economic and social trends varies widely between places according to their inherited characteristics, their geographical location and their responsiveness to changing circumstances (Cooke, 1986). At least four major dimensions – the north-south divide, differences in industrial structure, the urban-rural shift and local decentralization – acted simultaneously during the 1970s and early 1980s to produce major changes in the distribution of people and prosperity (Champion *et al.*, 1987). An index of local economic performance developed by Champion and Green (1985, 1987) to compare the relative standing of Britain's 280 Local Labour Market Areas (LLMAs) demonstrated the particular advantages accruing from proximity to London, and from the lack of any substantial manufacturing base, in helping places to weather the national economic recession.

Other geographical studies of economic, social and demographic trends during the 1970s (Fothergill and Gudgin, 1982; Goddard and Champion, 1983; Breheny, Hall and Hart, 1986; Danson, 1986; Martin and Rowthorn, 1986; Damesick and Wood, 1987; Hall *et al.*, 1987; Martin, 1987) highlighted the continued strong growth of medium-sized cities and towns in the South East round London, the resilience of what are traditionally thought of as cathedral cities and market towns, the revival of the flagging fortunes of the more remote rural zones, and the emergence of new industrial growth areas, particularly the 'sunbelt' focused on the M4 corridor. They also noted a number of more localized sites such as those associated with the electronics industry in the Cambridge area and central Scotland and with the oil-related developments of north-east Scotland. The other side of the coin, made worse by the poor performance of the national economy, was shown to be the increasing deprivation visited upon once-prosperous areas. These comprised not just the seedbeds of Britain's 19th-century industrial wealth in the inner parts of the largest cities, and across the major northern conurbations: they also included places that benefited greatly from the main 20th-century growth industries such as motor vehicles, petrochemicals and a restructured iron and steel industry, and indeed those that were the focus of the wave of international investment that brought welcome jobs to the Assisted Areas and New Towns in the 1960s.

The state and nature of the British economy have changed considerably since 1981. The massive levels of redundancies produced by the shake-out of Britain's manufacturing industries during the height of the recession (Townsend, 1983) have now eased in most sectors, as improved competitiveness resulting from streamlined processing and more flexible working practices have encouraged renewed investment by both British and overseas companies (Martin, 1986a). As shown in Chapter 5, increasing recognition is now being given to the role of business services in both local and national economic growth (Marshall, 1985a; Gillespie and Green, 1987; Howells and Green, 1988), with particular attention being focused on the growth of the financial, banking and insurance sector in the run-up to the deregulation of the London Stock Exchange in October 1986 (Marshall and Bachtler, 1987; Thrift, Leyshon and Daniels, 1987). A major surge in house prices in the London region had opened up a wide gap between north and south by the mid-1980s, as shown in Chapter 4 by Hamnett, while the accumulation of trends has placed the larger British cities below most of their continental rivals in a ranking of European cities (Cheshire, Carbonaro and Hay, 1986).

In this chapter, measures indicative of the strength and dynamism of places are identified and the performance of each place on each indicator is recorded. An aggregate score is then calculated for each place by summing the performances on each indicator, and the places are ranked according to this aggregate score. The next section of the chapter outlines the methodology adopted in more detail, while subsequent sections deal successively with the range of performance on the constituent variables, and the ranking of places on three different indices.

Methodology

Two sets of methodological decisions are required. The first relates to the geographical units that are to be used as synonymous with 'places' and for which the statistics for the key indicators of local prosperity are to be calculated. The second concerns the method for measuring the economic performance of each place.

Places and scores

The geographical units adopted for this study are the 280 Local Labour Market Areas (LLMAs) of the Functional Regions framework (Coombes *et al.*, 1982). This urban-centred functional approach divides the country up into a set of real places that are relatively independent and on which the quality of life of the local inhabitants largely depends. For present purposes this specially-defined set of areas is much preferred over the standard official statistical areas like counties and districts, the boundaries of which pay scant attention to the functional realities of Britain's settlements.

In providing a score for LLMAs on each indicator, we use a measure that takes account of the distribution of individual places between the maximum and minimum values. The LLMA with the best value on an indicator is allocated the score of 1.000, that with the worst value is allocated the score of 0.000 and intermediate values are calibrated on their position over the intervening range. The overall index is calculated by summing the scores on all indicators for each place and then dividing the result by the number of indicators used, so as to give a final index within the range 0.000 to 1.000. An overall index of 1.000 is possible only when an LLMA is consistently the best performer on all indicators, and vice versa for an LLMA scoring 0.000 overall. It is critical to note that all variables are given equal weighting.

Choice of variables

Variables were drawn from a wide range of data sets in order to provide the most up-to-date picture possible of patterns of, and recent trends in, local economic prosperity.

From the unemployment records, we extracted the unemployment rate in July 1987, levels of change in the unemployment rate between July 1984 and July 1987, and a measure of the duration of unemployment (the median duration of completed unemployment spells in July 1987). Unemployment is by far the most widely-used measure of labour-market performance at both national and local scales, but it needs to be complemented by other measures at local level because the relationship between unemployment rates and the strength of the local economy can be distorted by differential rates of labour migration, school-leaving, retirement and participation in the labour force by people of working age (Owen, Gillespie and Coombes, 1984). From the 1984 *Census of Employment* we calculated the proportion of total employment that is accounted for by the two sectors given most attention in recent years as the bases of Britain's future prosperity: high-technology industry (Butchart, 1987) and producer (or business) services, including finance, banking and insurance. We also derived a measure of change in employment in these two sectors combined for 1981–4, as well as the percentage change in the total number of jobs in each area for the same period.

The other variables selected are less direct measures of local economic buoyancy. The economic-activity rate in 1981 (the most recent date for which accurate local data is available) was chosen as a partial reflection of the degree of 'tightness' in the local labour market, on the assumption that greater labour scarcity will force up wages and encourage more people of working age to offer their services to employers. Rates of population change for 1981–5 were chosen as a key indicator of confidence in the opportunities in a town since, even where retired people are involved, its effect feeds through into further job growth because of extra spending on local services. Average house prices in 1986, and rates of change in the price of housing floorspace between 1982 and 1986, were selected as further indirect measures of local prosperity and buoyancy. This was not only because to some extent they reflect the immediate pressures on local accommodation and the wealth of those seeking to purchase housing, but also because they demonstrate the degree of longer-term confidence in an area, bearing in mind that nowadays house purchase is considered more of an investment item than an article of consumption for its role as shelter (Healey, 1987a).

In all, therefore, ten variables (see Table 3.1) were generated in order to gauge the relative performance of the 280 LLMAs during the 1980s. The first five variables relate to the conditions found in these places at particular points in time, in each case the latest available date and generally relating to the 'mid-1980s'. These will be used to calculate a Static Index. The second five variables measure change over time and will be used to calculate a Change Index that gives an indication of the recent dynamism of local economies. Finally, all ten variables are used to generate an Amalgamated Index that combines both static and change measures into a single score. First, however, we examine the range of performance on individual indicators.

Performance on the key variables

For most of the ten variables there is found to be an extremely wide range between the LLMA recording the highest level of economic strength and the one with the lowest level (Table 3.2). There is also a clear north-south pattern to this list of extreme cases; only Oldham provides an exception in that it exhibited the highest economic activity rate in Britain in 1981 despite being in the northern half of the country (in Greater Manchester). Nevertheless, a more rigorous analysis is needed

Table 3.1   Variables used for the indices (and their sources)

Static Index
  1. Unemployment rate, July 1987, % (Department of Employment via NOMIS).
  2. Median duration of completed unemployment spells, July 1987, weeks (source as for 1).
  3. Employment in producer services and high-technology (PSHT) industries as % of all employment, 1984 (*Census of Employment* via NOMIS).
  4. Economic activity rate for persons of working age, 1981, % (*Census of Population*).
  5. Mean house price, 1986, £000s (based on market-price approvals made by the Nationwide Anglia Building Society).

Change Index
  6. Change in unemployment rate, July 1984 to July 1987, % point (source as for 1).
  7. Change in total employment, 1981–4, % (source as for 3).
  8. Change in employment in PSHT industries, 1981–4, as % of employment in all industries, 1981 (source as for 3).
  9. Population change, 1981–5, % (CACI Market Analysis).
 10. Change in the unit price of housing floorspace, 1982–6, % (based on the price per square foot of market-price approvals made by the Nationwide Anglia Building Society, excluding flats and extreme sizes of houses).

to test the significance of the north-south divide and, in particular, to compare its role with that of the urban-rural dimension that has been noted as a dominant force in the 1970s. In this section, aggregate data are examined for each variable on the basis of LLMAs grouped according to location in either north or south (where the boundary runs broadly between the Severn Estuary and Lincolnshire) and according to size and urban status, supplemented by map evidence in a number of cases.

The 'static' variables

The unemployment rate for July 1987 exhibits an extremely-wide range between the two extreme LLMAs of Consett (Co. Dur.) and Crawley (W. Sussex). The likelihood of an economically-active person being unemployed in Consett is almost nine times the figure for Crawley. Table 3.3 shows that the north-south divide is a dominant feature, with none of the four LLMA categories in the south exceeding any of those in the north and with the urban-rural dimension spanning a relatively-small range in both north and south. Areas with particularly-high unemployment rates occur in central Scotland, north-east England and South Yorkshire, whereas the lowest rates are located within, or on the fringes of, the London metropolitan region. On the other hand, there are some notable exceptions from the general pattern. North of the Severn Estuary–Lincolnshire line, the dole queues are relatively short in Kendal (Cumbria) and Harrogate (N. Yorks.), 5.9 and 7.2 per cent respectively, and in southern England unemployment is particularly severe – even by the standard of northern Britain – in Deal (Kent) and Redruth & Camborne (Corn.), 20.3 and 19.8 per cent respectively.

Table 3.2   Extreme values on the ten variables

Variable (brief title)	Best-performing LLMA		Worst-performing LLMA		Median LLMA
Static variables					
1. Unemployment rate	Crawley	2.7	Consett	24.0	11.6
2. Duration of unemployment	Cambridge	6.4	Smethwick	26.0	16.8
3. Employment in PSHT industries	Bracknell	36.6	Peterlee	2.2	9.8
4. Economic activity rate	Oldham	80.9	Cardigan	68.3	75.6
5. Mean house price	High Wycombe	70.1	Keighley	19.4	34.9
Change variables					
6. Change in unemployment rate	Corby	−5.8	Banff & Buckie	+4.6	−0.8
7. Change in total employment	Milton Keynes	+21.7	Ellesmere Port	−23.4	−0.4
8. Change in PSHT employment	Thetford	+7.9	Woodbridge	−8.0	+0.8
9. Change in population	Milton Keynes	+18.1	Burnley	−5.8	+0.9
10. Change in price of housing	London	+86.3	Merthyr Tydfil	+0.6	+43.3

Note

See Table 3.1 for variable specifications (including dates and units of measurement) and sources. Particular care is needed for interpreting variable 8; see text.

Table 3.3 The five component variables of the Static Index, by LLMA group

LLMA group	1	2	3	4	5
South	8.7	14.0	18.2	76.6	43.2
Large Dominants	9.2	16.7	22.2	77.9	49.1
Cities	8.4	14.8	15.9	76.4	44.3
Towns	8.1	13.6	15.7	75.6	44.1
Rural Areas	10.0	14.4	11.5	73.8	38.9
North	14.1	18.6	11.2	76.0	31.1
Large Dominants	14.6	21.0	14.2	77.0	31.7
Cities	14.6	19.1	10.6	76.0	28.9
Towns	13.3	17.9	9.4	75.6	31.1
Rural Areas	12.9	17.1	7.7	73.4	33.8

Key to variable names (abbreviated): 1. Unemployment rate; 2. Duration of unemployment; 3. Employment in PSHT industries; 4. Economic activity rate; 5. Mean house price.

Notes
Weighted means for variables 1, 3 and 4; median LLMA for variables 2 and 5.
See Table 3.1 for the full names of variables, including dates and units of measurement.

The mean duration of completed unemployment spells is also sharply differentiated between north and south (Table 3.3). The line between the Severn Estuary and Lincolnshire emerges very strongly from the data for individual LLMAs mapped in Figure 3.1(a). Places with the lowest median duration highlight two of the main axes of job opportunity in southern England along the M11 and M3 corridors, while among the worst-off LLMAs on this indicator are places in the West Midlands, Merseyside, the coalfields and some remote rural areas. London, the lower Thames corridor and the coastal areas of Essex and Suffolk appear more disadvantaged on this indicator than on overall unemployment rate, as is also true of large parts of the Midlands and northern England. Parts of northern Scotland, by contrast, appear in a more favourable light in terms of the duration measure, indicating that turnover on the dole is more rapid than the overall rate of unemployment would suggest.

Bracknell (Berks.) and Stevenage (Herts.) head the list of LLMAs in terms of the proportion of employment in producer services and high-technology industries. Southern England again dominates the map through the shape of a cross comprising the M23 and M11 corridors as well as the lower Thames corridor and the M3/M4 sector west of London (Figure 3.1(b)). Over the rest of Britain the pattern is generally more varied than in the case of the unemployment indicators, with certain LLMAs in the Midlands, such as Rugby (War.), and the North West, such as Preston (Lancs.) showing high levels. At the other extreme, Peterlee (Co. Dur.), Llanelli (Dyfed) and Barnsley (S. Yorks.) have under 4 per cent of workers in these sectors, only a tenth of Bracknell's level (Table 3.2). In all, the north has 11.2 per cent of its workers in these industries compared with the south's 18.2 per cent, the latter boosted considerably by the major concentration in London, but there is also a clear urban-rural dimension to this variable in both halves of the country (Table 3.3).

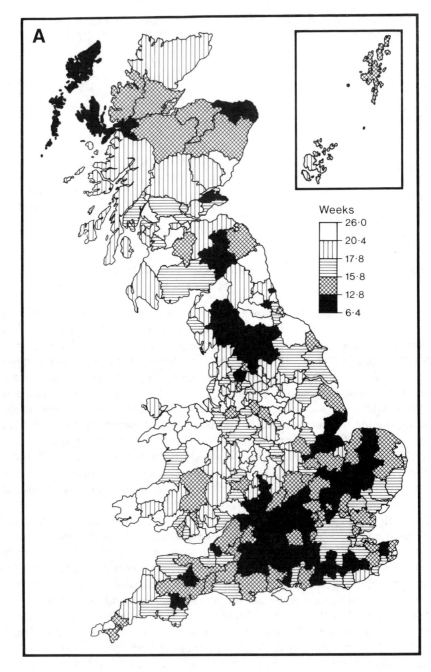

Figure 3.1   Measures of local economic strength in the mid-1980s: (a) Median duration of completed unemployment spells, July 1987

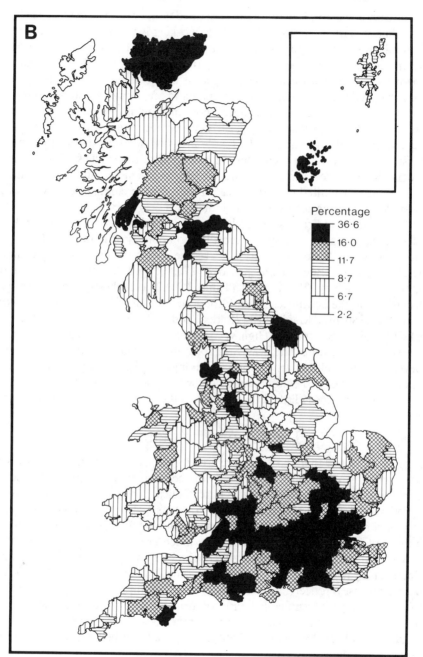

Figure 3.1 (cont.): (b) Proportion of employment in producer services and high-technology industries, 1984

In the case of economic activity rates, defined as the proportion of working-age people that are either employed or seeking work, it is the urban-rural dimension that dominates; there is comparatively little difference between north and south either in aggregate or for each size category of LLMA (Table 3.3). The importance of the urban-rural factor arises partly because of the higher costs of living in the more urbanized regions, which on the one hand encourage greater labour-force participation and, on the other, prompt those outside the labour market to move elsewhere, particularly people taking early retirement. Areas with a long tradition of female employment, such as the textile areas of north-west England and the Scottish borders, also have high rates, with Oldham (Gtr Manchester) and Hawick (Borders) heading the national ranking. By contrast, remoter rural areas continue to offer relatively limited opportunities for paid female employment, with places in west Wales scoring lowest on this indicator.

Of all the static indicators, mean house prices indicate the north-south divide most strikingly. At the extremes, according to analysis of data provided by the Nationwide Anglia Building Society, the average price of an owner-occupied house in High Wycombe (Bucks.) was just over £70,000 in 1986, compared to under £20,000 for Keighley (W. Yorks.) (Table 3.2). The highest-priced areas were concentrated in the South East round London, with Guildford (Surrey), Woking & Weybridge (Surrey), Maidenhead (Berks.) and St Albans (Herts.) and Bracknell (Berks.) heading the list after High Wycombe. The highest priced area north of the Severn–Lincolnshire line was Stratford-upon-Avon (War.), but even this achieved only 36th place in the national rankings. In the aggregate figures (Table 3.3), London is clearly the dominant factor within the south as well as nationally, whereas there is relatively little difference across the size categories within the north.

The 'change' variables

It is to be expected that the five measures reflecting change in local economic opportunities in the 1980s will present less coherent patterns than the 'static' variables just described. Whereas the latter indicate the position reached over a long period of time as well as recent trends, the 'change' variables relate to changes over a maximum of four years. As a result, developments that may seem relatively unimportant in the long term may assume much greater significance, especially for smaller, local, labour markets where the opening or closure of individual businesses may loom large at one particular time. Problems of interpretation can also arise because of differences between areas in their initial standing on a variable, for instance, large percentage increases occurring where the original base is very small. Therefore, it is not wise to place too much attention on the identity of the top and bottom LLMAs, shown in Table 3.2; instead, it is better to discern general patterns in the data.

On the criterion of 'percentage-point change' in the unemployment rate (July 1987 *minus* July 1984), the north and south were evenly matched in their scale of improvement between 1984 and 1987. For separate size groups the largest falls took place in the Cities and Towns of the south, and at the other extreme Rural Areas in the north experienced an increase in their overall unemployment rate (Table

3.4). More detailed figures reveal that, despite the much-quoted resurgence of the national economy, some seventy LLMAs recorded an increase in unemployment rate over this three-year period. This list is headed by Banff & Buckie (Grampian) and includes other areas in north-east Scotland, where the decline in oil-related

Table 3.4   The five component variables of the Change Index, by LLMA group

LLMA group	6	7	8	9	10
South	−0.83	1.5	1.38	1.6	58.6
Large Dominants	−0.53	−1.5	1.11	−0.6	68.9
Cities	−1.07	3.1	1.56	2.6	61.3
Towns	−1.05	3.9	1.65	2.9	60.1
Rural Areas	−0.93	5.8	1.22	2.8	44.8
North	−0.83	−3.3	0.45	−0.5	33.8
Large Dominants	−0.77	−4.5	0.63	−1.6	34.5
Cities	−0.95	−3.4	0.11	−0.6	32.6
Towns	−0.92	−2.4	0.63	0.1	35.8
Rural Areas	0.19	0.3	0.69	1.2	27.6

Key to variable names (abbreviated): 6. Change in unemployment rate; 7. Change in total employment; 8. Change in PSHT industries; 9. Change in population; 10. Change in the price of housing.

Notes
Weighted means for variables 6–9; median LLMA for variable 10.
See Table 3.1 for the full names of variables, including dates and units of measurement.

activities since the oil-price collapse of 1984 will have played a part. A substantial block of LLMAs in Yorkshire and the northern East Midlands also experienced increased unemployment rates, embracing both rural and coal-mining localities. The largest improvements were recorded by places on the fringes of the South East region and in the southern part of the Midlands, but areas in the north that suffered badly during the recession years of 1979–81 (West Midlands conurbation, south Wales, the North West and north east England) also experienced large falls in their rates of joblessness. Other factors besides local economic growth can, however, be held partly responsible for the wide spread of lower unemployment rates, including Special Employment Schemes, out-migration and changes in the rules for claiming Unemployment Benefit.

Indeed, the data on percentage change in total employment by workplace – the most direct way of measuring the dynamism of local economies – reveals much greater regional and sub-regional variation, though admittedly relating to the period 1981–4 rather than the more recent three-year period (because of the time required to process the *Census of Employment* returns). At this time there was a major contrast between the 3.3 per cent decline in jobs in the north and the 1.5 per-cent growth recorded by the south. The latter took place despite a considerable loss of jobs in London, while in the north only the Rural Areas, in aggregate, managed to avoid employment decline. In both parts of the country a clear urban-rural redistribution was in evidence at this time (Table 3.4). Strong economic growth was still taking place in northern Scotland, as well as in some of the more rural parts of northern England, Wales and the South West, while the recession and related industrial rationalization were continuing in some smaller or more specialized places, with Ellesmere Port (Merseyside) Neath and Port Talbot (W. Glam.) all losing around one in every five of the jobs they had in 1981. Meanwhile, the largest single concentration of growth occurred in a broad zone stretching from Dorset and Hampshire to Norfolk and the Fens, with offshoots to the Sussex coast, the Severn Estuary and Northamptonshire.

These regional contrasts are also plain in terms of the growth of the producer services and high-technology (PSHT) industries that are generally held up as the brightest hopes for Britain's economic resurgence. (In order to overcome the problem that many areas had very small numbers in these industries in 1981, our data relates the 1981–4 change in numbers employed in PSHT industries to the level of total employment in all sectors in 1981.) While the national growth in PSHT industries during 1981–4 amounted to a 0.9 per cent addition to the country's total employment, the equivalent figure for the south was 1.4 per cent, nearly three times the increase for the north. This contrast between north and south was much wider than that across the size categories within the two halves of the country, though northern Cities performed particularly badly and southern Cities and Towns fared relatively well (Table 3.4). Most favoured among the latter was the same broad area of growth in southern and eastern England noted for overall employment change, in this case led by Thetford (Norfolk) and also including Cambridge, Harlow (Essex), Hertford, Corby (Northants), Milton Keynes (Bucks.), Basingstoke (Hants) and Newbury (Berks.). Elsewhere the patterns are more varied and, despite the general pattern of growth, as many as 80 of the 280 LLMAs recorded losses in this sector.

Population change over the period 1981–5 exhibits the same broad patterns as total employment change, though somewhat less pronounced – growth in the south, decline in the north and a counterurbanization shift within both north and south (Table 3.4). Figure 3.2(a) reveals rapid growth through most of the south except London and its immediately adjacent LLMAs. Milton Keynes heads the list with a growth rate of 18 per cent for the four-year period, whereas the best that the north can show is 6.9 per cent for Northallerton & Richmond (N. Yorks.).

Finally, trends in the price of housing provide the most clear-cut patterns of the five 'change' indicators. The LLMAs with the steepest price rises are massively concentrated in the south-eastern corner of Britain (Figure 3.2(b)). London itself tops the list, with a massive 86 per cent increase in the price of housing floorspace between 1982 and 1986 at current prices, while at the other extreme the data indicate virtually no change for Merthyr Tydfil, representing a significant fall in the real price of housing there (Table 3.2). None of the size groups in the north comes close to any in the south in terms of the housing-price increase of their median LLMA (Table 3.4). This four-year period has obviously been characterized by a vast increase in an already-significant north-south differential, which has had the effect of magnifying the steepness of the gradient away from the London region both within the south and across the whole country.

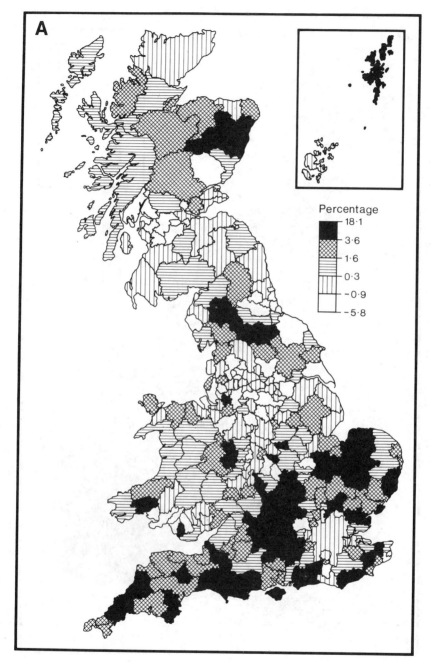

Figure 3.2   Measures of local economic change in the 1980s: (a) Population change, 1981–5

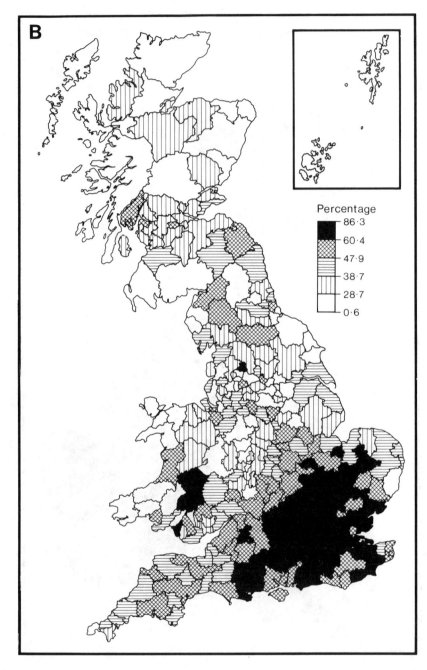

Figure 3.2 (cont.): (b) Change in the unit price of housing floorspace, 1982–6

Static, Change and Amalgamated Indices

The first five of the ten variables listed in Table 3.1 provide the basis for calculating a Static Index representing the relative level of local prosperity reached by each of the 280 LLMAs by the mid-1980s. The second group of five variables are used in the calibration of a Change Index measuring changes taking place during the early to mid-1980s. Finally, all ten variables are used in the compilation of an Amalgamated Index.

The Static Index

The relative standing of each LLMA in a league table of local prosperity around the mid-1980s is calculated on the basis of the unemployment rate, the mean duration of completed unemployment spells, the proportion of workers employed in producer (business) services and high-technology (PSHT) industries, the economic activity rate, and the average price of an owner-occupied house. Hence we are measuring the average inherited status of each place.

The results are presented in Figure 3.3 and Table 3.5. The boundary of the south, defined on the basis of the Severn Estuary–Lincolnshire line, is very clear and encloses all but nine of the top 70 LLMAs (scores of over 0.525), of which three (Stratford-upon-Avon, Rugby and Loughborough) lie immediately over the line (Figure 3.3(a)). Even more impressive than this, however, is the concentration of the 35 most prosperous places (scores of 0.636 and over) in a single and fairly compact zone, dominated by the block of LLMAs west and south west of London, but also embracing London and its surrounding LLMAs (except for the lower Thames corridor) and extending south-westwards to Salisbury and Cheltenham, and northwards via Welwyn and Stevenage to Cambridge and Huntingdon (Figure 3.3(a)). This area constitutes the pressurized 'heart' of the British economy in the mid-1980s in terms of the squeeze on the labour force, the importance of key industrial sectors and the demand for housing. Amongst the top ten towns on the Static Index (Table 3.5), the performance on the five separate measures is above the national median in all cases, except for the economic activity rate for Guildford (Surrey), which is only marginally below the median. Economic activity rates for the working-age population are particularly high in the New Towns of Crawley, Stevenage and Welwyn, while unemployment rates are less than half the median in all but Stevenage, Bracknell and Maidenhead. PHST industries employ around a third of the workforce in Bracknell, Stevenage, Welwyn and Didcot, while house prices average over £60,000 in all but Didcot, Crawley and Stevenage.

The 35 LLMAs with the lowest scores on the Static Index are a much more scattered set. They include some of the westernmost places in Britain in the far South West, west and north Wales, and south-west Scotland, as well as a number of places with mining and manufacturing traditions in south Wales, South Yorkshire/north Nottinghamshire and parts of north-east England. Merseyside appears as another large concentration of low-scoring LLMAs, while Tamworth scores very poorly in the West Midlands (Figure 3.3(b)). The characteristics that have produced the lowest ten places on the Static Index are shown in Table 3.5,

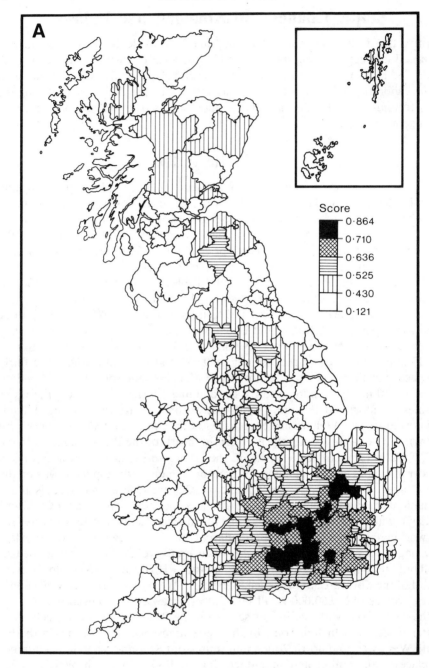

Figure 3.3   The Static Index: (a) Above median

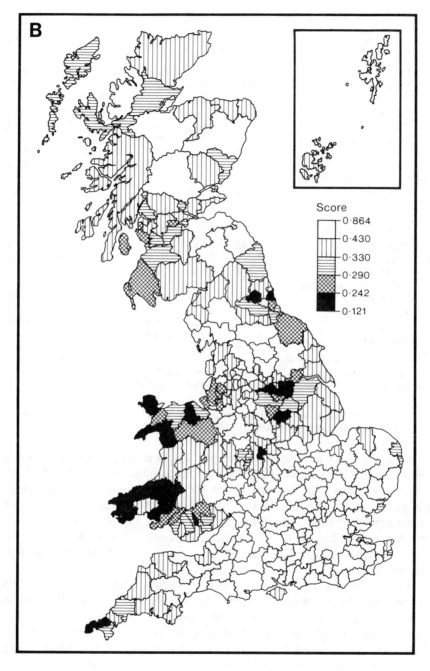

Figure 3.3 (cont.): (b) Below median

Table 3.5   Highest and lowest scores on the Static Index

Rank	LLMA name	Score	1	2	3	4	5
Top ten LLMAs							
1	Welwyn	0.864	4.7	11.2	33.8	79.0	69.8
2	Bracknell	0.835	5.9	12.7	36.6	77.7	65.0
3	Woking & Weybridge	0.804	4.4	8.3	23.1	76.0	69.0
4	Crawley	0.796	2.7	9.1	17.7	80.2	56.2
5	Didcot	0.788	4.5	10.6	33.0	77.2	51.9
6	Maidenhead	0.768	6.9	9.5	22.6	76.4	68.2
7	Aldershot & Farnborough	0.768	5.2	8.8	21.9	77.1	60.6
8	Stevenage	0.762	7.4	13.4	35.7	79.3	46.8
9	High Wycombe	0.750	4.7	9.5	16.5	75.7	70.1
10	Guildford	0.749	3.9	10.5	20.2	74.5	70.1
Bottom ten LLMAs							
271	Rhyl & Prestatyn	0.223	13.8	24.5	8.4	71.3	26.4
272	Mansfield	0.222	13.9	25.8	4.7	74.2	23.9
273	Penzance	0.221	15.9	21.9	7.6	69.5	32.8
274	Pembroke	0.214	18.0	21.0	7.7	70.7	28.7
275	Redruth & Camborne	0.191	19.8	20.6	7.1	70.1	29.6
276	Barnsley	0.179	17.1	25.1	3.2	74.0	21.6
277	Mexborough	0.143	23.3	19.7	5.4	71.5	20.2
278	Consett	0.130	24.0	23.6	7.5	72.9	19.8
279	Holyhead	0.129	22.8	19.5	5.8	69.1	24.1
280	Cardigan	0.121	21.5	25.4	8.3	68.3	33.7

Key to variable names (abbreviated): 1. Unemployment rate; 2. Duration of unemployment; 3. Employment in PSHT industries; 4. Economic activity rate; 5. Mean house price.

Note
See Table 3.1 for the full names of variables, including dates and units of measurement. See Table 3.2 for the median and range of LLMA scores on each variable.

with no instance of an above-median performance. Unemployment rates are particularly high in Consett (Co. Dur.), Mexborough (S. Yorks.), Holyhead (Gwynedd) and Cardigan (Dyfed), with the duration of completed unemployment spells greatest in Barnsley (S. Yorks.), Mansfield (Notts.), Cardigan and Consett. The proportion employed in producer services and high-technology industries is particularly low in Barnsley and Mansfield. Economic activity rates are lowest in the more rural areas, while house prices tend to be lowest in the mining and industrial LLMAs.

It is clear that while the LLMAs at the extremes of the index tend to score uniformly well/badly on each variable, the fact that they display higher/lower scores on some variables than on others indicates that the exact reasons for good/poor performance do vary in importance between LLMAs. Even within regions there is often considerable variation in scores on the Static Index (Table 3.6). All parts of Britain except Wales have at least one LLMA within the top fifth of the national ranking (i.e. 56th place or above), while all regions bar none have a representative in the bottom 56. However, it is important not to lose sight of the dominant north-south pattern. The median LLMA for the south comes in 66th place in the national rankings, compared with only 186th place for its

Table 3.6 Range of scores on the Static Index, by standard regions

Region (no. of LLMAs)	Median score	Highest LLMA		Lowest LLMA	
		Name	Rank	Name	Rank
South East (59)	0.636	Welwyn	1	Clacton	243
South West (30)	0.492	Cheltenham	33	Redruth & Camborne	275
East Anglia (14)	0.489	Cambridge	12	Yarmouth	229
East Midlands (23)	0.457	Northampton	48	Mansfield	272
North West (29)	0.430	Macclesfield	39	St Helens	263
West Midlands (23)	0.422	Stratford-upon-Avon	37	Tamworth	266
Scotland (34)	0.377	Hawick	50	Coatbridge & Airdrie	261
Northern (19)	0.365	Kendal	43	Consett	278
Yorkshire & Humb. (22)	0.362	Harrogate	53	Mexborough	277
Wales (27)	0.291	Brecon	145	Cardigan	280

Note
Regions are ranked according to their median LLMA score.

northern equivalent, and the south has more than twice as many representatives in the top 70 LLMAs as would be expected, while the north has less than a quarter of its fair share in this group (Table 3.7). This contrast is apparent for all four size groups, though the margin of the difference is relatively small for the Rural Areas, which are the least favoured LLMA type in the south.

Table 3.7   Performance on Static, Change and Amalgamated Indices by LLMA group

LLMA group	Median score			Chance of LLMA being in top 70		
	Static	Change	Amalgamated	Static	Change	Amalgamated
South	0.534	0.549	0.535	2.14	2.21	2.21
Large Dominants	0.604	0.523	0.563	4.00	2.00	2.00
Cities	0.556	0.562	0.567	2.73	2.54	2.55
Towns	0.542	0.552	0.554	2.20	2.37	2.48
Rural Areas	0.451	0.507	0.495	1.05	1.26	0.84
North	0.378	0.430	0.399	0.22	0.17	0.17
Large Dominants	0.381	0.420	0.416	0.00	0.00	0.00
Cities	0.354	0.419	0.380	0.00	0.00	0.00
Towns	0.380	0.448	0.405	0.38	0.19	0.24
Rural Areas	0.383	0.426	0.391	0.12	0.36	0.24

The Change Index

By comparison with the Static Index, there is greater consistency amongst the Change Index's best-performing places both in geographical terms (Figure 3.4(a)) and to a large extent in terms of their growth characteristics (Table 3.8). They are concentrated in two large blocks west and north of London, the latter stretching as far as Thetford (Norfolk) and Corby (Northants). Chichester & Bognor (W. Sussex), Milton Keynes (Bucks.), and Aylesbury (Bucks.) lie apart from these two blocks, but in reality they form part of a single extensive 'crescent' stretching from Chichester (W. Sussex) and Guildford (Surrey) in the south to Salisbury (Wilts.), Swindon (Wilts.) and Stroud (Glos.) in the west and swinging north-eastwards in a broad band extending to Thetford and Kings Lynn (Norfolk) at the end of London's main growth corridor into East Anglia. Apart from Crawley, Haywards Heath, Hastings (Sussex) and Southend (Essex), only three other places in the country have performed as strongly as this on the Change Index, these being Tiverton (Devon), Stratford-upon-Avon (War.) and Northallerton & Richmond (N. Yorks.).

Table 3.8 lists the top-ten performers on the Change Index and gives details of their performance on the five indicator variables. It is clear that Milton Keynes (Bucks.) is by far the fastest-growing place in Britain. It has the highest percentage rates of increase in both population and employment of all the 280 LLMAs as well as strong growth in PSHT jobs, a fall in unemployment rate since 1984 and vigorous growth in house prices. Even so, all the other places in the top ten have also experienced strong employment growth, both generally and in PSHT

Table 3.8   Highest and lowest scores on the Change Index

Rank	LLMA name	Score	6	7	8	9	10
Top-ten LLMAs							
1	Milton Keynes	0.835	−1.1	21.7	4.6	18.1	72.3
2	Huntingdon	0.754	−1.3	16.0	4.5	10.6	74.7
3	Newbury	0.741	−1.9	16.5	5.5	5.6	75.5
4	Thetford	0.709	−1.2	16.4	7.9	3.6	62.3
5	Hertford & Ware	0.703	−0.8	20.7	5.3	4.7	64.6
6	Corby	0.685	−5.8	11.1	4.5	−3.1	66.4
7	Basingstoke	0.671	−2.2	6.5	4.8	5.8	64.7
8	Cambridge	0.667	−1.0	12.4	5.6	2.2	71.2
9	Reading	0.666	−1.3	8.5	4.4	6.1	67.5
10	Aylesbury	0.660	−1.1	12.3	2.2	3.6	79.9
Bottom-ten LLMAs							
271	Sheffield	0.327	0.4	−8.5	−0.6	−1.5	23.2
272	Arbroath	0.323	1.8	−5.6	0.1	1.1	14.1
273	Hartlepool	0.315	−3.2	−12.1	−2.3	−3.5	11.2
274	Holyhead	0.308	1.5	−8.4	0.3	2.3	5.0
275	South Shields	0.305	−1.4	−14.3	−2.5	−2.8	24.4
276	Smethwick	0.301	−0.3	−8.3	−3.9	−2.2	25.7
277	Stranraer	0.301	0.3	−15.3	−2.2	−0.2	28.3
278	Banff & Buckie	0.299	4.6	4.3	1.5	−0.5	6.4
279	Stafford	0.286	0.2	−4.8	−7.6	1.4	23.8
280	Burnley	0.284	−1.6	−15.1	−1.4	−5.8	20.3

Key to variable names (abbreviated): 6. Change in unemployment rate; 7. Change in total employment; 8. Change in PSHT industries; 9. Change in population; 10. Change in the price of housing.

Note
See Table 3.1 for the full names of variables, including dates and units of measurement. See Table 3.2 for the median and range of LLMA scores on each variable.

industries, all have seen the cost of housing rise by two-thirds or more between 1982 and 1986, and all have recorded falls in unemployment rate, even though most of them already had very low rates at the outset. Corby (Northants) is perhaps the most notable LLMA in this list, because it has seen a major transformation in its labour-market conditions since the early 1980s, when it was reeling from the closure of its steel works. Between 1981 and 1984 its employment situation improved markedly, and since 1984 its unemployment rate has dropped by a substantial 5.8 per-cent points (though it is clear that this restructuring has exerted a price in terms of people 'getting on their bikes' in search of jobs elsewhere).

It is, however, more difficult to generalize about the places that score poorly on the Change Index. Figure 3.4(b) and Table 3.8 show that the worst performers are a scattered and mixed bunch, though they include some well-known cases such as Hartlepool (Cleveland) and Sheffield (S. Yorks.) in the top ten, with Liverpool coming in eleventh place. Also clear is the dimension of remoter rural areas, reinforced in north-east Scotland by Banff & Buckie, Peterhead and Arbroath (Figure 3.4(b)). Banff & Buckie's poor performance is no doubt directly attributable to the change in the fortunes of the oil industry in 1984 for, while it achieved

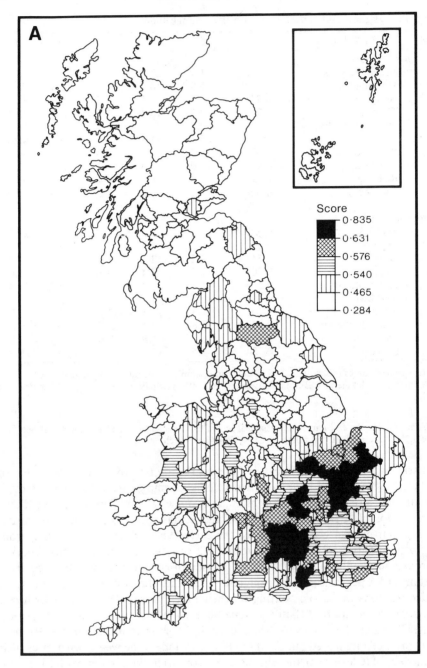

Figure 3.4   The Change Index: (a) Above median

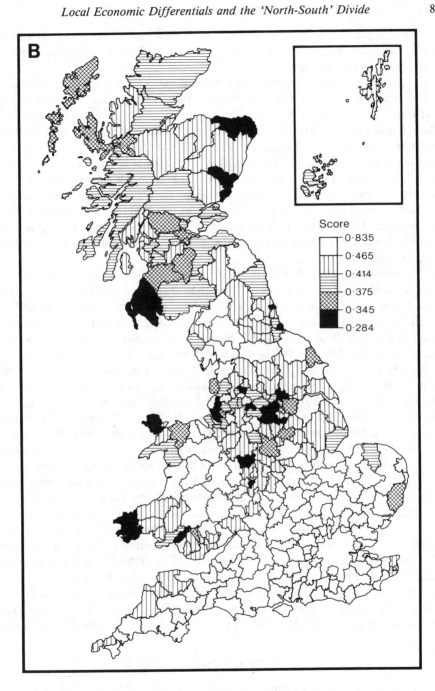

Figure 3.4   (cont.): (b) Below median

considerable job growth in the three years up till then, this area experienced a major rise in unemployment in the following three years, along with a substantial fall in the real price of housing.

The over-riding impression of the changes taking place in local economies since 1981 is clearly of the division between north and south. The map evidence (Figure 3.4) shows how few are the places south of the Severn–Lincolnshire line with a Change Index score below the median, though it also reveals that more buoyant local labour-market conditions extend across this boundary in the English Midlands and into parts of central and north Wales. At the other end of Britain, Scotland appears to present a fairly uniform picture of economic sluggishness, though the fact that Clydeside has recently been performing better than much of rural Scotland is remarkable in itself. The north of England, as made up by a diamond with Hull, Birmingham, Liverpool and Newcastle upon Tyne at its corners, also appears as a relatively-poorly performing area, sharing more in common with Scotland than with southern England.

The principal qualification to this generalization relates to the great degree of variation within these broad regions. Even in the south, several LLMAs fall below the median on the Change Index, particularly in east Kent, East Anglia and the South West, while even in the heart of the north there is a fair number of more dynamic places or 'Northern Lights' to use the terminology of Breheny, Hall and Hart (1987). On the basis of the Change Index, these include Northallerton & Richmond (N. Yorks.), Buxton (Derby.), Penrith (Cumbria) and Macclesfield (Ches.). When the standard regions are ranked according to the score of their median LLMA (Table 3.9), clear geographical groupings emerge: the three southern regions; the three regions comprising the Midlands and Wales; and the three remaining regions of northern England with Scotland some way behind in last place. On the other hand, it is fortunate that we have been able to draw upon sub-regional data to show that there is no uniform gradient in local economic performance across the country, but rather that each Standard Region exhibits a broad range from best to worst. Even so, there is a danger of over-emphasizing the importance of the brighter features of the north. It puts things into their proper perspective if it is noted that the place with the most dynamic record of change in the Northern region can manage only 74th place in the national rankings and that for the North West only 85th place. Moreover, the median LLMA in Britain north of the Severn–Lincolnshire line manages only 191st place in the national rankings, compared with 63rd place for its southern counterpart. Just as with the Static Index, the south contains over twice its share of representatives in the nation's top 70 places, with all four size categories outdoing any of the size categories in the north (Table 3.7).

The Amalgamated Index

The Amalgamated Index measures the overall performance of each LLMA across all ten variables. A clear north-south divide in the distribution of scores is indicated in Figure 3.5; the 166 LLMAs lying to the north of a Severn–Lincolnshire line concentrate very largely below the national median of 0.430 and exhibit a fairly 'normal' distribution, while the majority of the 114 LLMAs to the south of the

Table 3.9 Range of scores on the Change Index, by Standard Regions

Region (no. of LLMAs)	Median score	Highest LLMA		Lowest LLMA	
		Name	Rank	Name	Rank
East Anglia (14)	0.581	Huntingdon	2	Woodbridge	261
South East (59)	0.559	Milton Keynes	1	Deal	247
South West (30)	0.508	Stroud	21	Penzance	196
East Midlands (23)	0.460	Corby	6	Mansfield	250
West Midlands (23)	0.458	Stratford-upon-Avon	22	Stafford	279
Wales (27)	0.450	Aberystwyth	45	Holyhead	274
Northern (19)	0.434	Penrith	74	South Shields	275
Yorkshire & Humb. (22)	0.424	Northallerton & Richmond	18	Sheffield	271
North West (29)	0.414	Macclesfield	85	Burnley	280
Scotland (34)	0.395	Berwick	123	Banff & Buckie	278

Note
Regions are ranked according to their median LLMA score.

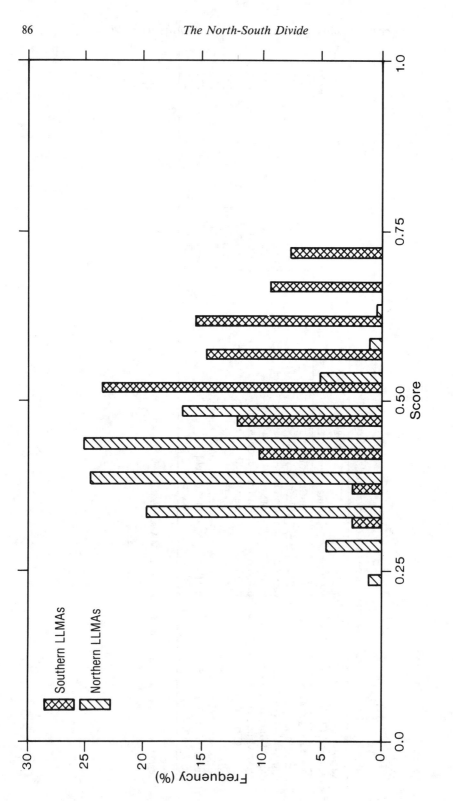

Figure 3.5   Amalgamated Index Scores

line have scores above the median, but display a much flatter and more wide-ranging distribution than the northern LLMAs. Clearly the south is not uniformly prosperous nor the north uniformly poor, but in statistical terms north and south do constitute very different 'populations' of LLMAs and in practice there is remarkably little overlap in scores between the two across the whole sample or even for individual size groups (Table 3.7).

The distinction between north and south can be demonstrated further by reference to a list of the highest- and lowest-scoring LLMAs (Table 3.10) and the map of the Index's geographical distribution across the country (Figure 3.6). Milton

Table 3.10 Highest and lowest scores on the Amalgamated Index

	Top LLMAs			Bottom LLMAs	
Rank	Name	Score	Rank	Name	Score
1	Milton Keynes	0.720	280	Holyhead	0.218
2	Newbury	0.716	279	Mexborough	0.249
3	Didcot	0.710	278	Barnsley	0.257
4	Welwyn	0.709	277	Pembroke	0.275
5	Aldershot & Farnborough	0.706	276	Cardigan	0.281
6	Cambridge	0.705	275	Stranraer	0.282
7	Huntingdon	0.705	274	Doncaster	0.293
8	Hertford & Ware	0.705	273	St Helens	0.298
9	Basingstoke	0.703	272	Mansfield	0.298
10	Woking & Weybridge	0.690	271	Neath	0.298
11	Crawley	0.690	270	Liverpool	0.302
12	Andover	0.682	269	Smethwick	0.307
13	Bracknell	0.682	268	Consett	0.308
14	Reading	0.679	267	Arbroath	0.310
15	Guildford	0.668	266	Ffestiniog	0.310

Keynes (Bucks.) and Newbury (Berks.) head the list of LLMAs with the highest scores on this index, but close behind them are Didcot (Oxon.), Welwyn (Herts.), Aldershot & Farnborough (Hants.), Cambridge, Huntingdon (Cambs.), Hertford & Ware (Herts.) and Basingstoke (Hants.), all with scores within the range 0.703–0.710 (Table 3.10). Inspection of the map of LLMAs scoring more than the national median (Figure 3.6(a)) not only confirms the southern domination of the highest-scoring LLMAs, but also reveals that the top 35 places (those above 0.610) fall into a single crescent-shaped zone extending round the western side of London from places like Crawley (W. Sussex), Chichester (W. Sussex) and Winchester (Hants.) in the south to Cambridge, Newmarket and Thetford in the north.

The list of weakest LLMAs is headed by Holyhead (Gwynedd), which is separated by a substantial gap from Mexborough (S. Yorks.) and Barnsley (S. Yorks.), with Pembroke (Dyfed), Cardigan (Dyfed), and Stranraer (Dumfries & Galloway) making up the next lowest group, all below 0.285 (Table 3.10). The 35 lowest scoring LLMAs shown in Figure 3.6(b) are scattered geographically, unlike the best-performing places of Figure 3.6(a), but most can be classified into one of four

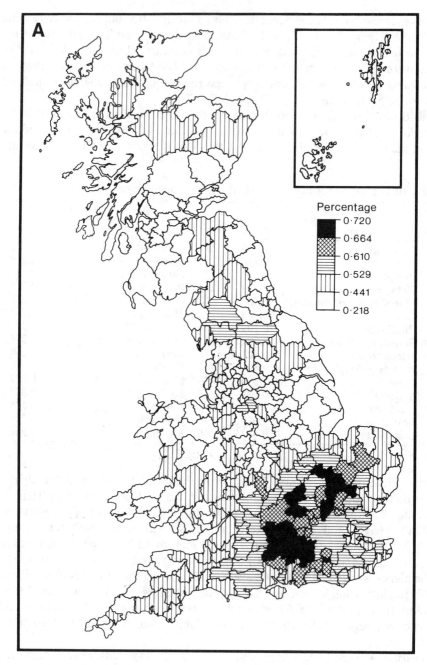

Figure 3.6   The Amalgamated Index: (a) Above median

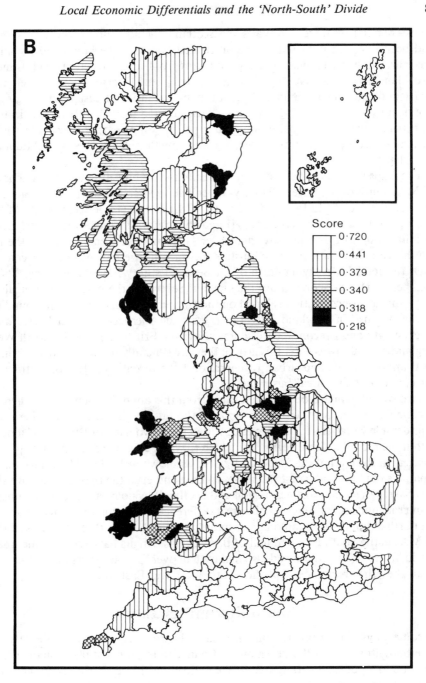

Figure 3.6 (cont.): (b) Below median

types – remoter rural areas in Wales and Scotland, including some whose prosperity had been temporarily lifted by the oil-related boom of the later 1970s; smaller specialized industrial towns suffering long-term problems of structural readjustment like Llanelli (Dyfed), Neath (W. Glam.), St Helens (Merseyside), Consett and Hartlepool (north-east England); coal-mining localities in east Durham, South Yorkshire and north Nottinghamshire, which suffered from further rationalization and strike action in the coal-mining industry; and all or parts of large cities with particular problems such as Liverpool and Smethwick (in the West Midlands conurbation).

The maps of the Amalgamated Index reveal the striking absence of low-scoring LLMAs south of the Severn Estuary–Lincolnshire line, and the predominance of these further north. In fact, only 16 of the 114 LLMAs (14 per cent) south of the line lie below the median score of 0.441 and all these are characterized by peripheral location and most by relatively small size. Their main concentration is in the far South West, but there are also clusters in Lincolnshire and on the east coast.

Of the 166 LLMAs lying north of the Severn Estuary-Lincolnshire line, 32 (or 19.3 per cent) have scores above the median. Several of these lie close to the line, and a further concentration is based on the northern Pennines and its surrounding market towns. In Scotland only Inverness and Aberdeen, and in Wales only Aberystwyth and Brecon, record scores above the British median. In North West England several towns enter this group; they are generally the smaller towns which road improvements and urban regeneration have recently made more attractive for commuters and local businesses.

Two overall conclusions can be drawn from this analysis, namely that there is a major contrast between north and south, but at the same time there are considerable variations in performance within these two parts of Britain and indeed within the more localized regions of which they are comprised. Both these points are clear at the level of the Standard Region, as shown in Table 3.11. A huge range separates the best and worst in the South East and even the two regions with the narrowest range (the Northern region and Scotland) by no means present an image of internal uniformity. Even so, the great differences in general performance across the north-south divide should not be under-estimated. Over three-quarters of the LLMAs in the South East and half of those in East Anglia have scores higher than any in Wales and Scotland and also higher than over three-quarters of the LLMAs in all the other regions except the South West and East Midlands.

Continuity and change

In some ways it is unfair to compare places in the north and south directly. It is perhaps little wonder that, even on the Change Index, the best places in the north show up in a poor light compared to the majority of places in the south, because many of the latter have a strong post-war foundation of investment and growth on which to build. It is much easier for a place to maintain a record of growth than to reverse an earlier trend of decline. In this section, therefore, each LLMA's recent performance is examined within its own terms of reference by comparing its Change Index with its Static Index.

Table 3.11   Range of Amalgamated Index scores, by Standard Region

Region (no. of LLMAs)	Median score	Highest LLMA		Lowest LLMA	
		Name	Rank	Name	Rank
South East (59)	0.613	Milton Keynes	1	Deal	241
East Anglia (14)	0.522	Cambridge	6	Lowestoft	213
South West (30)	0.501	Salisbury	37	Redruth & Camborne	261
East Midlands (23)	0.461	Northampton	42	Mansfield	272
West Midlands (23)	0.433	Stratford-upon-Avon	32	Smethwick	269
North West (29)	0.426	Macclesfield	47	St Helens	273
Yorkshire & Humb. (22)	0.398	Northallerton & Richmond	51	Mexborough	279
Northern (19)	0.391	Kendal	60	Consett	268
Scotland (34)	0.377	Hawick	89	Stranraer	275
Wales (27)	0.375	Aberystwyth	103	Holyhead	280

Note
Regions are ranked according to their median LLMA score.

Correlation of the two Indices against each other for the 280 LLMAs yields a coefficient (*r*) of 0.66. The positive sign of the correlation is as would be expected from the earlier descriptions of the Static and Change Indices, with places scoring higher on the one generally having high scores on the other. Of course, it could be argued that the two are directly related because the Static Index measures the situation at the end of the period on which the Change Index has been calibrated, but in fact the three-to-four-year period covered by the change indicators cannot be responsible for more than a relatively-small proportion of the variation in the Static Index across the country. In any case, in this section our primary interest is in those places that have a Change Index that is significantly out of line with their Static Index, and the relatively-modest level of correlation suggests that a considerable number of places fall into this category.

Table 3.12 gives fuller information about the distribution of the Static and Change Indices against each other, with LLMAs ranked into eight equal-sized

Table 3.12 Cross-tabulation of LLMAs by scores on Static and Change Indices

Position on Change Index by octile	Position on Static Index by octile								Row total
	Highest	2	3	4	5	6	7	Lowest	
Highest	17	9	2	6	0	1	0	0	35
2	11	8	8	3	3	1	1	0	35
3	5	8	9	4	7	0	1	1	35
4	2	6	6	4	3	4	5	5	35
5	0	3	4	4	6	11	4	3	35
6	0	0	4	4	5	7	6	9	35
7	0	0	2	6	7	6	7	7	35
Lowest	0	1	0	4	4	5	11	10	35
Column total	35	35	35	35	35	35	35	35	280

groups on both scores. If there had been a perfect relationship between the two rankings, so that each LLMA held the same rank for its Change Index as on its Static Index, the table would merely contain a diagonal line running from top left (high on both scores) to bottom right (low on both scores), with 35 cases in each of the eight cells. In fact, only 68 LLMAs fall in the same octile on both scores. We will ignore small shifts in rank, including movements between adjacent octiles. Thus, a total of 113 LLMAs (two in five) have their Change Index in a cell in Table 3.9 that is two or more octiles removed from its position on the Static Index, while there are 53 (almost one in five) with a difference of three or more octiles, and 13 with one of four or more.

The places on or close to the diagonal line can be considered to be fuelling the geographical divides that exist in Britain. Seventeen LLMAs crowd into the cell in the top-left corner that represents the brightest places on both scores. They all lie to the south of the Severn–Lincolnshire line, particularly to the west of London (for example, Reading and Newbury (Berks.), Basingstoke and Andover (Hants.) Salisbury (Wilts.), Didcot and Oxford (Oxon.), but also located to the south and south-west of London (Crawley and Haywards Heath (Sussex) and Guildford

(Surrey)), to the north-west (Aylesbury (Bucks.) and St Albans (Herts.)) and to the north-east (Hertford & Ware and Letchworth (Herts.) and Cambridge and Huntingdon (Cambs.)). These are all highly-privileged areas in terms of their economic situation in the mid-1980s and they have made great strides during the first half of the decade.

The other cells in the top row of Table 3.12 contain places that have grown similarly rapidly in the 1980s, but do not command – as yet – such high status in terms of labour-market characteristics. In this sense, they can be treated as examples of the emerging centres of economic strength. The nine in the second octile of the Static Index include areas that have benefited in the past from New or Expanded Town Status (e.g. Milton Keynes (Bucks.) and Swindon (Wilts.)), places on the rapidly-growing M11 corridor (e.g. Bishops Stortford, Newmarket, Thetford) and some older-established centres like Stratford-upon-Avon (War.), Stroud (Glos.) and Chichester & Bognor (W. Sussex). Amongst other LLMAs occupying a significantly-higher rank on the Change than on the Static Index are Corby and Kettering (Northants), Tiverton (Devon) and Kings Lynn (Norfolk), Wisbech and Peterborough (Cambs.).

The places further down the first column under the top-left cell in Table 3.12 can be considered to be the more mature of the economically-privileged places in Britain. These include several of the earlier New Towns (Bracknell (Berks.), Harlow (Essex) and Hemel Hempstead, Stevenage and Welwyn (Herts.)), as well as several dormitory towns on the fringes of London now hemmed in by green-belt restrictions (including Watford (Herts.) and Reigate & Redhill (Surrey)), together with places somewhat further afield (such as Winchester (Hants.) and Horsham (W. Sussex)). Impressively, it also includes London, which – despite the undoubted problems faced by some of its localities – has proved extremely dynamic for its size.

The over-riding geographical feature behind this description, of the places ranking highest on either Index, is the domination by the south. Of all the places in the first column and first row, only two lie north of the Severn–Lincolnshire line: Stratford-upon-Avon, on the north-south boundary, and Northallerton & Richmond. A number of places have not been growing as rapidly as their mid-1980s standing would suggest, so to that extent they could be seen as contributing to a narrowing of the north-south divide. On the other hand, the rates of change recorded by some prosperous places have to some extent been pulled down by their high initial bases. It is evident from the identity of the most dynamic places that the zone of most rapid growth is extending beyond the traditional 'Home Counties' round London to affect some once relatively-inaccessible places in Norfolk and Lincolnshire to the north and Wiltshire and Devon in the west, but so far the outcome of this trend is to sharpen up the north-south divide rather than to blur it.

If these places represent the geography of 'boom' in Britain, then LLMAs in the bottom row of Table 3.12 should be considered as representatives of Britain in 'gloom', certainly the ten places in the bottom-right cell. The latter comprise Liverpool and St Helens (Merseyside), Stranraer (Dumfries & Galloway), Holyhead (Gwynedd), Pembroke (Dyfed), Neath (W. Glam.), Barnsley, Mexborough and Doncaster (S. Yorks.) and Mansfield (Notts.) – all depressed cities, remoter rural areas or coal-mining areas.

Although the bottom quadrant of Table 3.12 is dominated by places in the north, this is not to say there are no positive signs here. In all, 25 of the 35 LLMAs with the lowest economic standing on the Static Index were ranked higher than this on the Change Index, with six displaying scores above the national median.

Summary and concluding comments

This chapter has sought to describe the geography of growth and decline in Britain in the mid-1980s. It has reported on the geographical patterns portrayed for Britain's 280 Local Labour Market Areas by ten key variables. Five of these constitute the latest available data for measuring various aspects of the strength of the local economy for these places, and by inference the level of economic opportunity available to their residents in the mid-1980s; while the other five relate to the dynamism and buoyancy of these places in the preceding three or four years. Since each variable presents a somewhat different picture owing to the multi-faceted nature of local economic conditions and change, we collapsed the information into three synthetic measures termed the Static, Change and Amalgamated Indices.

The most striking result that continually emerges from these analyses is the great extent of the north-south divide. All the 35 highest-scoring places on the Amalgamated Index, headed by Milton Keynes (Bucks.) and Newbury (Berks.), have been found to lie on or south of a line between the Severn Estuary and Lincolnshire and to form a continuous crescent around London from Crawley, Chichester and Winchester in the south to Cambridge, Newmarket and Thetford in the north. Over the rest of the country, the poor performance of the principal industrial concentrations, noted in previous studies, remains evident, though some improvement appears to have taken place in the West Midlands, Clydeside and north-east England. By contrast, the mid-1980s have seen a sharp deterioration in the South Yorkshire area and in many of the more remote rural areas in Wales and western Scotland. These findings confirm the evidence of those reports that have identified 'the London factor' as the dominant force leading Britain's economic recovery; they also suggest that events in the rest of the country have been influenced by the maturing of the North Sea oil boom, the downturn in agricultural prosperity and the further rationalization of – and strike action in – the coal-mining industry.

The patterns conveyed separately by the Static and Change Indices both reinforce this impression in large measure. In particular, the Static Index highlights a massive block of LLMAs extending across central-southern England from London and the Home Counties in the east westwards towards Wiltshire and Gloucestershire. Here lie Britain's strongest combinations of low unemployment, high labour-force participation rates, specialization in advanced industries and high-salary employment and expensive housing. The main zone of most-rapid economic growth, as measured by changes in population, employment, unemployment and house prices, excludes London itself and most of the adjacent areas traditionally dominated by London in the south-eastern corner of England. Instead, it stretches in a broad crescent round the western and northern sides of London, similar to that shown by the Amalgamated Index but stretching further northwards, particularly into East Anglia and the southern margins of the East Midlands. This northward extension, however, does nothing to redress the north-south divide, but rather makes even clearer the sharp break between the two along the line between the Severn Estuary and Lincolnshire.

This overall conclusion would seem to be at variance with some recent studies and statements that have attempted to portray the situation of the north and its future prospects in a better light (e.g. Breheny, Hall and Hart, 1987; McLoughlin, 1987; Wilsher and Cassidy, 1987). Our analyses, however, do not rule out the existence of brighter spots north of the Severn Estuary–Lincolnshire line. Indeed, they demonstrate the wide range of variation in scores on all three indices that exists not only north of this line but also south of it, and not only at this broad two-region level but also within each of the ten Standard Regions. By cross-tabulating rankings on the Static and Change Indices we have shown that a number of the places with the lowest economic standing in the mid-1980s – mostly places in the north – have actually performed quite strongly over the last few years. Equally, several places that rank among the most prosperous in Britain according to the available data have apparently seen relatively sluggish growth since 1981.

Nevertheless, the main weight of the evidence points to the north-south divide as the primary dimension in variations in economic health across Britain at the LLMA scale, with a general tendency in the 1980s for a widening of this gap. The analyses of differential performance by LLMA size groups bear witness to the legacy of the urban-rural shifts that were so powerful in the 1970s. They also reveal that 'counter-urban' tendencies were still being felt in terms of population and employment change in the first half of the 1980s. However, the scale of the urban-rural shift in the 1980s is completely overwhelmed by the size of the contrasts between north and south. Moreover, the 'Northern Lights' identified by Breheny, Hall and Hart (1987), and other similarly-fortunate places identified in this chapter, tend to be drawn from amongst the smaller places in this part of Britain and they do not compare favourably with the size, degree of concentration or absolute level of economic dynamism of the growth leaders in the south. More important still is the fact that their achievements in the 1980s pale considerably when set against the massive size of the principal cities in the north and against the scale of their problems. In reality, many of these more fortunate northern places have been constrained in their recent development, not merely by shortages of indigenous and inward investment but also by the availability of suitable sites and labour. Nor does it make the outlook more promising to find that some of the more remote rural areas outside southern England, especially in Wales and Scotland, now look decidedly less healthy in economic terms than a few years ago. Their contribution to solving the broader regional problems of the north is likely to be only small.

The analyses presented in this chapter have not aimed to rank places according to their future economic potential, but rather to measure recent performance and current standing. The results have been based on historical data relating to the resolution of local economies in terms of such indicators as employment change and house prices, rather than on the levels of investment and business development that have produced these effects, or on the aspects of the local business environment such as quality of local services or availability of sites and premises. Moreoever, we have been concerned with the performance of the local economy rather than any wider concept of living standards for individuals. While the results provide an indication of the level of job opportunities for residents, they say very little about the cost of living in financial terms or about the quality of life in terms of ease of access to attractive facilities for education, shopping, recreation and so on, on which many northern places score favourably (Breheny, Hall and Hart, 1987; Rogerson, Findlay and Morris, 1988). It remains to be seen whether the recent widening of the gap in living costs for residents (Reward Regional Surveys, 1987) and in operating costs for industrialists and business people (Hillier Parker, 1987a, 1987b) will provoke a strong self-correcting reaction. By encouraging a significant northward movement of business investment beyond the outer reaches of the metropolis, this would help towards a return to greater regional balance in the longer term.

Acknowledgements

This chapter is based on a report entitled *Local Prosperity and the North-South Divide: Winners and Losers in 1980s Britain*, by Tony Champion and Anne Green, January 1988 (see references). The authors are grateful for the help they received in obtaining data. The data on employment and unemployment were derived with the help of Alan Townsend from the Department of Employment's National On-line Manpower Information System, programmed by Robert Nelson and Peter Dodds, of the Durham University Geography Department. These data are Crown copyright. The data on economic activity rates was extracted from aggregations of 1981 Population Census data to the CURDS Functional Regions framework, originally set up by Stan Openshaw and David Owen. The data on population change were calculated from local-area population updates provided by CACI Analysis and made available by Keith Dugmore and Roger Bracewell. The data on house prices were calculated from data tapes supplied by Barry Bissett, Housing Statistics Manager of the Nationwide Anglia Building Society, and processed by David Owen. The methodology for deriving the indices was originally developed by Pam Lewis, then at the Department of Economics, University College of North Wales, Bangor. The maps and diagrams were initially prepared by the authors using GIMMS and GHOST. The authors are also very grateful to Marilyn Champion who undertook the typing.

4

THE OWNER-OCCUPIED HOUSING MARKET IN BRITAIN : A NORTH-SOUTH DIVIDE?

Chris Hamnett

Introduction

In 1982 Thorns published an important paper on the links between industrial restructuring and changes in the labour and property markets in Britain. He argued that the older industrial regions of the Midlands and the north were characterized *both* by high levels of job losses and unemployment compared to the more prosperous areas of the South East, *and* by a depressed owner-occupied housing market in which prices and rates of house-price inflation were much lower than in the South East (prices might actually be falling). He argued that the property market was reinforcing and reflecting labour-market conditions in north and south and that, as a result, a process of cumulative and progressive regional disadvantage was operating. This was opening up a growing gap between the affluent and depressed regions, which was simultaneously providing jobs and equity accumulation in the south and locking the residents of the depressed regions into declining labour and housing markets in which they were effectively trapped. As he put it (p. 759):

> The changes... which have occurred since the early 1960s and have led to a considerable restructuring of the labour and property markets, have produced considerable wealth transfers. These transfers have been in the same direction and have given rise to a firmly entrenched 'middle class' group, increasingly regionally concentrated in the South East, regional centres, and new towns.

Thorns was the first commentator to attempt systematically to link changes in both labour and owner-occupied housing markets to an analysis of regional disadvantage and his paper represents a major conceptual advance. The weakness of his argument lay in the limited empirical evidence he provided to support his claim that the owner-occupied market in the north was static or declining during the 1970s. As shown elsewhere (Hamnett, 1983, 1984), analysis of the period 1969–81 provides no evidence for this. But the rapid house-price inflation in London and the South East, and the very limited inflation in the northern regions since

1983, have led to considerable media attention regarding the existence of marked regional differences in average house prices and house-price inflation in Britain. The main focus of interest has been on the growing house-price differential between the South East and the rest of the country and its consequences for access to, and mobility within, the owner-occupied market in Britain. It has been suggested that the differences in regional rates of house-price inflation are likely to prove permanent and, therefore, that the house-price gap will widen further.

Some of the media comment seems to reflect metropolitan satisfaction on the part of the authors at the rapid increase of London house prices and the increase in their owners' equity, and perhaps even a degree of concealed pleasure at the plight of the hapless northern owners: it has been suggested by more concerned commentators that these differences have had a number of adverse consequences. These can be briefly listed as follows:

1. The house-price gap has created a dual owner-occupied housing market between north and south, paralleling the differences in regional employment, incomes and prosperity and reinforcing the social and geographical division of Britain into 'Two Nations' (Penycate, 1987; Foley, 1987).
2. The growing regional house-price gap inhibits labour mobility from areas of high unemployment in the north to areas of lower unemployment in the south because of the huge difference in cost, size and quality of housing available for a given price in the south compared to the north (Champion, Green and Owen, 1987; Healey, 1987b; Parsons, 1987). These problems are said to have been compounded by the difficulties of gaining access to the council sector and the virtual disappearance of affordable private-rented accommodation (Minford, Peel and Ashton, 1987). It has also been argued (Hogarth, 1987) that these problems have led to the growth of long-distance weekly commuting from north to south by those with a job in the south but who cannot afford to live there.
3. High house prices in the South East have inflated the cost of living and intensified the difficulties of access to housing in the region, either squeezing out lower-income, potential buyers or increasing housing costs or both. This has led to difficulties in staffing services such as education (*The Times Educational Supplement*, 1987) and transport, to shortages of some types of skilled labour (Incomes Data Services, 1988) and have forced employers to increase cost-of-living allowances (*The Independent*, 1987) and to offer special financial packages to job applicants from elsewhere.
4. Rapid house-price inflation in the South East has generated rapid equity-accumulation for existing owners, has increased the inequalities in wealth ownership, and allowed migrants from London to outbid local residents in other areas for scarce housing.

This chapter examines some of these issues, but first it is necessary to examine critically the evidence for the emergence of a permanent and widening north-south divide in house prices and house-price inflation. It will be argued that while house prices have risen far faster since 1983 in the south than in the north, it is necessary to set these changes in a longer-term context to understand the dynamics of regional house prices and inflation.

The house-price gap: the recent evidence

There is strong evidence that house-price inflation has been far higher in London and the South East than elsewhere in Britain during the mid-1980s. The index of house prices published by the Halifax Building Society reveals that the average price of houses mortgaged to the society in London in the third quarter of 1987 was £75,483 – an increase of 23 per cent on the third quarter of 1986. In the South East, the average price was £66,882 – an increase of 23.5 per cent over the year. In the northern region, on the other hand, the average house price in the third quarter of 1987 was just £30,074 – an increase of 6.6 per cent over the year. In Yorkshire & Humberside, average prices in the third quarter of 1987 were £30,074, an increase of 7.9 per cent over the year. On the basis of these figures, average house prices in London were some 2.5 times greater than those in the north.

Similar figures for the second quarter of 1987 from the Nationwide Building Society show average house prices in London of £73,360 – 30 per cent greater than a year earlier, compared to £28,930 in the North – a 4 per cent increase over the year and a gap of 2.5 times. Also, the 5 per cent joint Building Societies Association and Department of Environment (BSA/DoE) sample of mortgage completions indicate an average house price of £63,626 in London in the second quarter of 1987, an increase of 19.5 per cent over the second quarter of 1986, compared to an average of £27,016 in the North, an increase of 11 per cent over the year and a gap of 2.4 times.

There is, of course, no such thing as the average house. The average house-price figures produced by both sources are statistical artefacts that aggregate houses and flats of very different types and sizes, the precise mix of which changes over time. But the same gap manifests itself when like is compared with like. Halifax figures for the third quarter of 1987 revealed that the average price of semi-detached houses in London was about £92,000 compared to £29,000 in Yorkshire & Humberside, £30,450 in the North and £31,800 in the North West. Similar differences are found for other house types.

The existence of these differences does not, of course, mean that the gap between north and south is a completely uniform one. There are some northern towns and cities such as Harrogate, York, Stockport, Glasgow, Edinburgh and Aberdeen where house prices are relatively high, just as there are some more peripheral parts of the South East such as Southampton, Colchester and Dover, where prices are below the regional average. But Halifax data for the third quarter of 1987 show that average prices in lower-price towns in the South East are still generally higher than average prices on the high-priced northern cities. Edinburgh is the only northern city where prices approach those of the South East.

This raises the related question of whether the house-price gap is best conceived in terms of London and the South East, on the one hand, and the rest of the country on the other, or between north and south more generally. It will be argued that London and the South East have consistently been the highest-priced regions in Britain, and that there has long been a big gap between London and the South East and the rest of the country. The South West and East Anglia are now firmly established as the third and fourth highest house-price areas in the UK, and are currently experiencing rapid price-inflation as a result a 'ripple effect' from South East prices and displaced demand. However, average prices in the two regions are 33 to 50 per cent less than i n London, and London and the South East have consistently led in each of the three rounds of house-price inflation in Britain since 1970. The concentration of high house prices in London and the South East in 1987 is clearly seen in Figure 4.1. Figure 4.1(a) uses Nationwide mean house-price data aggregated into local labour-market areas by Champion, Green and Owen (1987) and Figure 4.1(b) is based on Halifax data on the average prices of semi-detached houses by county.

The importance of cyclical variations in house-price inflation

It is clear from the figures given above that the house-price gap between the highest- and lowest-priced regions grew rapidly in 1986–7, and is currently of considerable proportions. But can we conclude from this, as many observers have done, that the gap between the 'two nations' in British house prices has grown steadily wider over time and will continue to increase?

While it is impossible to predict the future with any accuracy, it is suggested that most commentators have not paid sufficient attention to the existence of past trends and have generalized on the basis of trends over the last three years. In particular, analysis of the BSA/DoE 5 per cent sample of mortgage completion data over the 18-year period 1969–86 shows the existence of marked cyclical variations in rates of regional house-price inflation, and in the size of the gap between the high- and low-priced regions. Whereas London and the South East have led each of the three major bursts of house-price inflation since 1969, they have also been the first to slow down. Conversely, house-price inflation tends to continue in the lower house-price regions long after it has stopped or slowed in London and the South East.

Both the regional rates of price inflation and the size of the house-price gap vary considerably depending on the period taken for calculation. Depending on the stages of the cycle being compared, it is possible to conclude that the size of the house-price gap between high- and low-priced regions was increasing or decreasing. Thus, an official review concluded that 'In all regions, average prices in 1976 as percentage of Greater London prices were several percentage points higher than in 1969 thus indicating a general *narrowing of the gap* between regional and London prices over the period (Royal Commission on the Distribution of Income and Wealth, 1977, p.148, *emphasis added*). This conclusion was correct for the period 1969–76, just as it is correct to conclude on the basis of data for the past few years that the size of the gap is increasing. But it is necessary to look at the structure of change over the longer term to obtain a comprehensive picture. It is accepted that the omission of bank mortgage lending limits the analysis, particularly after 1981, and probably understates house prices in London and the South East. However, in the absence of regional data on the price of houses mortgaged by the banks, the BSA/DoE sample is the only source of reliable comparative long-term data.

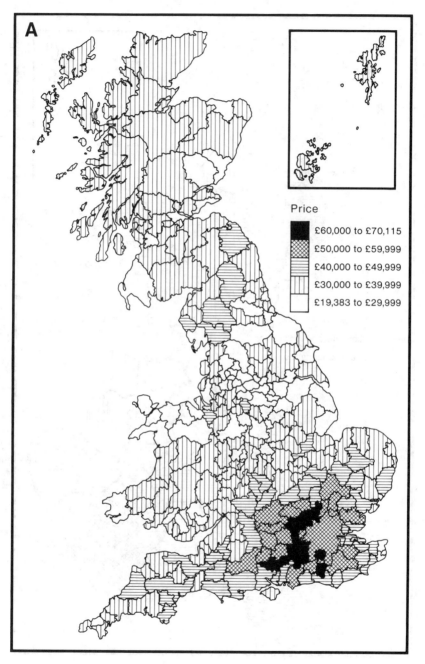

Figure 4.1   Mean house prices: (a) By LLMAs, 1985

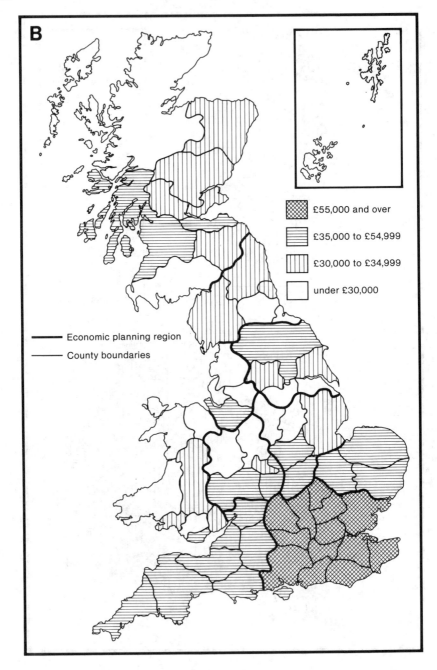

Figure 4.1   (cont.): (b) Mean price of semi–detached houses by counties, 1987

Regional variations in house prices, 1969–86

One way of comparing changes in regional house prices over time is by calculating individual regional prices as a percentage of the national average for each year and plotting the results. This is done in Figure 4.2, which shows the average price on completion of houses mortgaged to building societies in comparison to the

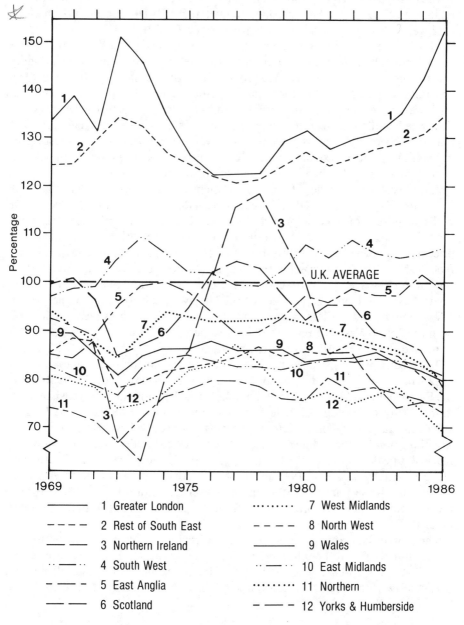

Figure 4.2   Regional house prices as a percentage of the UK average, 1969–86

national average for each of the 18 years 1969–86. This shows the marked and persistent differences between the regions. At the top end, average house prices in London and, to a lesser extent, the South East, have consistently run 25 to 50 per cent higher than the national average. The South West has run about 5 per cent above and East Anglia 5–10 per cent below the national average, though both have exhibited a general upwards trend since 1978. At the bottom end, the Northern region and Yorkshire & Humberside, stand at about 70–80 per cent of the national average, with a general downwards trend since 1977.

This pattern of regional differentials remained basically stable over the period. There were only limited fluctuations in the rank order of different regions. London was the highest region in every year followed by the South East, the South West and East Anglia, while the North and Yorkshire & Humberside consistently had the lowest prices. The major exception to this pattern was Northern Ireland, which fluctuated wildly from eighth-ranked region in 1969 to the lowest region in 1973, only to rise rapidly to third place in 1977–9 and to fall back to the lowest region in 1984. The principal explanation for these differences is to be found in the changes in building-society lending practices in the province.

Although the rank order of regional house prices has remained relatively stable over time, Figure 4.2 shows that there have been distinct and consistent fluctuations in the magnitude of regional price differentials. Four points particularly stand out. First, it is clear that the gap between London and the South East and the lower-price regions opened up sharply during the first major bout of house-price inflation from 1970 to 1973. Average house prices in London rose from just over 130 per cent of the UK average in 1971 to 150 per cent in 1972 and average prices in the South East rose from 120 per cent of the UK average in 1970 to 135 per cent in 1972. Similar, though less marked and slightly later, increases were recorded in both the South West and East Anglia in this period. All the other regions showed a marked decline relative to the UK average.

The second point to stress is that the size of the gap narrowed considerably from 1972 to 1977–8. During this period, average prices in London, the South East, the South West and East Anglia all fell relative to the national average while prices in the low-priced regions all rose relative to the national average. By 1977–8 the size of the gap had fallen back to what it was prior to the first house-price boom. The third point is that while average house prices in London and the South East reached a peak relative to the UK average in 1972, and prices in the South West and East Anglia peaked in 1973 and 1974 respectively, prices in the other regions continued to rise relative to the national average until 1976–7. Relative price movements in these regions were sufficiently 'lagged' as to be partly counter-cyclical.

The final point is that the magnitude of the regional price gap between the four southern regions and the other regions increased in the second house-price boom of 1977–9, and closed slightly in 1980–1 when house-price inflation fell sharply, particularly in the four southern regions. Since then it has continued to widen.

Changes in regional house prices relative to Greater London

Given the wide variation in regional house prices and rates of inflation, UK averages are clearly a rather artificial construct. And because the current debate is focused on the magnitude of the gap between London and the South East and the northern regions, Figure 4.3 compares regional price changes to prices in London for each year between 1969 and 1986. Two features in particular stand out: first, the consistent gap between London and the South East and the rest of the country; and, second, the marked cyclical variations in regional house prices relative to London prices. Average house prices in most regions fell sharply relative to prices

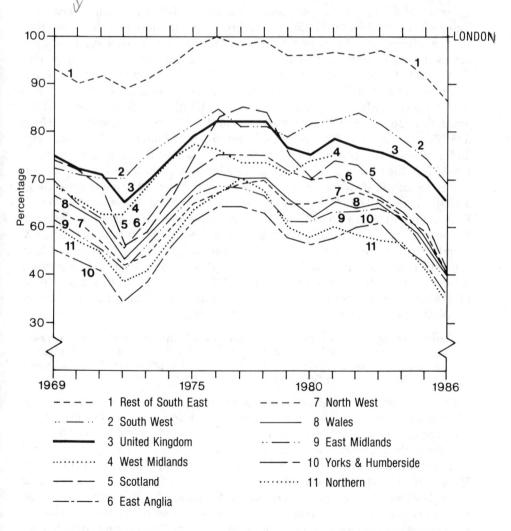

– – – –	1 Rest of South East	– – – –	7 North West
·· — ··	2 South West	———	8 Wales
———	3 United Kingdom	·· — ··	9 East Midlands
··········	4 West Midlands	—— –	10 Yorks & Humberside
— —	5 Scotland	··········	11 Northern
—·—·—	6 East Anglia		

Figure 4.3   Regional house prices as a percentage of London's, 1969–86

in London from 1969 to 1972 when the regional house-price gap reached a maximum. Average regional house prices then rose consistently from 1972 to 1976 relative to London prices, and from 1976 to 1978 the regional house-price gap was at its smallest. The gap then widened from 1978 to 1980, narrowed slightly from 1980 to 1982–3 and has continued to widen from 1983 to 1987. It is clear that although the regional house-price gap is a continuing phenomenon, the *size* of the gap has been highly cyclical depending on the rate of inflation in the different regions.

Regional variations in house-price inflation, 1970–86

The differences in regional price movements relative to the national average are a product of differential rates of regional house-price inflation. It can be seen from Table 4.1, which shows the individual regions' rates of house-price inflation, that the four highest-priced regions effectively led the process of house-price inflation during the 1970s. They were the first to rise, they rose most sharply and they were the first to fall back. Thus, the burst of house-price inflation that occurred in 1971–2 was most marked in Greater London, where prices increased 50 per cent in one year, followed by East Anglia (41 per cent), the South West (40 per cent) and the South East (36 per cent). The Northern region, Yorkshire & Humberside, the East and West Midlands and Wales all experienced rates of inflation between 21 and 28 per cent whilst the North West and Scotland had rates of just over 15 per cent. By 1972–3, the rate of inflation had declined to just over 30 per cent in London and the South East, while all the other regions experienced rates of between 37 and 46 per cent. By 1973–4 inflation had virtually ceased in London, the South East and South West (3, 6 and 7 per cent respectively) while inflation in the other regions varied from 12 per cent in East Anglia to 17 per cent in Yorkshire & Humberside. These differentials persisted through 1975 and 1976 as the four southern regions all marked time while the other regions caught up. A similar, if less marked, pattern emerged in the late 1970s house-price boom and the slump of 1980–2. This relationship has also been observed by the Building Societies Association (1981 p.5):

> During these periods in which prices are rising rapidly throughout the country, prices in the Southern regions have tended to increase faster than the national average; conversely, in times when prices nationally are rising slowly, prices in the Northern regions tend to 'catch up', rising more rapidly than the national average.

One consequence of these cyclical variations in regional house prices is that rates of regional house-price inflation differ considerably depending on the time periods used for calculation. Table 4.1 shows that if we take the period 1969–86 (when the size of the regional house-price gap was at its greatest) the rates of regional house-price inflation range from 760 per cent in London, 732 per cent in the South West, and 700 and 704 per cent in East Anglia and the South East to 555 per cent in the Northern region and 492 per cent in Scotland. But if we take the period 1969–81 (when the regional house-price gap was at its smallest), the variations in rates of regional house-price inflation were much smaller, ranging from 464 per cent in the South West, 459 per cent in Yorkshire & Humberside to 417 per cent in the South East, 396 per cent in London and 383 per cent in Wales. If we take the period 1969–84, the rate of house-price inflation averaged 527 per cent for the UK as a whole. The regional rates varied from 455 per cent in Scotland and 475 per cent in Wales and the West Midlands to 558 per cent in East Anglia, and 581 per cent in the South West. The rates in London (535 per cent) and the South East (545 per cent) were little above the national average. The overall rate of house-price inflation in London and the South East was not consistently higher than in the northern regions from 1969–84. It varies depending on the stage in the cycle of regional variations.

There are parallels with the race between the tortoise and the hare. The gap between the high and the low house-price regions widens or narrows depending on the stage in the race. The gap was greatest in both 1971–3 and 1979–80 when the average price in London was double the average price in the North and Yorkshire & Humberside. In 1976–7 the gap was only 55–60 per cent but it has been rising from 1981 and today it is 120 per cent. The difference is that in the house-price race the tortoise never overtakes the hare. But, until 1984 at least, the hare has not continued to gain on the tortoise. On the contrary, the long-term gap between the two remained broadly constant. Thorns' theory of the cumulative and progressive process of regional inequality in the owner-occupied housing market, paralleling growing economic inequalities, can thus be seen to be empirically incorrect over the period from 1969–83. But from 1983 to 1987 the evidence does seem to support Thorns' interpretation.

A permanent widening of the gap?

The crucial question is whether the gap will continue to widen, whether it will stabilize at its current level, or whether it will narrow once again as it has done in the past. At the heart of this question is a debate about the effects on the owner-occupied housing market of the marked changes that have occurred in the geographical structure of British economic activity since 1979. Champion, Green and Owen (1988) have shown that there is a strong positive relationship at the local labour-market level between house prices in 1985 and indicators of economic performance derived from the 1971 and 1981 censuses (but this link is cross-sectional and not the result of longitudinal analysis). The Henley Centre for Economic Forecasting (1988) argue that the main determinant of house prices is personal disposable income, and they suggest that, largely as a result of the mortgage lending to income multiplier, a rise of 1 per cent in real incomes is reflected in a 2.5 per cent increase in house prices. Regional differences in real income growth are therefore of major importance for house prices.

It can be argued, on the basis of the regional incidence of job loss and unemployment over the past few years, that house prices in the Northern regions (including the Midlands) will continue to remain depressed. The *BSA Bulletin of Information* for January, 1987, suggested that while long-term rates of house-price inflation have been very similar between regions, this pattern may now have come to an end. This would be the result of the growing importance of banking, finance

Table 4.1   Annual regional rates of house-price inflation, 1970–86

	Northern	Yorks. & Humber.	East Midlands	East Anglia	Greater London	South East
1969–70	6.1	5.8	4.6	5.0	11.1	7.4
1970–1	11.3	10.7	10.7	10.0	7.5	17.0
1971–2	23.3	21.3	28.0	41.5	50.2	36.1
1972–3	37.0	44.6	45.7	40.7	30.0	32.8
1973–4	13.9	17.4	12.2	11.6	2.8	5.9
1974–5	13.7	9.3	8.7	4.8	0.4	5.1
1975–6	8.9	10.3	6.6	2.8	4.3	6.0
1976–7	12.6	7.3	6.8	2.7	7.6	5.9
1977–8	10.8	12.8	12.7	14.7	14.4	14.9
1978–9	18.4	24.0	23.6	32.2	34.6	30.4
1979–80	14.7	17.9	19.5	23.5	20.1	20.9
1980–1	5.0	8.5	2.8	1.1	0.7	0.5
1969–81	401	459	413	436	396	417
1981–2	− 2.8	− 5.3	+ 0.1	− 1.3	− 0.1	− 1.0
1982–3	10.8	14.8	13.0	10.6	12.8	13.8
1983–4	11.4	7.1	10.7	9.5	13.0	10.6
1984–5	0.8	4.4	4.8	11.9	12.6	8.4
1985–6	6.8	8.8	9.5	8.6	20.2	15.0
1969–84	509	551	543	558	535	545
1969–86	555	639	637	700	760	704

and insurance in the economy and its concentration in the South East, the prosperity reportedly brought to the South East as a result of the M25 and the proposed Channel Tunnel, the permanently-lower level of unemployment in the South East compared to other regions, and resistance to new house building in the Green Belt. Foley (1986, p.3) reached similar conclusions:

> In previous cycles, prices in the rest of the country seem to have followed those in London and the South-East, suggesting that they may soon start to rise more rapidly. However, there is now more regional variation in economic performance than previously, so it is by no means certain that prices will respond in the typical fashion, though some pick up in prices outside the South-East corner does seem probable.

There can be no clear-cut answer to this question. However, on the basis of past evidence, rapid house-price inflation in London and the South East is a relatively short-lived phenomenon, lasting only two to three years and then quickly subsiding as house prices rise to levels at which increases can no longer be sustained by incomes, even if mortgage finance is available. At this point house prices stabilize, but as real incomes continue to rise, new inflationary pressures build up resulting in a further burst of house-price inflation. Halifax Building Society figures show that average prices in London rose by 22 per cent in 1986 and 26 per cent in 1987, and that by the end of 1987 they were 114 per cent higher than in 1983. It is questionable how far this rate of increase is sustainable. The Nationwide Building Society (1987) showed that the ratio of house prices to household income in London and the South East rose from 4.0 in 1983 to 5.25

Table 4.1 (cont.)

South West	West Midlands	North West	Wales	Scotland	Northern Ireland	UK
8.5	3.3	6.7	6.4	8.5	11.3	7.2
14.0	4.7	18.3	8.3	8.1	6.0	13.2
39.7	26.5	15.7	23.6	15.3	6.1	30.9
39.8	40.8	36.9	41.2	37.9	25.3	34.8
6.8	16.8	13.4	12.1	13.7	40.9	10.5
4.2	6.0	9.9	7.2	13.9	15.0	7.2
7.5	6.9	7.5	10.4	16.5	28.3	7.8
4.2	7.8	9.7	4.9	9.7	22.2	7.4
14.4	14.5	16.4	14.6	13.4	17.0	14.2
32.2	28.9	26.0	27.6	20.0	18.6	27.9
23.4	17.1	18.9	13.5	12.3	8.4	18.4
0.3	0.4	2.3	4.1	5.8	15.9	2.5
464	400	424	383	399	404	421
− 0.6	− 3.5	+ 1.1	− 2.4	− 2.1	+ 1.4	− 2.2
9.7	10.2	7.9	14.7	5.3	3.4	11.9
9.3	8.0	6.9	6.2	8.0	2.9	9.9
7.6	3.5	2.9	5.6	4.2	7.3	6.9
13.6	6.2	6.0	8.3	2.4	11.6	12.4
581	474	522	475	455	444	527
732	531	579	557	492	552	653

at the end of 1986. This exceeded the level reached in 1973 and it was highly unlikely that this could continue to increase for much longer as house prices became unaffordable. If the rate of house-price inflation slowed considerably in London and the South East, as seemed likely, the size of the regional house-price gap would stabilize. Whether it will shrink again is partly dependent on the rate of house-price inflation outside the South East. It is perhaps indicative of future trends that the Halifax Building Society (1987, p.1) noted of the fourth quarter of 1986 that

> There are signs that the rate of increase in Greater London and the South East has levelled off... . The most noticeable feature of the fourth quarter was a relative recovery in house prices in the East and West Midlands regions, East Anglia and the South West as house price inflation radiates out from the south east corner of the United Kingdom.

The Halifax report on the third quarter of 1987 confirmed these trends. It noted that the annual rate of house-price inflation in both East Anglia (26.7 per cent) and the South East (23.5 per cent) exceeded that of London (23.2 per cent), with the rate reaching 20.1 per cent in the South West, and 14.3 per cent in both the East and West Midlands. The report on the first quarter of 1988 provided further convincing evidence of this process. It showed that the annual rate of inflation in East Anglia (39 per cent), the South West (27.7 per cent) and the South East (26 per cent) was already substantially higher than in London (22.7 per cent), and that the rate of inflation in the West Midlands (22 per cent) was approaching that in London. Whether this is solely the result of a 'ripple effect' in the southern regions, as first-time buyers are priced out of London and find it easier and cheaper to commute in, or whether it heralds the onset of a generalized shift in house-price inflation away from London and the South East, in line with previous cyclical variations, remains to be seen. It may be that we are witnessing a shift from a division between London and the South East and the rest-of-the-country market to a wider division between a southern and a northern market. What is clear is that the size of the regional house-price gap between London and the South East and the rest of the Midlands and the south is already beginning to narrow.

Regional variations in accumulation and access

It is clear from the evidence discussed above that while house-price inflation during the period 1969–81 as a whole was broadly similar across different regions, over the last few years average house prices have risen much more rapidly in London and the South East than they have in the rest of the UK. This has had a number of important implications. The first is that existing owners in London and the South East have seen the market value of their houses increase much more rapidly than owners in other regions. According to Halifax lending data, the average price of houses in the UK rose by 60 per cent between 1983 and the fourth quarter of 1987. But prices in London rose by 115 per cent, by 98 per cent in the South East and by 96 per cent in East Anglia, against 26 per cent in the North, 30 per cent in Scotland, and 35 per cent in the North West and in Yorkshire & Humberside. Because prices in London and the South East were considerably higher to begin with, this has meant that absolute capital appreciation has been far greater in London and the South East.

There are at least two ways of measuring capital appreciation in the housing market. The first is to subtract the average mortgage amount from the average price paid by existing owners in different regions to give a measure of implied equity. Using data from the BSA/DoE 5 per cent sample for 1986, this yields an *average implied equity* of approximately £30,000 in London, £25,600 in the South East and £9–10,000 in the North, the North West and Yorkshire & Humberside.

But this method is indirect and does not take account of either 'equity removal' or 'equity injection' on purchase. It also aggregates all second-time and subsequent buyers, irrespective of when they first purchased. A second and more reliable method calculates the average implied capital appreciation for existing owners between any two dates, by simply subtracting the price of an average house in a region in one year from the average price in a later year. Using Halifax average house-price data by region for 1983 and the third quarter of 1987, the average implied capital appreciation for all owners who bought or already owned in 1983 ranged from £38,662 in London, £30,924 in the South East and £22,656 in the East to £7,291 in Yorkshire & Humberside and £6,069 in the Northern region.

The average implied capital appreciation in London over the last four years has been 6.4 times the level in the North and 5.3 times the level in Yorkshire & Humberside. This has major implications for regional variations in the ownership of personal wealth, and it has enabled many home owners in London and the South East to gain far more from house-price inflation than they would have been able to save out of earned income. If the same calculations are made on the basis of earlier years, the disparity is less but still significant. Taking 1976 as the base and using BSA/DoE data, average absolute capital appreciation in London was £48,060 – 2.8 times the £16,945 in Yorkshire & Humberside. Taking 1970 as the base, the figure for London was £56,774 – 2.4 times the £23,315 in Yorkshire. These differences are reflected in the average value of housing inheritance across the country.

The owner-occupied housing market has proved a major source of personal wealth accumulation for existing owners in London and the South East since 1983. But gains for existing owners have been achieved only at the expense of rapidly-rising house prices and housing costs for those trying to enter the owner-occupied housing market in the South East. Bramley and Paice (1987) have calculated that, even assuming that potential buyers can raise a 95 per cent mortgage on three times their income, one in three families living in the South East cannot afford to enter owner occupation. Detailed evidence from the Nationwide Building Society on regional variations in house-price/income ratios from 1975 to 1986 reveals the sharp disparities that exist. The ratio of house prices to the average household income of all working households (Figure 4.4 shows the considerable variations in house-price/income ratios between regions over time. In 1986, the average working household in London and the South East would have had to pay 5.2 their average

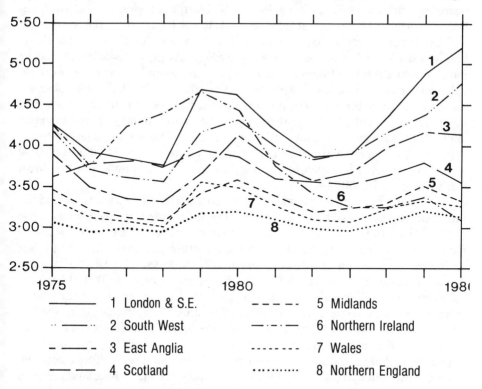

Figure 4.4   Ratio of house prices to incomes (a) All households, 1975–86 (first quarter); (b) Borrowers of the Nationwide Building Society, 1975–87 (first quarter) (Source: Nationwide Building Society, 1987)

income to purchase the average house, compared to between 3.0 and 3.5 in Northern England, Wales, Northern Ireland and the Midlands. While the ratio has remained stable in Northern England since 1975, it has increased from 4.0 to 5.2 in the South East since 1983. This has obviously squeezed many potential lower-income buyers out of the market and those who have been able to buy have faced much higher mortgage repayments as a proportion of income. The Nationwide also point out that this has been achieved by the increasing tendency in the South East for a higher proportion of borrowers (44 per cent) to have joint incomes compared to just 28 per cent in Yorkshire & Humberside. This has not only meant an increase in working spouses/partners, but the emergence of shared house purchase by unrelated persons. Owner occupation is much more affordable in the north than it is in the south despite the lower incomes in the north.

Regional differences in use and exchange values

These regional differences in average house-price/income ratios are compounded by the marked differences in the type of property that can be purchased for the same money. The Nationwide (1987) show that if the average purchaser paid the current average UK price of £43,350, this would buy a modern three- to four-bedroom detached house or bungalow in the Northern region, a modern three-bedroom detached house or bungalow in Yorkshire & Humberside, the North West and the East and West Midlands, a modern two-bedroom detached house or three-bedroom semi-detached in East Anglia and the South West, a two-bedroom modern flat or an older three-bedroom terraced house in the South East or a one-bedroom older converted flat in a few cheaper areas of London. As the Nationwide observe, the level and value for money of housing acquired in London and the South East is, on average, markedly lower than in the rest of the country. This has major implications for labour mobility, as the owner of a £30,000 semi-detached house in the north east or the North West is very unlikely to be able to afford the £100,000 needed to replace it in London; nor are they likely to be willing to move down market into a £50,000 one-bedroom flat.

This reveals an interesting contradiction between the current-use value and the future-exchange value of housing in different regions. In general, there is an inverse relationship between the two values. The greater the current-use value purchased for a given sum of money, the less the potential future-exchange value. This raises an interesting question as to who is better off, the buyer of a £43,000 modern detached house in the north of England or the buyer of a £43,000 older, one-bedroom converted flat in a cheap area of London. In terms of current-use values, there is clearly no contest. But in terms of future-capital appreciation, there is also no contest. The flat-buyer is likely, on the basis of trends over the last three years, to see the value of his or her flat to increase by £11,000 a year, compared to perhaps £2,500 for the detached house in the north. There is therefore a potential trade-off between current-use and potential future-exchange values in the British owner-occupied housing market at present. Nor are the future-exchange values merely potential ones. If the owners in London and the South East move out of the region, they can either release some of their accumulated equity for general consumption or they can purchase a higher standard of housing than would have been possible on the basis of income. Alternatively, the beneficiaries of their estates stand to inherit a far larger sum of money.

Conclusions

There is currently a large difference in regional house prices and rates of house-price inflation. This has resulted in marked regional variations in rates of capital gains, access to ownership and value for money in housing. At present there is undoubtedly a dual owner-occupied housing market between the north and south of Britain. But it has been argued that while the regional house-price gap is of long standing, its size has varied considerably over time depending on the stage of the cycle of regional house-price inflation. If, as seems very likely, the rate of house-price inflation has peaked in London and rates of inflation continue to increase in the rest of the south and the Midlands, then the gap between London and the rest of the south will stabilize or even reduce over the next few years. This will reduce the disparities in access and accumulation within the south but it is unlikely to reduce the problems of migration from north to south or the wider north-south disparities in access and accumulation.

5

SOUTH GOES NORTH? THE RISE OF THE BRITISH PROVINCIAL FINANCIAL CENTRE

Andrew Leyshon and Nigel Thrift

Introduction

This chapter examines one aspect of the north-south divide, the rise of financial services to a position of some prominence in the British economy. According to some commentators (for example, Gillespie and Green, 1987; Howells and Green, 1988), the growth of financial and producer services has only strengthened the north-south divide in terms of employment, occupational mix and a host of other indicators. We take limited issue with this interpretation of the British space economy by considering the rise of the provincial financial centre in the 1970s and 1980s. It may seem a strange idea to talk of the provincial financial centre. The term conjures up an image of all but outmoded practices of commerce, such as the provincial stock-exchange, but the evidence is there. The provincial financial centre is on the rise and not just in the south.

The evidence is set out in the first section in which we identify the leading urban centres of financial and producer service activity in Great Britain and chart their growth from the mid-1970s to the mid-1980s. However, the explanation for the rise of the provincial financial centres is paradoxical. Although part of the explanation lies in the strength of certain regional economies and their emergent demand for financial services, another important determinant has been decentralization processes emanating from Central London. Office decentralization is one of these processes. Another is the expansion of London-based firms in opportunist searches for new business. These firms have also acted as a catalyst for local financial-service activity. In the second section we consider both indigenous expansion and these two 'south goes north' processes. The last section documents some of the local impacts of financial and producer service growth, paying particular attention to the consequences of the in-migration of offices of large London-based financial and producer service firms.

The growth of provincial financial centres in Great Britain, 1974–84

Defining financial centres

There are several ways in which the relative importance of a financial centre may be determined. These include the number of key financial functions located within a centre; the demand for office space in a centre as reflected in local office-rental values; the importance of finance-related occupations within the overall employment structure of a centre; and total employment within financial and producer service industries.

First, the relative importance of financial centres may be assessed by way of an examination of the spatial distribution of key financial functions (Table 5.1). Only six British cities – London, Birmingham, Manchester, Liverpool, Glasgow and Edinburgh – possess stock exchanges. It is not surprising that these centres of capital formation and exchange also contain relatively large proportions of stockbroking firms. The headquarters of the ten British clearing banks are based in only four cities – London, Edinburgh, Glasgow and Manchester. Merchant banks are overwhelmingly located in the City of London and only seven such banks were actually located outside the capital. Other banks and deposit-taking institutions are also predominantly located within London, although they displayed a greater level of spatial dispersal, with Manchester, Edinburgh and Nottingham containing important concentrations. The functional importance of a financial centre will also be influenced by the number of institutional investors that are located there, given that such organizations are the principal users of stock exchanges and are the most important clients of stockbrokers. The spatial distribution of the headquarters of insurance companies, investment trust companies, unit trust managers, pension fund management groups and self-investing pension funds is illustrated in Table 5.2. These too are primarily located in large cities with London and Edinburgh containing by far the largest concentrations of investment institutions. Smaller concentrations occur in Liverpool, Norwich, Birmingham, Bristol, Croydon and Manchester.

A more indirect measure of the relative importance of financial centres may be derived from the level of demand for office space as reflected by office-rental values. Of course, rental values give only a very broad indication of a centre's functional importance since many activities other than financial and producer services occupy office space within urban areas. Nevertheless, financial and producer service firms are major occupiers of office space in towns and cities and one would intuitively expect the prevailing rental value of office property to be related to the demand for floorspace generated by such firms. In 1986 the demand for office property in England and Wales was considerably greater within centres located within the south. Rental values in Central London were £35 per square foot per annum. In the rest of Greater London they averaged £11 per square foot per annum, while in suburban cities of the South East the mean annual rental value was £10.25 per square foot. The highest annual rental values outside the South East were recorded in Birmingham and Bristol where office property was valued

Table 5.1 Locations containing stock exchanges or at least two headquarters of British stockbroking firms, clearing banks, merchant banks and other banks and deposit-taking institutions

Centre	Stock exchanges	Stockbrokers	Clearing banks	Merchant banks[1]	Other banks, deposit-taking institutions	Total number of firms
London	1	108	6	64	194	372
City of London	1	106	6	61	128	301
Rest of Central London	0	2	0	3	66	71
Manchester	1	12	1	0	8	21
Birmingham	1	10	0	1	1	12
Edinburgh	1	3	2	3	4	12
Glasgow	1	7	1	1	3	12
Liverpool	1	6	0	0	2	8
Bristol	0	3	0	0	3	6
Nottingham	0	2	0	0	4	6
Leeds	0	4	0	0	1	5
Bournemouth	0	3	0	0	2	5
Bradford	0	2	0	0	2	4
Aberdeen	0	2	0	0	1	3
Cardiff	0	1	0	0	2	3
Croydon	0	0	0	0	3	3
Exeter	0	1	0	0	2	3
Harrow	0	0	0	0	3	3
Norwich	0	1	0	0	2	3
Sheffield	0	2	0	0	1	3
Hull	0	1	0	0	1	2
Leicester	0	1	0	0	1	2
Lincoln	0	1	0	0	1	2
Newcastle	0	2	0	0	0	2
Slough	0	0	0	0	2	2

Notes
1. Members of Issuing and Accepting Houses Committees.

(*Source: The City Directory*, 1984–5.)

Table 5.2 Locations containing at least four headquarters of institutional investment organizations

Centre	Insurance companies	Investment trust companies	Unit trust managers		Pension fund management		Pension funds (self-investing)		Total firms
			No.	Funds (£m)	No.	Funds (£m)	No.	Funds (£m)	
London	229	154	72	21,928	34	90,898	37	45,500	526
City of London	193	126	58	19,762	30	88,552	12	12,566	419
Rest of London	36	28	14	2,166	4	2,346	25	32,932	107
Edinburgh	9	33	14	2,857	13	13,344	1	428	70
Liverpool	7	1	1	98	0	0	2	349	11
Birmingham	5	5	0	0	0	0	0	0	10
Glasgow	4	0	3	119	3	2,538	0	0	10
Norwich	8	0	1	353	1	769	0	0	10
Bristol	2	0	1	228	2	281	4	2,213	9
Croydon	7	0	0	0	1	400	1	173	9
Manchester	5	0	3	119	0	0	0	0	8
Dorking	6	0	1	61	0	0	0	0	7
Tunbridge Wells	4	0	1	36	1	68	0	0	6
Bournemouth	4	0	1	61	0	0	0	0	5
Dundee	0	5	0	0	0	0	0	0	5
Exeter	2	0	1	43	1	350	1	83	5
Milton Keynes	4	0	0	0	0	0	1	250	5
Aberdeen	0	4	0	0	0	0	0	0	4
Halifax	3	0	0	0	0	0	1	260	4
Perth	3	0	0	0	0	0	1	352	4
Stratford-upon-Avon	2	0	1	9	1	350	0	0	4

(*Source: City Directory*, 1984–5; *Crawford's Directory of City Connections*, 1986; Pensions Management, 1987.)

at £8.50 per square foot. The only other provincial centre outside the South East where office property values exceeded £8.00 per square foot per annum was Swindon.

Third, some indication of the functional significance of a financial centre may be gauged by the relative importance of key 'financial occupations' within the employment structure of the travel-to-work area (TTWA) within which centres are based. The extent to which the occupational groups of 'chartered and certified accountants', 'underwriters, brokers, investment analysts', 'taxation experts' and 'economists, statisticians, actuaries' formed a greater proportion of the resident workforce than was the case in Great Britain as a whole can be judged with the Location Quotient (LQ).[1] Out of a total of 322 TTWAs in Great Britain, financial-service occupations were over-represented in only 40, according to the residence of respondents to the 1981 Population Census. Of these, 30 TTWAs were located in the south (defined here as the South East, South West, East Anglia), and 20 were based in the South East region. The seven highest concentrations of financial-service occupations were all in the South East, with Tunbridge Wells (LQ = 3.15), Crawley (2.62), Southend (2.38), London (2.10) and Chelmsford and Braintree (2.06) possessing the largest over-representations. Of the ten northern TTWAs containing over-representations of financial-service occupations, the highest-ranking northern centres were Harrogate (LQ = 1.68), Warwick (1.37) and Edinburgh (1.29). However, these were ranked only 8th, 15th and 17th respectively. Therefore, not only was there an over-representation of financial service occupations in more southern centres than northern centres, but also the relative concentration of such employees tended to be greater in the south than in the north.

Although such data may be indicative of the functional importance of a centre, it is important to bear in mind that the location quotients indicate only the relative importance of financial and producer service occupations and say nothing about the absolute numbers of employees. More importantly, the data used are residence-based and allowances need to be made for people working in one labour-market area and commuting to another. This problem is of particular significance within the South East region. For example, while the Tunbridge Wells TTWA contained the highest proportion of financial-service occupations within its overall employment structure, it is located firmly within the City of London commuter zone (see Thrift, Leyshon and Daniels, 1987). Indeed, the 'London effect' is probably a major determinant of the over-representation of financial and producer service occupations in many of the South East TTWAs.

The most direct measure of the functional importance of financial centres is the number of employees directly employed within financial and producer services. Financial-service industries are those that are fundamental to the functioning of a financial centre. Using the 1980 revision of the Standard Industrial Classification these industries include Banking and bill discounting (Activity Heading 8140), Other financial institutions (8150), Insurance (8200), Activities auxiliary to banking and finance (8310), Activities auxiliary to insurance (8320), and Accountants, auditors and tax experts (8360)[2]. Producer service industries in this context are taken to be secondary business services that assist in the successful functioning of a financial centre. These include House and estate agents (Activity Heading 8340), Legal services (8350), Advertising (8380), Computer services (8394) and Business services (8395). Following Reed (1981), the 25 leading centres have been classified as either pre-eminent, regional or sub-regional financial centres[3]. Although Reed's original analysis of international financial centres was multi-dimensional, time and data availability constraints forced our classification to be posited solely upon the numbers employed within either financial or producer services. Nevertheless, despite the one-dimensional character of the classification it served to confirm our earlier attempts to arrive at a functional definition of financial centre by possession of key financial operations.

Figure 5.1 reveals the extent to which London is Britain's pre-eminent financial and producer service centre in terms of numbers employed within such industries. In 1984 the city contained around 14 times as much financial and producer service employment as the next largest financial centre. Consequently, over 60 per cent of all financial and producer service employment within the 25 centres in 1984 was located within London. The supremacy of London resulted in large part from the importance of the international financial enclave that is the City of London. Some 37 per cent of the 560,000 people employed within financial and producer services in the capital worked in the City. However, other areas of the capital were also important centres of financial and producer service employment. For example, if component employment-office areas of London were considered as separate financial centres in their own right then – after the City of London – Westminster, Marylebone, King's Cross and Croydon would respectively rank as the second, fourth, ninth and tenth largest such centres in Britain. Over 148,000 employees worked in financial and producer service industries in these employment-office areas in 1984. London's pre-eminent status in terms of financial and producer service employment is a product of not only its sheer size – one in seven of Britain's entire population live in the capital (Champion *et al.*, 1987, p.10) – but also of its importance as a locational base of key international financial and producer service organizations (Leyshon, Daniels and Thrift, 1987; Leyshon, Thrift and Daniels, 1987).

Financial-service employment is clearly a major component of overall producer service employment in a centre. Figure 5.1 reveals that financial-service employees outnumbered other producer service employees in 23 of the 25 centres. Financial-service employment was particularly important in Bootle, Southend and Norwich where over three-quarters of financial and producer service employees were employed within financial-service organizations, while over two-thirds of financial and producer service employees were employed in financial-service industries in Brighton, Northampton, Bradford and Bournemouth.

Despite London's clear pre-eminence as a centre of financial and producer service employment, its relative dominance in Britain has in fact been in decline in recent years. This has resulted not from employment decline in the capital but from rapid employment growth in certain regional and sub-regional financial centres. The following section analyses the processes of financial and producer service employment change within the largest 25 centres in Britain between 1974 and 1984.

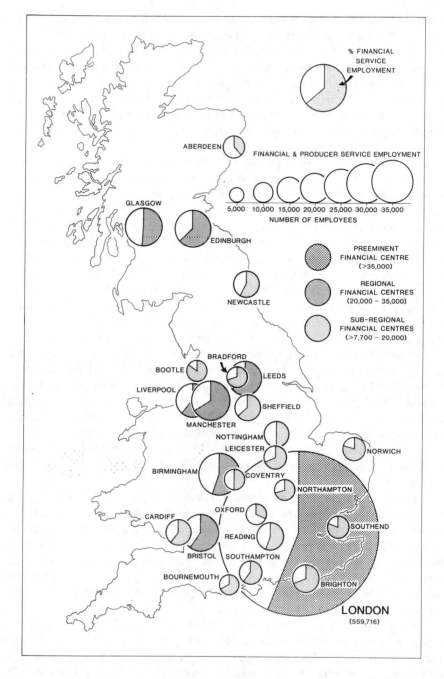

Figure 5.1   Distribution of financial and producer service employment, 1984 (Source:
Census of Employment, *1984, as from the National Online Manpower*
Information System)

Financial and producer service employment change in Britain's leading financial centres, 1974–84

The economic history of urban Britain during the 1970s and 1980s has been dominated by the twin themes of large-scale job loss and sharply-increased levels of unemployment. These phenomena have been caused by the over-riding processes of restructuring and de-industrialization that have characterized most western capitalist economies in recent years (Hausner, 1987). However, amidst the widespread economic contraction and employment shrinkage, the major provincial cities of Britain have enjoyed more than a decade of continuous growth in financial and producer service employment. For example, some 931,251 people were employed in financial and producer service industries within the leading 25 British 'financial centres' in 1984, representing an increase of 12.9 per cent from 1981 and 16.9 per cent since 1974.

While London remains by far the most dominant financial centre within Great Britain, its relative dominance among provincial financial centres has been undermined. Relatively-slow employment growth within financial and producer service industries meant that whereas in 1974 the capital contained 63 per cent of all financial and producer service employment within the 25 leading centres, by 1981 this had fallen to 59.5 per cent, although more vigorous employment growth during the early 1980s saw this share recover slightly to just over 60 per cent by 1984. London's share of purely-financial service employment similarly declined from 61 per cent to less than 58 per cent between 1974 and 1981, only to rise marginally between 1981 and 1984. Nevertheless, over the decade London's relative supremacy *vis-à-vis* the remaining 24 centres was measurably reduced, for while London experienced only modest rates of employment growth in financial and producer service industries from the mid-1970s onwards, many of Britain's provincial financial centres enjoyed quite phenomenal rates of growth (Table 5.3 and Figure 5.2). For example, between 1974 and 1981 employment within financial and producer services overall expanded by more than one quarter within as many as 12 centres, while within three centres such employment increased by more than 50 per cent.

Differential rates of employment growth between 1974 and 1984 ensured a marked reshuffling of the rank ordering of financial centres in terms of the numbers employed within financial and producer service industries during the period, although the distinctiveness of the pre-eminent, regional and sub-regional centres remained intact throughout the period (Table 5.4). Nevertheless, there were clear 'winners' and 'losers' among the regional and sub-regional centres. The 'losers' amongst the regional centres were Manchester, Liverpool and Leeds. The loss of over 5,000 financial and producer service jobs in Manchester between 1974 and 1984 meant that the city lost its status as the largest regional centre in Britain. Liverpool also experienced a decline in financial and producer service employment and in its relative status as a financial and producer service centre, losing over 1,000 jobs and falling from fourth-largest regional centre in 1974 to sixth in 1984. Leeds, meanwhile, became the smallest regional centre in 1984, even though its financial and producer service employment base actually expanded by more than

Table 5.3   Financial and producer service employment change, British provincial
centres: (a) 1974–81

Financial and producer service employment change			Financial-service employment change		
Rank	Centre	(% change)	Rank	Centre	(% change)
1	Bootle	(88.8)	1	Bootle	(78.0)
2	Coventry	(55.1)	2	Sheffield	(56.3)
3	Aberdeen	(51.0)	3	Brighton	(50.2)
4	Brighton	(39.9)	4	Bournemouth	(44.2)
5	Southend	(38.9)	5	Aberdeen	(43.5)
6	Norwich	(38.2)	6	Southend	(41.8)
7	Bristol	(37.6)	7	Bristol	(40.1)
8	Sheffield	(35.0)	8	Reading	(36.7)
9	Northampton	(34.2)	9	Norwich	(38.2)
10	Leeds	(31.2)	10	Southampton	(29.2)
11	Bournemouth	(30.1)	11	Northampton	(26.5)
12	Southampton	(21.5)	12	Coventry	(22.2)
13	Oxford	(20.8)	13	Edinburgh	(21.3)
14	Reading	(20.1)	14	Newcastle	(20.5)
15	Leicester	(17.8)	15	Leeds	(16.9)
16	Birmingham	(16.9)	16	Oxford	(15.9)
17	Cardiff	(16.8)	17	Glasgow	(12.5)
18	Edinburgh	(16.7)	18	Birmingham	(10.7)
19	Glasgow	(9.8)	19	Leicester	(10.6)
20	Newcastle	(9.4)	20	Bradford	(6.7)
21	Bradford	(7.8)	21	London	(4.8)
22	London	(2.5)	22	Manchester	(4.1)
23	Liverpool	(−2.4)	23	Cardiff	(2.9)
24	Manchester	(−8.9)	24	Nottingham	(−9.8)
25	Nottingham	(−10.8)	25	Liverpool	(−11.1)

Table 5.3   (cont.): (b) 1981–4

Financial and producer service employment change			Financial-service employment change		
Rank	Centre	(% change)	Rank	Centre	(% change)
1	Aberdeen	(38.0)	1	Southend	(18.6)
2	Oxford	(32.6)	2	Brighton	(16.0)
3	Reading	(26.0)	3	Cardiff	(15.7)
4	Southend	(21.6)	4	Southampton	(14.3)
5	Northampton	(20.5)	5	Northampton	(13.8)
6	Birmingham	(19.9)	6	Reading	(13.4)
7	Edinburgh	(18.2)	7	Aberdeen	(11.2)
8	Brighton	(17.1)	8	Edinburgh	(10.8)
9	Newcastle	(15.8)	9	Coventry	(9.8)
10	Cardiff	(15.7)	10	Birmingham	(9.1)
11	Southampton	(15.0)	11	Leeds	(8.0)
12	Nottingham	(14.6)	12	Bradford	(7.8)
13	Coventry	(14.4)	13	Oxford	(7.0)
14	London	(14.1)	14	London	(6.6)
15	Bournemouth	(9.7)	15	Bournemouth	(5.6)
16	Leeds	(7.7)	16	Bootle	(4.8)
17	Bristol	(6.4)	17	Norwich	(4.3)
18	Bradford	(6.1)	18	Nottingham	(3.0)
19	Norwich	(6.1)	19	Newcastle	(2.4)
20	Liverpool	(4.8)	20	Leicester	(0.3)
21	Glasgow	(4.4)	21	Bristol	(−0.1)
22	Bootle	(3.3)	22	Liverpool	(−1.5)
23	Manchester	(1.3)	23	Glasgow	(−4.3)
24	Sheffield	(−3.5)	24	Sheffield	(−6.6)
25	Leicester	(−5.0)	25	Manchester	(−6.8)

(*Source: Census of Employment*, 1974, 1981, 1984, as from the National Online Manpower Information System.)

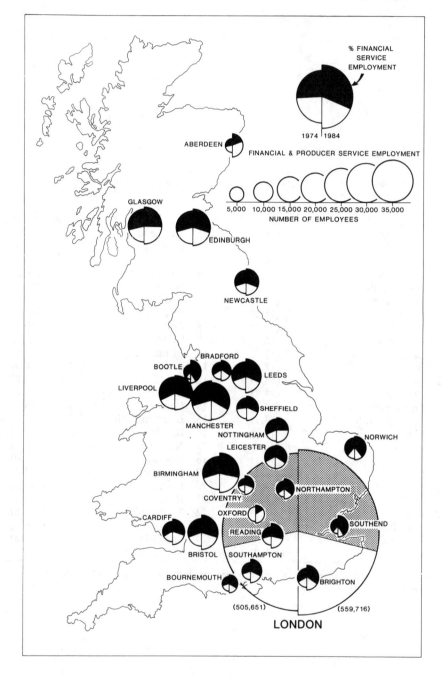

Figure 5.2 Change in the distribution of financial and producer service employment, 1974–84 (Source: Census of Employment, 1974, 1984, as from the National Online Manpower Information System)

Table 5.4   Rank order of British provincial centres by financial and producer service employment, 1974–84

1974		1981		1984	
1	*London*	1	*London*	1	*London*
2	Manchester	2	Manchester	2	Birmingham
3	Birmingham	3	Birmingham	3	Manchester
4	Glasgow	4	Glasgow	4	Glasgow
5	Liverpool	5	Edinburgh	5	Edinburgh
6	Edinburgh	6	Bristol	6	Bristol
7	Leeds	7	Liverpool	7	Liverpool
8	*Bristol*	8	*Leeds*	8	*Leeds*
9	Nottingham	9	Sheffield	9	Newcastle
10	Newcastle	10	Newcastle	10	Reading
11	Sheffield	11	Brighton	11	Brighton
12	Cardiff	12	Cardiff	12	Cardiff
13	Leicester	13	Nottingham	13	Nottingham
14	Reading	14	Norwich	14	Sheffield
15	Norwich	15	Reading	15	Norwich
16	Brighton	16	Leicester	16	Southampton
17	Bradford	17	Southampton	17	Aberdeen
18	Southampton	18	Portsmouth	18	Leicester
19	Northampton	19	Bradford	19	Southend
20	Southend	20	Aberdeen	20	Northampton
21	Bournemouth	21	Bootle	21	Bradford
22	Oxford	22	Southend	22	Bootle
23	Coventry	23	Northampton	23	Coventry
24	Hull	24	Hull	24	Oxford
25	Guildford	25	Bournemouth	25	Bournemouth

(*Source: Census of Employment*, 1974, 1981, 1984, as from the National Online Manpower Information System.)

23 per cent between 1974 and 1984. However, Bristol, the smallest regional centre in 1974, experienced a 49 per cent expansion in financial and producer service employment in the period up to 1984. This growth resulted in the creation of almost 8,000 additional jobs in the city. Birmingham became the largest regional centre in 1984, benefiting from the creation of almost 7,500 financial and producer service jobs between 1974 and 1984. The other principal 'winner' among the regional centres was Edinburgh, where the creation of over 7,000 additional financial and producer service jobs elevated the city from fifth to fourth-largest regional centre between 1974 and 1984.

Among the sub-regional centres the re-ordering of centres by numbers employed within financial and producer service industries was even more pronounced, and a fairly-distinctive north-south division emerged in the relative fortunes of sub-regional centres between 1974 and 1984. The largest sub-regional centre remained non-southern throughout the period, as Nottingham, the largest sub-regional centre in 1974, was supplanted by Sheffield in 1981, which in turn was replaced by Newcastle in 1984. Employment in financial and producer services in Newcastle expanded by over 28 per cent over the period. However, the southern boom-towns of Reading and Brighton emerged as clear winners among the sub-regional centres.

Financial and producer service employment in these towns increased by 59 and 67 per cent respectively between 1974 and 1984, elevating them to second and third place among Britain's sub-regional centres. Other southern centres to expand their financial and producer service employment bases and to increase their relative standing among sub-regional centres included Southampton. However, those centres that experienced a decline in their relative standing among sub-regional centres were predominantly non-southern towns and cities. For example, while the financial and producer service employment bases of Nottingham, Sheffield, Leicester, Bradford and Northampton all increased over the period, all five centres were relatively less important in terms of such employment in 1984 than they were in 1974.

Therefore, a considerable re-ordering of regional and sub-regional financial centres took place between 1974 and 1984, in terms of financial and producer service employment. Although 'winners' and 'losers' could be identified, within only 2 of the 25 leading centres – Manchester and Liverpool – did employment within financial and producer service industries actually decline.

A closer analysis of employment change within the component industries of the financial and producer service industries indicated that those centres that grew fastest were dependent initially upon the rapid growth of usually just one financial sector. First, there were those towns and cities that grew fastest in terms of financial-service employment between 1974 and 1981 – centres such as Bootle, Sheffield and Southend were dependent largely upon the expansion of the banking and bill-discounting sector. The number of employees within this sector in the three centres increased by 84, 127 and 62 per cent respectively. Financial-service employment growth in Bootle has been caused almost exclusively by the *in situ* expansion of the operations of the national Girobank, while Southend is now the administrative centre of the Access credit-card organization (owned jointly by the major clearing banks). Second, centres such as Bournemouth, Bristol, Reading and Norwich, on the other hand, had their financial-service employment growth fuelled by the expansion of the insurance sector, within which employment increased by 122, 57, 98, 45 and 37 per cent respectively. The insurance labour-market in these centres is dominated by a relatively small number of large employers. For example, a handful of large nationally-orientated insurance companies – Phoenix, Sun Life, Clerical Medical and General, London Life and the insurance subsidiary of NatWest – accounted for over half of all insurance employment in Bristol in 1983 (Boddy, Lovering and Bassett, 1986). The insurance labour-market in Norwich is concentrated to an even greater extent. Although Sedgewick, the UK's largest insurance broking firm, operates within the city, local insurance employment is dominated by the Norwich Union insurance company. The firm has been based in the city since the 18th century and is now one of the world's *premier* insurance companies. The company employs around 4,000 people making it Norwich's largest private-sector employer (Reeves, 1987b). Some 60 per cent of all those employed within the insurance industry in Norwich work for Norwich Union, as do 42 per cent of all those who work within financial-service industries. Finally, much of the financial-service employment growth in Brighton was dependent upon the expansion of the 'other financial institutions sector', where employment increased by more than 132 per cent over the period. One component of this growth is the expansion of the Alliance and Leicester Building Society, which is headquartered in the town.

However, while between 1974 and 1981 financial-service growth in the fastest-growing centres could be attributed to the influence of employment expansion in just one financial-service industry, between 1981 and 1984 growth seems to have been more equitably distributed across the range of financial-service sectors. For example, Brighton, Southend and Reading also figured among the ten fastest-growing centres between 1981 and 1984. However, in each case the relative specialization of their financial-service employment base actually declined, and within each centre the level of dependence upon one, key, growth sector was reduced.

Determinants and mechanisms of growth

This section attempts to identify both the determinants and mechanisms of financial and producer service employment growth within British provincial centres since the mid-1970s. Accordingly, the section is in two parts. The first part considers the implications of an elementary regression model that measures the degree to which local levels of consumer and business demand are linked to the level of financial and producer service employment within provincial centres. The second part of this section identifies the processes of financial and producer service employment growth within the provincial centres of Britain.

Determinants of financial and producer service employment growth within provincial centres: an exploratory analysis

Using employment data for 1984, an attempt was made to determine the extent to which the level of financial and producer service employment in provincial centres was related to the local level of local consumer and business demand. A proxy for 'consumer demand' was calculated by multiplying the 1984 average, gross weekly income of full-time male and female employees (*New Earnings Survey*, 1985) by the respective number of male and female employees employed within the TTWA in which the centre was located (*Census of Employment*, 1984). A proxy for 'business demand' was derived from the relevant county Gross Domestic Product figures for 1984 as calculated by the Central Statistical Office (CSO, 1988). The use of these variables is, of course, fraught with problems and it must be stressed that this is merely an exploratory analysis. The interpretative value of the analysis is tempered by a quite considerable list of caveats[4]. In addition to these caveats the analysis omitted two centres: London, because its relative size would have distorted the analysis and because, in any case, the functional importance of London's financial and producer service industries beyond local demand levels can be taken as read, given the importance of the city as an international financial centre; and Bootle, because of the impossibility of deriving meaningful values of local consumer or business demand from the data available, in the light of its dependence on the national demand for the services of the Girobank.

The regression analysis revealed that the local level of consumer demand and business demand was an extremely good predictor of the level of financial and producer service employment within provincial centres (Figures 5.3 and 5.4). The level of consumer and business demand was found to explain 65.2 per cent of the variation in financial-service employment and 76.3 per cent of the variation in financial and producer service employment in British provincial centres. It was, therefore, not surprising to discover financial and producer service employment increased fastest in those centres that were for the most part located within TTWAs and counties where consumer and business demand experienced the greatest increases (Table 5.5).

Having established that the level of financial and producer service employment within British provincial centres appears to be closely related to prevailing levels of local demand, the next section outlines the three major processes by which financial and producer service employment has grown within these centres. First, employment has increased as a consequence of the growth of local financial and producer service firms. A second process of employment growth has been the in-migration to provincial centres of offices belonging to large London-based multi-locational financial and producer service firms. The third process of financial and producer service employment growth has been the decentralization of offices from central London.

Mechanisms of financial and producer service employment growth

Growth of local firms

The most immediate effect of rising regional demand for financial and producer services has been to stimulate the growth of financial and producer service firms 'indigenous' to provincial centres. It is clear that the local business-service communities of many provincial centres have undergone something of a renaissance in recent years, and an important component of this renaissance has been the willingness of local firms to extend the range of services they offer. Anyone who regularly reads the British financial and business press cannot have failed to notice the recent eagerness with which financial journalists have reported the growing confidence – and growing profitability – of provincial financiers and business professionals. In this respect there is no north-south divide since the growing prominence of local financial and producer service firms is as evident in the provincial cities of the north as it is in those of the south. Indeed, this has created something of a paradox in the writings of several financial journalists. On the one hand, they continue to transmit the prevailing governmental line that unfavourable socio-economic conditions in the north are due in large part to the absence of a suitable entrepreneurial culture among the people who live there (see Massey, 1988). Yet much of the credit for the resurgence of provincial financial centres is attributed

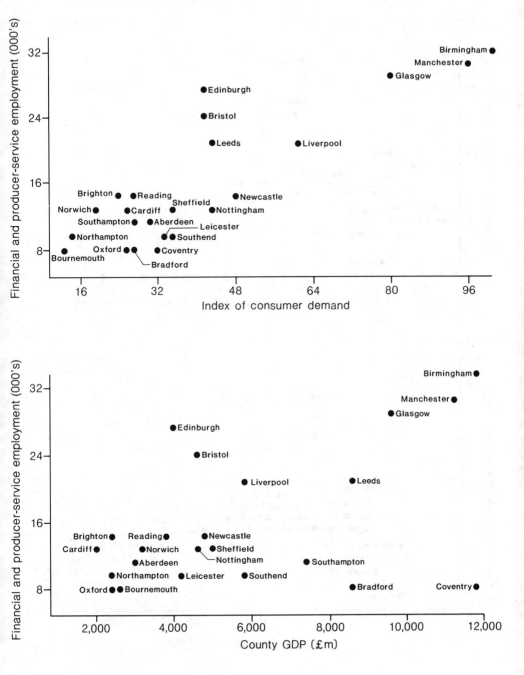

Figure 5.3 Relationship of financial and producer service employment to measures of demand

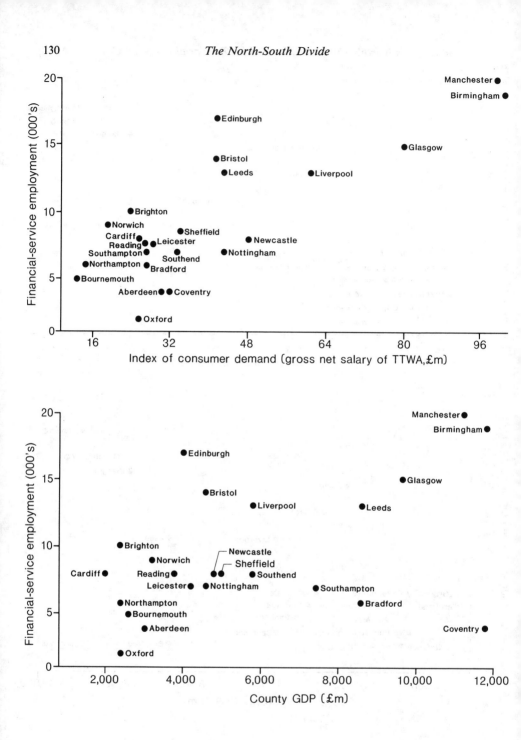

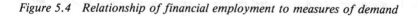

Figure 5.4   Relationship of financial employment to measures of demand

Table 5.5 Indices of change in producer service employment and demand, 1977–84, 23 leading centres

Centre	Producer service employment[1]			Consumer demand[2]			Business demand[3]		
	1977	1981	1984	1977	1981	1984	1977	1981	1984
Aberdeen	100.0	154.8	213.6	100.0	213.7	331.5	100.0	184.5	255.7
Birmingham	100.0	110.4	132.3	100.0	163.3	216.3	100.0	141.7	175.0
Bournemouth	100.0	114.9	126.0	100.0	185.5	248.4	100.0	171.4	223.4
Bradford	100.0	105.8	112.2	100.0	157.8	211.3	100.0	157.1	195.2
Brighton	100.0	115.2	134.9	100.0	191.3	286.3	100.0	185.7	221.9
Bristol	100.0	113.8	121.1	100.0	171.0	211.5	100.0	168.2	217.0
Cardiff	100.0	116.1	134.6	100.0	156.2	207.8	100.0	159.2	210.4
Coventry	100.0	137.0	156.8	100.0	145.8	192.5	100.0	141.7	175.0
Edinburgh	100.0	111.6	132.0	100.0	182.7	240.2	100.0	165.9	212.5
Glasgow	100.0	139.8	148.0	100.0	152.7	195.5	100.0	154.4	184.9
Leeds	100.0	113.1	121.8	100.0	168.0	223.1	100.0	157.1	195.2
Leicester	100.0	103.2	98.0	100.0	179.9	240.5	100.0	173.8	226.1
Liverpool	100.0	103.9	108.9	100.0	153.6	188.8	100.0	148.2	175.7
Manchester	100.0	101.0	102.3	100.0	165.0	209.8	100.0	155.8	187.8
Newcastle	100.0	110.4	127.8	100.0	150.0	195.4	100.0	154.4	182.5
Northampton	100.0	126.2	152.0	100.0	178.9	247.2	100.0	160.9	219.9
Nottingham	100.0	120.9	117.9	100.0	169.6	211.7	100.0	170.1	203.5
Norwich	100.0	122.9	130.3	100.0	178.3	242.9	100.0	166.9	219.8
Oxford	100.0	114.7	152.2	100.0	174.7	242.2	100.0	169.3	212.0
Reading	100.0	139.9	175.1	100.0	201.0	304.8	100.0	169.3	212.8
Sheffield	100.0	118.3	114.1	100.0	161.9	194.9	100.0	156.1	173.8
Southampton	100.0	127.8	146.9	100.0	173.6	246.4	100.0	177.9	212.0
Southend	100.0	140.4	170.7	100.0	181.7	246.5	100.0	175.9	210.7

Notes
1. Number of producer service employees by amalgamated employment office area (*Census of Employment*).
2. Number of male and female employees and relevant TTWA multiplied by gross average income in relevant county (*Census of Employment; New Earnings Survey*).
3. Gross domestic product in relevant county (Central Statistical Office).

(*Source: Census of Employment*, 1977, 1981, 1984 as from the National Online Manpower Information System.); *New Earnings Survey*, 1977, 1981, 1984; Central Statistical Office, 1988.

to the efforts of northern-based financiers and professionals, who have responded to the increasing level of demand for financial and producer services by enterprisingly extending the range of services on offer. For example, the following statements were both included within a recent report on Sheffield:

> The worry among professionals is that many of the manufacturing workforce ... are not going to be entrepreneurial enough. They have been too used to being employees in big corporations. ... What is ... apparent from doing the rounds of Sheffield's professional and financial community ... is that this community contains some impressive entrepreneurs in their own right. What other explanation is there for the survival of firms of solicitors such as Rogers and Howe which has been in continuous business in the same building since 1800?
>
> (Hamilton Fazey, 1987a, p.4)

That financial and producer service firms are able to survive and even thrive in regions more commonly associated with processes of economic decline should not really be surprising. For example, a still-important component of accountancy practice is insolvency work, where firms earn fee income from the management of company receiverships and liquidations. Insolvency also creates work for solicitors who are employed by creditors to act on their behalf in presentation of winding-up petitions to the court. Therefore, such firms are able to remain profitable in times of economic downturn as well as in times of growth. However, in recent years local financial and producer service firms, even in northern provincial centres, have been faced with sharply-growing levels of demand for a whole suite of business services. Firms have responded by extending the range of their existing services while at the same time new firms have emerged to fill market niches.

There would seem to be three important causes of the upsurge in demand for financial and producer services within provincial centres. First, there is the general trend within the economy towards externalization and the vertical disintegration of production (Marshall, 1988), where activities that were previously performed in-house are contracted out to specialist firms. For example, economic pressures have forced many companies to dispense with specialist management advisory positions, preferring instead to buy in such services as and when they are needed, a development that has benefited the management consultancy departments of accountancy firms in particular (see Leyshon, Daniels and Thrift, 1987).

Second, advances in communications technologies have had the effect of undermining the functional importance of location for certain financial-service activities. For example, the installation of the automated SEAQ (Stock Exchange Automated Quotations) system in London in October 1986 has allowed regionally-based stockbrokers to participate within the domestic securities market on a more or less equal footing with firms based in the City of London. Witness the comments of a Manchester-based financial professional quoted in a recent press report:

> 'The Big Bang has been very good for Manchester and has brought business back. Local stockbrokers are working all the hours there are and doing very good business.' With Manchester Britain's most important financial centre after London, the electronics revolution has given it direct, instantaneous contact like never before. Anyone wanting to deal might as well be in Manchester 1 as London EC4.
>
> (Hamilton Fazey, 1987b, p.3)

The third cause of growing demand for financial and producer services in provincial centres also results from changes taking place within the City of London. The restructuring of the City in 1986 confirmed its new role alongside New York and Tokyo as one of the three transactional centres of the New International Financial System (Thrift, Leyshon and Daniels, 1987; Thrift and Leyshon, 1988). In the hours between the closing of the Tokyo financial markets and the opening of the New York markets, London is the international financial centre of the world economy. As the volume of capital flowing through London has increased so some City-based organizations have increasingly tended to concentrate upon satisfying the demand for their services emanating from multinational corporations and international financial institutions, and many City firms have embarked upon substantial internal expansion programmes in an effort to keep up with demand. However, in the scramble for highly-valued internationally-orientated business, the needs of smaller domestic clients have become very much of secondary importance. Therefore, the functional take-off of the City has presented regionally-based financial and producer service firms with the opportunity to fill the growing lacunae in local financial and business-service markets. And local firms are indeed responding to the opportunities that have arisen from the increasing scale of operations in London. For example, take the case of Manchester:

> Increasingly when companies in the [North West] issue their company reports or prospectuses, the addresses of their professional and financial advisers are Manchester ones. When it comes to flotations and buy-outs in the North West, the list of advisers will be Manchester-based. Partly it is a question of scale. While Manchester ... is a big league player in financial circles, even £100m companies are small by London standards ... . A Northern industrialist visiting his (*sic*) London merchant bank will nowadays find it difficult to see much of a senior partner, if at all. But he can reach Manchester from almost anywhere in the North-West in less than an hour – and be guaranteed the attention he wants and deserves.
>
> (Hamilton Fazey, 1987b, p.3)

However, the best illustration of the benefits that have accrued to many local financial and producer services firms as a result of the transformation in the City has been the spectacular growth of regionally-based corporate legal practices. The largest corporate legal practices in Britain are all based in London, and the largest of these in the City of London. These firms have long provided corporate legal advice to companies throughout Britain, and are hired as much for the prestige their appointment brings as for the quality of their services. Interviews conducted with partners of City law firms by the authors in the summer of 1987 confirmed their increasing orientation towards the international capital markets. Although the City firms had all expanded rapidly in the face of growing demand, several of the partners interviewed admitted that they had been forced to turn work down since they were already overloaded. Regional lawyers have not been slow to seize the market opportunities this presents. They have quickly tapped into the regional demand for corporate legal services and are beginning to cut off the flow of business that traditionally has gone to London:

> 'The London firms are so bombed out with work for very large national companies or international clients that even a £10m capitalised Yorkshire company is pretty small beer

to them. Yorkshire directors quickly catch on – 200 miles is a long way to go to see a newly qualified solicitor different from the one they saw last time.'
                        (Bradford solicitor, quoted in Hamilton Fazey, 1987c, p.5)

Indeed, the orientation of City law firms towards very large-scale corporations has meant that provincial corporate legal practices are not only shoring up their own regional markets for legal services, but in some cases are also encroaching into the medium-sized firm corporate legal market within London and the South East where firms too are feeling neglected by their former advisers. For example, Bristol legal practice Osborne Clark possesses many London-based clients. A recent review of corporate legal practice in Scotland suggested that in the near future Scottish law firms would soon begin to expand into London to 'stop the more lucrative Scottish business haemorrhaging out to the English jurisdiction' (Fennell, 1987b, p.36). Two trends that are becoming increasingly important are those of centralization and spatial expansion both within and between provincial centres. With regional demand for corporate legal services increasing as City-based firms move off into the distance of the international markets, so local firms are eschewing organic growth in favour of more rapid accretional expansion so as to pool those resources necessary for the provision of services of the scope and sophistication required by their increasingly-numerous clients. There are many examples of centralization among corporate legal practices within provincial centres. For example, merely within the first half of 1988 two new enlarged firms were created in Leeds as A. V. Hammond merged with Last Suddards (to form Hammond Suddards) and Walker Morris & Coles merged with Scott Turnbull & Kendal (to form Walker Morris Scott Turnbull) (Fennell, 1987a). In many cases, merger activity is combined with spatial expansion providing the firms with more comprehensive geographic coverage. Thus, Liverpool-based practice Alsop Stevens expanded the spatial extent of its operations by opening an office in Manchester in 1984 (Hamilton Fazey, 1987b), while Bristol firm Burges Salmon is forging an office network running parallel with the M5 from Plymouth to Birmingham (Alexander, 1987). In Scotland, Glasgow firms are increasingly looking for Edinburgh practices with which to merge because the location in the capital of the Supreme Court allows firms located there direct access to counsel. This was an important motive in the recent creation of the Glasgow–Edinburgh practices of Bishop and Robertson Chalmers in 1986 and Bird Semple in 1987 (Fennell, 1987b).

However, it would be wrong to assume that the vigorous growth displayed by provincial corporate legal practices is paralleled by all provincial financial and producer service firms. Although there is an undoubted increase in demand for financial and professional business services in such centres, provincial lawyers have enjoyed the comparative luxury of being free from the very real competitive pressures exercised by the regional operations of multi-locational London-based financial and producer service firms. In other sectors, local financial and producer service firms have not been so fortunate to find themselves in competition only with one another. As demand for financial and producer services has grown in provincial centres, local firms have been forced to compete for market share with branch offices of large international practices. Therefore, while there has most assuredly been a renaissance of financial and producer service activity within provincial centres, it would be wrong to overstate the importance in this movement of locally-based firms.

The geographical expansion of large multi-locational financial and producer service firms

The extent to which large London-based financial and producer service firms have embarked upon the construction of branch-office networks varies quite markedly between sectors. At one extreme are the corporate lawyers who operate almost exclusively out of their London offices. In contrast, there are the large accountancy firms who have relentlessly pursued a policy of geographical expansion so that most now possess almost comprehensive national coverage. Below we examine the spatial impacts of the expansion of the office networks of large accountancy firms and of large firms within two other sectors – commercial property agencies and merchant and investment banking.

The accountancy profession in Britain is characterized by a three-tiered organizational structure. The bottom two levels are characterized by many thousands of small firms (usually consisting of no more than two or three partners) and a decreasing number of medium-sized firms. The upper strata of the accountancy profession is characterized by a handful of international practices that dominate the accountancy market worldwide (Bavishi and Wyman, 1983). Between 1978 and 1986 the British operations of these large accountancy firms experienced substantial growth in fee-income, professional employment and profitability. As these firms have grown internally they have also comprehensively extended their office networks throughout the UK. For example, in 1985 the 20 leading firms collectively operated some 492 offices in the UK, an increase of over 62 per cent from 1975 (Leyshon, Daniels and Thrift, 1987). Between 1975 and 1985 the leading firms entered 128 previously-unserved locations while consolidating their position in established markets, and in 1985 12 cities contained the offices of at least 11 of the leading 20 firms (Table 5.6).

There were four interrelated spatial determinants of large accountancy-firm office growth during the period. First, offices were opened by firms in an attempt to claim UK market share through the construction of nationwide office networks that include most of the major cities. In 1975 some of the leading firms still ran their UK operations solely out of their London office. Cities such as Glasgow and Edinburgh, for example, have particularly benefited from this process of office-network development. Second, offices have been opened in response to business opportunities that arise in areas of industrial expansion. Aberdeen, the Thames Valley and Cambridge all witnessed a significant increase in the number of offices operated by the leading firms as they moved in to secure new clients. Third, the stagnation of the audit market during the period encouraged many large accountancy firms to cast their client-net wider to encompass the small-firm sector. The desire to capture an increased share of the small-firm accountancy market

Table 5.6   UK office distribution of large accountancy firms, 1975–85; cities with
             largest number of offices of 20 leading firms

| 1975 | | 1985 | | |
City	Offices	City	Offices	Change 1975–85
1 London	20	1 London	20	0
2 Birmingham	16	2 Birmingham	19	3
3 Manchester	15	3 Glasgow	17	6
4 Leeds	13	4 Leeds	16	3
5 Glasgow	11	5 Manchester	16	1
5 Liverpool	11	6 Edinburgh	15	8
5 Newcastle	11	7 Bristol	14	4
8 Bristol	10	7 Newcastle	14	3
9 Belfast	9	9 Cardiff	12	4
9 Nottingham	9	9 Liverpool	12	1
11 Cardiff	8	11 Aberdeen	11	6
11 Leicester	8	11 Belfast	11	2
13 Edinburgh	7	11 Nottingham	11	2
14 Douglas	6	14 Norwich	9	7
15 Southampton	5	14 Southampton	9	4
15 Aberdeen	5	16 Leicester	8	0
15 Sheffield	5	16 Reading	8	5
18 Bradford	4	18 Sheffield	7	2
19 Hull	3	19 Bradford	6	2
19 Reading	3	19 Douglas	6	0

(*Source:* Leyshon, Daniels and Thrift, 1987, Table 18.)

encouraged large accountancy practices to lower the generally-accepted population
threshold of a town that will support the operation of an office and to begin to
open offices in locations where they have no existing clients (*The Accounting
Bulletin*, 1983, p.8-9). Finally, accountancy firms now have greater opportunities
in the public-sector market and this development has helped to reinforce the
justification of office openings in some major cities (Leyshon, Daniels and Thrift,
1987).

Although large firms within the accountancy sector have demonstrated the most
vigorous expansionary growth among financial and producer service organizations,
they have not been alone in extending their operations throughout the country.
Commercial property firms have also steadily encroached into regional markets
since the mid-1970s. These firms have also undergone substantial organizational
growth as the increasing commercialization of the property market and its planned
securitization have forced many firms to rethink their operational structures. A
number of firms, such as Michael Laurie (now Morgan Grenfell Laurie) and
Richard Ellis, have forged links with investment banks to integrate respective skills.

These pressures for organizational change have occurred at a time when
commercial property firms are undergoing the beginnings of geographical expansion
throughout the UK. The 20 largest general-practice firms of chartered surveyors
in the UK are all headquartered in London, and the capital has long constituted
the most important market for these firms. However, the period between 1976

and 1986 saw these firms begin to break out of London and during the period the number of UK offices operated by them increased from 99 to 134. By 1986 the leading firms operated in 52 locations, an increase of 15 per cent on 1976 (Leyshon, Thrift and Daniels, 1987). Nevertheless, despite this growth, most offices remained concentrated within the wider South East region, and in both 1976 and 1986 over half of all those offices operated by the leading general-practice firms were based in that region. Cities such as Edinburgh, Glasgow, Leeds and Manchester all experienced increases in their share of large firms during the period (Table 5.7). However, London remained the only city within which over half of the leading 20 firms ran an office.

Table 5.7   UK office distribution of large commercial property firms, 1975/76–1985/86

1975		1985		
City	Offices	City	Offices	Change 1975–85
1 London	20	1 London	20	0
2 Edinburgh	6	2 Edinburgh	9	3
3 Glasgow	5	3 Glasgow	7	2
4 Birmingham	3	4 Leeds	5	3
5 Bath	2	5 Birmingham	3	0
5 Canterbury	2	5 Manchester	3	2
5 Cardiff	2			
5 Hereford	2			
5 Leeds	2			

(*Source:* Leyshon, Thrift and Daniels, 1987, Appendix 2.)

The continued predominance of London and the South East as a locational centre for leading firms of chartered surveyors can be attributed to the importance of the London commercial property market. For example, in 1985 a survey of institutional property holdings revealed that some 51 per cent of such holdings were based in London, with a further 19 per cent in the rest of the South East. There is evidence to suggest that London's pre-eminence as an outlet for property investment funds may be in decline as the property markets of other domestic centres increase in value.

A third example of a sector where firms have enjoyed considerable internal growth is that of investment (merchant) banking. UK investment banks have experienced considerable growth in the past decade as demonstrated by their burgeoning balance sheets and rising profit levels. However, unlike accountancy and commercial property firms, an analysis of the spatial expansion of their domestic office networks between 1975 and 1985 revealed that the total number of offices actually underwent a reduction of 5 per cent, despite a 140 per cent increase in the size of their overseas office networks. Moreover, an analysis of the location of the offices in Great Britain of all overseas banks between 1981 and 1986 also revealed a reduction in foreign-banking activity outside London (*The Banker*, 1981, p.113; 1986, p.74). The overall reduction in the number of domestic regional offices operated by UK investment banks and overseas banking conceals important trends towards a concentration and a transformation within banking activity in the regions. For example, Birmingham increased its share of UK investment-banking offices and remained the most important location for the offices of overseas banks outside London, while Manchester maintained its three UK investment-banking offices and experienced an increase in the number of foreign-banking offices operating there, as did cities such as Leeds, Glasgow and Liverpool. The fall in foreign bank offices in the regions was due almost entirely to radical cutbacks in the branch networks of institutions such as the Bank of Pakistan, the Habib Bank and particularly the Muslim Commercial Bank, organizations that largely provide commercial-banking facilities for ethnic segments of the banking market. Between them these organizations closed 31 offices between 1981 and 1986, predominantly in towns within the North West and Yorkshire & Humberside regions. If these banks are removed from the analysis the picture is somewhat different (Figure 5.5). Moreover, although the number of locations that contained overseas bank branch offices fell by some 23 per cent between 1981 and 1986, the number of foreign banks operating within the regions actually increased from 35 to 44. In addition, there was evidence of a change in the composition of overseas banks operating in the regions. Banks that opened regional UK offices between 1981 and 1986 included both Sumitomo Bank and Fuji Bank (in Birmingham and Manchester) who were the largest and fifth largest capitalized banks in the world in 1986 (*Euromoney*, 1987).

Therefore, large firms within the accountancy, commercial property and investment-banking sectors have experienced substantial internal growth since the mid-1970s that, for the most part, has been accompanied by a marked expansion in the domestic office networks of these firms. The cumulative locational impact of the spatial expansion of the office networks of large organizations within these three financial and producer service sectors can be assessed from Table 5.8. The table reveals those locations in Great Britain that contained the highest concentrations of 47 large accountancy firms, investment banks and commercial property firms in 1985-6 and indicates those locations where the in-migration of large multi-locational firms between 1975 and 1976, and 1985 and 1986, was strongest. The analysis clearly demonstrates the continued hegemony of London as a centre for financial and producer service activity as the only location within which all the 47 firms ran an office. The table also indicates those regional financial centres and sub-regional financial centres that were the sites of office expansion and, with the exception of Leicester, in all the provincial financial centres the number of offices operated by large financial and producer service firms increased. Among the regional centres, Edinburgh demonstrated the highest level of corporate in-migration with some 11 large producer service firms opening offices there between 1975 and 1976, and 1985 and 1986. This 70 per cent expansion in offices ensured that in 1985-6 Edinburgh contained the second highest number of large firms within the three producer service sectors. Meanwhile, the number of large firms operating in Glasgow also increased sharply, making it the third most important locational centre for such activity. Indeed, with the exception of Liverpool, the number of offices operated by the 47 large producer service firms in regional financial centres increased by at least 16 per cent.

Table 5.8   Office expansion of 47 large producer service firms in Great Britain[1], 1975/76–1985/86

City	Number of firms operating in city 1985/86	Increase 1975/76–1985/86	
		No.	%
London	47	0	0
Edinburgh	27	11	69
Birmingham	25	4	19
Glasgow	25	9	56
Leeds	22	6	38
Manchester	22	3	16
Bristol	15	4	36
Newcastle	15	3	25
Cardiff	14	4	40
Liverpool	13	1	8
Aberdeen	11	6	120
Nottingham	11	2	22
Norwich	10	8	400
Southampton	9	4	80
Leicester	8	0	0
Reading	8	5	167
Sheffield	8	2	33
Bradford	6	2	50

Note

1. 20 accounting firms; 20 commercial property firms; 7 UK investment banks.

(*Source*: Authors' research.)

The expansion of the domestic office networks of large producer service firms in the UK would therefore seem to correspond broadly with the pattern of employment growth in producer services in provincial financial centres outlined earlier. However, an adequate elucidation of the true nature of the relationship between multi-locational firm office growth and employment change would require access to comprehensive firm-based employment data that is not yet available. Nevertheless, the partial data that does exist would lead us to suggest that the opening of offices by large producer service firms is an important component of financial and producer service employment growth in provincial financial centres. For example, employment within large accountancy firms comprises a significant proportion of all accountancy employment within regional economies. Using both firm-based and Department of Employment data we estimate that, with the exception of East Anglia, the leading 20 accountancy firms provide at least one third of all accountancy employment within each regional economy. In the South East and Scotland the 20 largest firms provide over half of all accountancy jobs. Within the provincial centres themselves, the large accountancy firms are even more important employers. For example, four of the leading firms employed over 10 per cent of all accountancy employment in Birmingham and over 19 per cent in Glasgow. In Bristol, seven large multi-locational firms provided over 36 per cent of all accountancy employment. Although no comparable data is available, we would expect similar levels of large-firm domination to be replicated across other producer service industries.

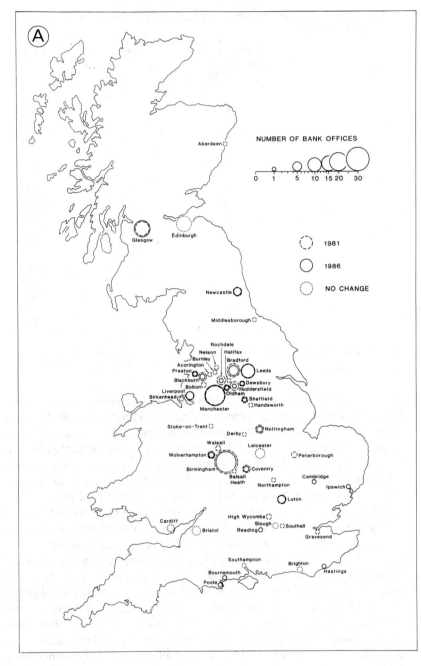

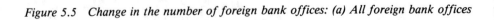

Figure 5.5 Change in the number of foreign bank offices: (a) All foreign bank offices

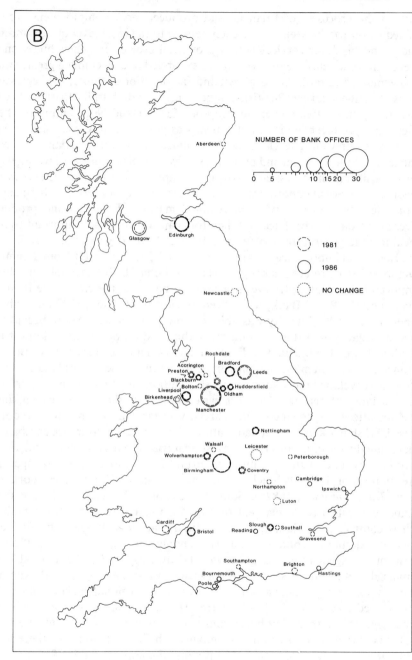

Figure 5.5   (Cont.):(b) Excluding banks catering for ethnic minorities

Both of the processes of financial and producer service employment growth discussed so far can be seen to be closely related to the local level of demand for financial and producer services within provincial centres and their hinterlands. However, in some centres employment has expanded to a level much greater than can be explained in terms of local-demand factors. For example, the regression analysis described earlier identified nine centres (Edinburgh, Bristol, Leeds, Norwich, Brighton, Reading, Southampton, Cardiff and Northampton) where financial and producer service employment was greater than would otherwise be expected given prevailing levels of local consumer and business demand. A closer examination of the financial and producer service organizations based within these centres reveals that the excess employment in many cases result from these centres possessing a functional importance that enabled them to export effectively financial and producer services beyond their regional markets. Financial and producer services are tradable over space and therefore can constitute an important source of local-income generation (Coffey and Polese, 1987; Beyers *et al.*, 1986).

The functional importance of these centres can be seen to result from a number of factors. First there are historical reasons. Edinburgh, for example, has been an important financial centre ever since the formation in the city of the Bank of Scotland and the Royal Bank, which were opened in 1695 and 1727 respectively (Draper *et al.*, 1988). The city was able to grow as a financial centre because of a separate legal system that, among other things, did not contain within it the protection afforded to the Bank of England that was enforced in the rest of Britain. Insurance companies emerged in the early 19th century to serve local markets and out of these developed the investment trusts that became of increasing importance during the late 19th century. The overseas experience of the insurance companies whose operations became international relatively early in their history, no doubt because English markets were already saturated with English insurance companies, was later highly advantageous to the investment trust groups (Draper *et al.*, 1988). The city is now one of the five most important international fund-management centres in the world, and is bracketed alongside London, Zurich, New York and Boston (*The Economist*, 1987b). Some £40 billion in funds are managed from Scotland (equivalent to 20 per cent of all British-managed money), the bulk of which is controlled by Edinburgh-based fund managers. Indeed, the financial district of Edinburgh contains what is arguably the highest concentration of investment management houses in the world (Edwards, 1988). The residual levels of financial and producer service in Norwich can also be seen to be due largely to the city exporting financial services beyond the regional market and to its historical pedigree as a financial centre. However, Norwich is a much less international centre than Edinburgh and is predominantly dependent upon one firm, the Norwich Union Insurance Company, which was established there some two-hundred years ago. Nevertheless, it is a major company and in 1987 it earned over 6 per cent of the premiums worldwide (Reeves, 1987a).

The second cause of residual levels of financial and producer service employment in centres would seem to result from certain large cities increasing their functional importance within the regional economies of which they are a part. This results both from the renaissance of local firms and from the influx of the offices of large financial and producer service organizations. For example, take the case of Leeds:

> the growing strength of the regional market is underscored by a remarkable explosion in financial and professional services in and around Leeds [which is] providing Yorkshire and Humberside with a self-sufficient financial capital city. There is almost no need for any Yorkshire company to go to London for financial service [because] almost every one of a company's professional advisors – accountants, solicitors, merchant banks, and stockbrokers – can be drawn from local ranks.
>
> (Hamilton Fazey, 1987c, p.5)

While Edinburgh is clearly the most important financial centre in Scotland, in Glasgow other producer service firms have undergone a resurgence as, for example, in the increasingly-expansionary behaviour of the corporate lawyers. In Manchester, while the level of financial and producer service overall is lower than would be expected given the prevailing level of demand, there is in fact a residual of purely financial-service employment. This residual employment results from a combination of the resurgence of local firms and of the influx of larger institutions that is helping to establish the city as the most important financial centre of the north of England:

> Finance has become a new lynchpin. The facts are readily wheeled out – over 40 different banks are represented; the Bank of England has its largest office outside London here; Henry Cooke Lumsden claims to be Britain's biggest regional stockbroker; the Manchester Stock Exchange is the settlement centre for all the northern exchanges.
>
> (Kennedy, 1988, p.54)

However, there is a group of provincial centres whose functional importance owes less to historical antecedents than to an increasing tendency of the organizations there to serve the wider regional economy. Centres such as Bristol, Reading and Brighton, for example, have benefited from becoming important destinations for office decentralizations from Central London. This has allowed these centres to engage in the export of financial services, either directly through the sale of services to the rest of the economy, or indirectly to other parts of the organization of which they are a part (Coffey and Polese, 1987).

Office decentralization from Central London

Since 1964 the process of office decentralization has transferred nearly 150,000 jobs out of Central London (Jones Lang Wootton, 1987a). Between 1979 and 1986 alone it is estimated that some 27,000 jobs were relocated from Central London in this way. Therefore, although much reduced in scale from the movements of the early-to-mid-1970s, office decentralization remains one source of mobile employment that would appear to have survived from the 'golden era' of employment redistribution in Britain that lasted from 1945 until 1973 (Morgan, 1986b). Unlike the geographical expansion of large financial and producer service firms described in the last sub-section, decentralized activities tend either to serve national markets or are key operational divisions of the organizations of which they are a part. The decentralization of financial-service firms is most commonly associated with the relocation of 'back office' activities, developments that are made possible by advances in communicative technology (Moss and Dunau, 1986; Nelson, 1986; van Dinteren, 1987). Decentralization from Central London seems to be primarily motivated by rising property costs (Jones Lang Wootton, 1987a), although labour costs may also be significantly reduced through decentralization – not only by moving out of the relatively high-wage London labour market but also by combining the move with the introduction of new technology, thereby facilitating productivity increases that enable firms to enter their new locations with reduced labour requirements (Boddy, Lovering and Bassett, 1986; Morris, 1986).

Decentralization can act as an important engine of financial-service employment growth within provincial centres, although it should be noted that only 28 per cent of all decentralizations from Central London between 1979 and 1987 involved financial and producer service firms. However, while the resurgence of local firms and the in-migration of the offices of large London-based multi-locational organizations were equally prevalent within northern and southern provincial centres, the employment benefits enjoyed by the recipient locations of office decentralization have been spatially constrained to the South East. Over 78 per cent of all decentralizations from Central London between 1979 and 1987 were directed towards locations within the South East region, with 43 per cent relocating merely within the Greater London area. Therefore, the impact of office decentralization from Central London upon financial and producer service employment growth outside the South East would seem to be limited to only certain provincial centres, given that only 22 per cent of relocations extended beyond that region.

A more detailed examination of the decentralization of offices of financial-service firms from Central London between 1983 and 1987 is illustrated in Table 5.9. The spatially constrained nature of these moves is once more clearly evident. Only four of the 26 moves listed were destined for locations outside the South East, all of which were in regions geographically contiguous to the South East. Three were destined for the South West and one for the East Midlands. It should be noted that those moves that did go beyond the South East did in fact tend to be larger – an average of 282 jobs per move compared to 239 overall – and were accompanied by a greater range of functions than were moves closer to London. Moves to Gloucester and Poole were accompanied by the entire suite of operational activities, while a firm that moved to Peterborough left behind only its investment department and two key officials. Nevertheless, such moves were relatively insignificant compared to the number of jobs transferred out of Central London and into the suburban towns of the South East.

The residual levels of financial and producer service employment identified by the earlier analysis within places such as Brighton and Reading are thus due at least in part to the locational impacts of decentralization. A clear example of the benefits that can accrue to a centre through decentralization is afforded by examination of the growth of insurance employment in Bristol. The city was the destination of a series of important insurance company decentralizations during the 1970s and early 1980s. Between 1972 and 1983, Phoenix, Sun Life, Clerical Medical and General and London Life all moved their administrative headquarters to the city, while the National Westminster Bank established its insurance subsidiary in the city during the same period (Boddy, Lovering and Bassett, 1986). Other centres in the south are increasingly benefiting from the advantages that accompany the decentralization of national administrative centres. For example, Southampton is now home to the headquarters of the Skandia Life company (Coopers & Lybrand, undated) and has been targeted as the location for the national centre of the Midland Bank's trustee division (Hampshire Development Corporation, per. comm.). Meanwhile, Brighton is the headquarters location of the Alliance & Leicester Building Society, one of the largest such organizations in Britain in 1988, and contains the administrative centre of the Legal and General Insurance Company and an operating division of American Express, the latter being decentralized in 1974 and now one of the largest ten employers within the city (SEEDS Association, 1987; Kennedy, 1988).

Although to date it has undoubtedly been provincial centres within the south that have most benefited from the injection of employment that decentralization brings, there are signs that office decentralization may indeed be creeping north and west as property prices in the south continue to rise. Therefore, provincial centres such as Northampton and Cardiff have already become the sites of financial-service administration centres. Northampton contains the Headquarters of Barclaycard, while in 1982 Chemical Bank moved its information and data-processing departments to Cardiff (Morris, 1988). However, interviews conducted by the authors with key employees in large investment banks based in the City of London in the spring and summer of 1987 did not really suggest that long-distance decentalization was a serious alternative for many of them. Most executives who were interviewed stressed that as financial markets became progressively more complex so the back-office activities also needed to become increasingly sophisticated. Many expressed a preference for keeping the back office in fairly close spatial proximity to the front-end activities so that settlement problems could more easily be ironed out, preferably by face-to-face communication. The furthest these firms seemed to be thinking of decentralizing was to Canary Wharf in the London docklands. It was clear that many whom we interviewed thought that for them even Bournemouth was somehow a wildly-eccentric location for financial services while Chemical Bank's move to Cardiff was scarcely comprehensible.

The impacts of financial and producer service growth in provincial centres

In this section we wish to consider some of the consequences of the increasing prominence of financial and producer service firms within provincial centres. The growth of these firms has had a range of impacts, of which we identify three as being of particular importance. The first is the growing importance of financial and producer service employment within the employment bases of provincial centres across the breadth of the country. Second, we wish to examine the implications of the growth of these activities upon other industrial sectors within regional economies. Third, and finally, we look at the impact of the growing importance

Table 5.9 Decentralization of financial services from Central London, 1983–7

Company	Classification	Origin	Destination	No. of jobs	Date of move
Bank of America	Bank	EC3	Bromley	350	1983
		Croydon	Croydon	350	1983
United Dominion Trust	Bank	EC3	New Barnet	200	1983
Commercial Union	Insurance	EC3	Croydon	700	1983
English & American Insurance	Insurance	EC3	Gloucester	170	1984
Lloyds Life Insurance	Insurance	EC2	Peterborough	180	1984
National Mutual Life of Australia	Insurance	EC2	Poole	180	1984
Brown & Shipley	Bank	EC3	Haywards Heath	100	N/a
Abbey National	Building society	W1	Milton Keynes	700	1985
Commercial	Insurance	EC1	Basildon	330	1985
Provident Life	Insurance	EC2	Basingstoke	250	1985
Chase Manhattan	Bank	EC2	Bournemouth	600	1986
Confederation Life	Insurance	WC2	Stevenage	250	1987
Allied Irish Banks	Bank	City	Uxbridge	1,000	N/a
Lombard North Central	Bank	WC	Redhill	350	1986
Sun Life of Canada	Insurance	SW1	Basingstoke	500	1987
Total				6,210	

Note
N/a = not available or not applicable.
(*Source*: Jones Lang Wootton, 1987a, Tables 4 and 5.)

Table 5.9 (cont.)

Type of move	Functions moved	Functions remaining	Reasons for move
Partial	Processing, servicing & admin. depts	Personnel, marketing, trading	Rationalization, consolidation
Partial	Most HQ functions	N/a	Cost reduction
Complete (small office)	All	N/a	Cost reduction
Complete (small office)	All	N/a	Cost reduction
Almost complete	All but –	Investment, MD, marketing director	Cost reduction, consolidation environmental amenity
Complete	All	N/a	Cost reduction, consolidation, environmental amenity
Partial	N/a	N/a	N/a
Almost complete	All but –	Finance, marketing	Consolidation, cost reduction
Partial	Support	HQ functions	Cost reduction
Complete (small office)	All	N/a	Cost reduction
Partial	Admin. operational	Marketing, finance	Expansion, accommodation, cost reduction, environmental
Almost complete	All but –	Investment	Cost reduction
Partial	HQ functions	N/a	N/a
Partial	HQ, banking	Deposit office	
Almost complete	All but –	Investment	Expansion

of financial and producer service employment upon the north-south dimension of the overall spatial division of labour within Britain. Much of the evidence used in this final section is anecdotal. Nevertheless, it seems to suggest that in many ways the growth engendered by the expansion of financial and producer services in provincial cities may well become self-generating.

The growing importance of financial and producer service employment within local and regional labour markets

One of the most important impacts of financial and producer service growth within the leading provincial centres of Britain has been the growing prominence of financial and producer service firms as employers. Between 1974 and 1984 the proportion of total employment that was within financial and producer service industries increased in every one of the leading financial centres in Britain. On average these industries accounted for almost 12 per cent of total employment within the leading provincial centres in 1984, compared to only 8 per cent in 1974. In 1984 financial and producer service industries were of above-average significance as employers in Bootle (26 per cent of total employment), Birmingham (20 per cent), Glasgow (18 per cent), London (16 per cent), Manchester (16 per cent), Edinburgh (15 per cent), Bristol (15 per cent), Bournemouth (14 per cent), Southend (14 per cent) and Brighton (13 per cent).

The multiplier impacts of financial and producer service employment growth within provincial centres

The growth of financial and producer service employment within provincial centres has had a wide range of beneficial impacts upon the local and regional economies in which they are based. These include the direct multiplier effects that result from increased corporate and employee spending and from the agency role that financial and producer service firms play in generating economic growth.

The increasing prominence of financial and producer service firms within provincial centres has significantly boosted the demand for ancillary services such as printing and publishing, temporary employment agencies, courier services, etc. The growing number of financial and producer service and ancillary firms in provincial centres has had a marked impact upon office rental values in provincial centres. Financial and producer service firms generate a quite specific type of demand for office space in that they prefer to occupy modern premises in central locations. The relative paucity of this type of property within provincial centres (Chesterton Research Department, 1988) has placed considerable upward pressure on rental values. Indeed, rental values are increasing to the level where the speculative funding of office developments will become increasingly economically viable within provincial centres, a phenomenon that has been of relatively little importance in provincial centres to date. This will have major beneficial impacts for the construction industry in these centres.

A further benefit to arise from the increased level of financial activity in the provincial centres derives from the multiplier effects of employee spending. The labour employed by financial and producer service firms is predominantly highly skilled and well renumerated. For example, an occupational breakdown of 18 leading accountancy firms in the UK in 1986 revealed that of the 39,500 employed, over 84 per cent were classified as 'professional staff' (*The Accountant*, 1986). Other financial and producer service firms such as corporate lawyers and commercial-property agencies similarly comprise relatively-high proportions of highly-qualified labour (Farmbrough and Jenkins, 1987; Leyshon, Thrift and Daniels, 1987). It should also be noted that the ratio of professional to support staff within the offices of multi-locational financial and producer service firms would appear not to vary spatially. This is important, for highly-qualified labour within producer service firms enjoy levels of remuneration that are much higher than average. Spending by well-renumerated, high-status staff within financial and producer service firms will have beneficial effects upon local markets of property, goods and services (for example, see Thrift, Leyshon and Daniels, 1987).

In addition to the very real impacts made by financial and producer service firms by way of corporate and employee spending, the increasing concentration of these firms within provincial centres may also be encouraging economic growth through the agency services they perform for capital. It is widely acknowledged by local financial and producer service firms that the in-migration of financial and producer service conglomerates has made a significant contribution to the increasing sophistication of many provincial financial centres. This is perceived as beneficial not only to the local firms themselves, who increasingly pick up referrals from larger firms, but it is also held to be beneficial to the wider regional economy. In northern centres this is seen to be of particular importance: 'It is not just that there is more profitable work for all of us. The fact that good professional advice and expertise is available locally helps keep the head offices and the decision-making here' (Lawyer with Yorkshire corporate legal practice, quoted in Hamilton Fazey, 1987c, p.5). The diminution of head offices and decision-making in the north (see Chapter 6) is in fact less to do with the degree of sophistication of the financial centres there than the short-term profit-seeking attitude of the large institutional investors who have actively encouraged the recent merger and acquisition boom in Britain (Scouller, 1987), and therefore also the process of capital centralization, by willingly selling their major shareholdings in British capital for the premiums offered by acquiring companies.

In another way, the increasing sophistication of the financial communities may well be bolstering the north's possession of key functions within the overall social division of production. Most venture-capital funds for new business operations in Britain are still by and large raised in the south for use by new ventures in the south (Mason, 1987). The bias towards the south holds true even for government-sponsored funding projects such as the Business Expansion Scheme (BES) (Mason and Harrison, 1987). Mason and Harrison suggest that one of the reasons for the lack of BES funds for new projects in peripheral regions may be the result of geographical biases in the risk perceptions of South-East-based fund managers, biases that discriminate against projects outside the buoyant economy of the south.

However, the burgeoning financial communities of provincial centres are rapidly developing local sources of venture funding that would overcome such a bias. Financial-service firms recognize that it is very much in their interest to encourage the growth of new firms so that sufficient management functions are retained to generate enough demand for the financial and business services they sell. Although Investors in Industry (3i) – the venture-capital organization owned by the clearing banks and the Bank of England – remains the most prominent organization of this type within Britain as a whole (Harris, 1988), it is facing increasing competition from a series of more localized venture-capital groups even within the provincial centres of the north. For example, take the case of Newcastle, where 3i's more recent competitors include 'Northern Industries, a £5m fund formed in 1984 as a private sector replacement for the government's wound-down British Technology Group, and the £5.25m Northumbria Unit Trust, one of Lazard's regional funds. Soon, the Newcastle office of Penny Easton will be launching a fund for equity deals under £50,000' (Hamilton Fazey, 1987d, p.3). This in a city that has not been noted for its entrepreneurial successes in the past. Similar examples may be found in many of the other provincial centres of the north. The development of local sources of venture capital such as these is considered to be essential for filling the 'equity gap' of under £250,000, which is below the threshold level of investment set by City of London venture-capital funds, a factor that is thought to explain the current paucity of small rapid-growth firms in the regions of the north (Mason, 1987).

In addition, the influx of the branch offices of larger financial organizations is allowing provincial centres to retain a local interest in larger financing deals that otherwise would have gone to London. For example, witness the comments of a Manchester-based director of the County NatWest investment bank:

> There comes a point when a transaction is too large for any of the locally represented investment banks to handle independently. Instead of sitting back and seeing that transaction directed to London, a number of development capitalists in Manchester get together and we now see local syndication of the large deals.
>
> (quoted in *Investors Chronicle*, 1987, p.12)

This may be particularly important in the case of large deals such as management buyouts. These deals have the added advantage for provincial financial-service firms in that they often increase the level of local decision-making within industry, a factor that is seen as crucial for the generation of future business. For example, County NatWest took advantage of the increasing sophistication of the Leeds financial community in its syndication of a £1.5 million management buyout of Holliday Dyes and Chemicals: 'It took a big risk here, buying 71 per cent of the equity itself and then selling it down to other investors. Something most observers would have thought inconceivable in an English region only a year ago' (Hamilton Fazey, 1987e, p.3).

These advances in corporate finance within provincial centres may hold out hope for an increasing level of local autonomy in industrial activity within the northern regions in particular. However, perhaps of more immediate significance for local levels of employment within such regions, the increasingly international character of the larger financial and producer service firms based in provincial cities may also be helping to attract overseas production units to the north through the agency services such firms provide to multinational capital. For example, in the four months between December 1986 and April 1987 three large overseas banks, two Japanese and one West German, opened offices in Manchester. The openings were stimulated both by a desire to penetrate local corporate finance markets and to promote foreign direct investment in the north of England (Hamilton Fazey, 1987f). The Japanese banks, especially, see Manchester as a regional financial centre within which they can act as gatekeepers to Japanese investment flowing into the north of England.

Therefore, financial and producer service firms based in provincial centres may be helping to boost employment levels, while also acting to improve the quality of such employment, by encouraging the growth of indigenous business through its corporate finance activities. Moreover, these firms may also be helping the effectiveness of industry by improving the quality of advice available in provincial centres, although of course this is an unmeasurable effect. A further point to consider in this context is the impact that the employment within financial and producer service firms actually has upon the overall spatial division of labour within Britain.

Corporate control and the spatial division of labour within financial and producer service firms

In recent years the concentration and centralization of capital within Britain has resulted in an increasing spatial polarization of social class. As the controlling functions within the overall social division of production have become increasingly concentrated within the south of the country, principally as a result of merger and acquisition activity, but also through a greater level of new-firm formation in the south, so managerial, professional and administrative occupations have become increasingly concentrated within the occupational structure of employment there (Massey, 1984; 1988). At the same time, these high-status occupations have become less important within the occupational structure of employment within northern regions. The increase in financial and producer service firms within the provincial cities of the north would seem to have had an ambiguous effect upon the general trend by which northern regions in general have lost key determining functions within the economy.

On the one hand, it is undoubtedly true that the growth of the offices of large multinational financial and producer service conglomerates within the provincial cities of the north has itself contributed to the extension of corporate control over financial and producer service activity. In this sense, the growth in the office networks of these large firms throughout the leading provincial centres can be seen as a way in which the influence of the City of London is being extended throughout the regional economies, and in this sense provincial financial centres are being increasingly integrated with national and even international financial markets. In addition, through the process of office decentralization, financial and producer service firms may even reinforce the growing spatial division of labour by relocating only the most routinized and low-wage functions within the overall work process (Boddy, Lovering and Bassett, 1986; Nelson, 1986).

However, it is also clear that an important component of financial and producer service growth has been the result of the resurgence of local firms. These firms freely acknowlege the role played by the influx of offices of larger firms in bringing a new financial 'respectability' to provincial centres that has in turn rubbed off on indigenous financial and producer service firms. Moreover, it is a notable feature of financial and producer service firms that their branch operations are endowed with levels of operational autonomy much greater than is normally the case in other sectors of the economy (Bertrand and Noyelle, 1986). This is because the success of financial services is 'increasingly dependent on product customization and individualized relationships with clients i.e. the production of a service has become far less important than its effective distribution and refinement. Tailoring sales or product development to client needs involves more autonomy, responsibility and decentralized decision-making than is typical for production' (Daniels, 1987, p.436). The relatively high degree of latitude afforded to the branch operations of financial and producer service firms has helped contribute to the growing functional cohesiveness of provincial financial centres as illustrated by the anecdotal examples presented above. The degree of operational independence does vary between sector, dependent upon the dominant form of organizational structure, with autonomy being highest where firms are organized as partnerships, as, for example, in the case of accountancy practices, while rather less independence is ceded to the branch operations of private or public limited companies, as, for example, investment banks.

Therefore, the malign local impacts that are commonly associated with the spread of the corporate economy in other sectors is not necessarily apparent within the financial and producer services sector. They pay higher than average levels of remuneration to the large numbers of professional staff they employ, which are passed into the local economy through employee spending. Furthermore, these firms possess relatively high levels of functional autonomy, enabling them to retain a greater degree of self-determination over their development than is the case for branch units within other sectors of the economy.

Conclusion

We have revealed that the leading provincial financial centres in Britain have, for the most part, enjoyed quite rapid growth in financial-service employment since the mid-1970s. Although the fastest-growing centres tended to be located in the south, northern provincial centres, too, experienced widespread employment growth within these industries. Employment growth was seen to be the result of three important processes. First, the expansion of indigenous financial and producer service firms; second, the in-migration of the offices of large multi-locational financial and producer service firms; and third, the decentralization of operating divisions of such firms from Central London. However, whereas the first two demand-led processes were of equal importance within both northern and southern centres, the third process was virtually exclusive to southern-based provincial centres. This has important implications for the creation of a spatial dichotomy between northern and southern centres in their ability to engage in the export of financial and producer services, either directly or indirectly (Coffey and Polese, 1987). Nevertheless, the growth of financial and producer service employment has meant that these industries have become increasingly important as employers, both within provincial centres and within the region in which the centres are based, and have conferred considerable economic benefits to local economies in both north and south.

We have paid particular attention to the expansion of large multi-locational financial and producer service firms into the major provincial financial centres of Britain, and this phenomenon has been an important component of producer service employment growth within such locations. The unique combination of autonomous operational behaviour linked to an ability to draw on the resources of a multinational service conglomerate has enabled these firms to penetrate regional markets successfully for financial and producer services. In doing so, the increased scale and scope of activity associated with their entry has also benefited indigenous financial and producer service firms who, where not in direct competition with the multi-locational organizations, have profited from the rising level of financial activity performed in provincial centres. There is more than a little justification in drawing a broad parallel between producer service employment growth in provincial financial centres and the growth in employment from the microelectronics industry in central Scotland: both provincial financial centres and 'Silicon Glen' have experienced employment growth through the in-migration of large multi-locational organizations. Moreover, just as Silicon Glen has reached a point of 'take-off' as an assembly point for imported components for redistribution in the international economy (Cooke, Morgan and Jackson, 1984), so the recent growth in and of provincial financial centres looks set to forge their full integration with the international financial system. However, unlike Silicon Glen, where employment is predominantly unskilled female labour working within the branch plants of US multinational corporations, the developing articulation of provincial financial centres in the world economy will be much more independent and will stimulate employment growth characteristic of the top end of the occupation hierarchy. There is increasing evidence to suggest that the influx of offices of international financial and producer service firms in provincial financial centres will soon breach London's virtual monopoly on the organization of cross-border business in financial and producer services. There will be a much greater integration of the 'local' and the 'international' in the organization of capital and informational flows, as financial and producer service firms in provincial financial centres respond to the growing international activities of regionally-based capital by allowing them direct access to the international financial system without recourse to London-based firms. The ability of financial and producer service firms directly to access the international financial system is greatly enhanced by the development and application of information-technology systems that have dramatically increased the locational flexibility of financial-service firms in particular.

However, it would be wrong to overstate the long-term role of local financial and producer service firms in this scenario. Although many local firms are currently thriving, many are doing so because of the limited geographical expansion of large London-based practices within particular sectors. The corporate lawyers are a case in point.

In addition, it is unlikely that all the leading provincial centres will continue to benefit from the growth of such activities. There is evidence to suggest that there is a process of regional centralization underway that is pushing just one centre in a region to prominence above all others. This process is most clearly evident amongst northern centres. For example, Leeds is increasingly becoming the financial centre for Yorkshire & Humberside and the Northern region and some large accountancy firms have even located national departments within the city. In this respect it is weakening the relative importance of the sub-regional centres of both Newcastle and Sheffield. Leeds is in battle with Manchester for the title of the provincial financial centre of the entire north of England. Manchester would seem to be better placed in this larger arena given its wider range of financial institutions and its ability to suck in functions from Liverpool. Liverpool seems to be in terminal decline as a regional financial centre, as it is outpaced by it larger rival. Similar examples of regional centralization can be seen elsewhere. Birmingham is growing rapidly, while Nottingham and Leicester experience relative stagnation. Bristol is the dominant centre for the West Country, and to a large extent for south Wales too. Despite the rapid growth in financial producer service employment in Cardiff (especially between 1981 and 1984), the city still lacks any important base of local financial institutions. More than any other large sub-regional centre, financial and producer service employment growth in Cardiff has been dependent upon the expansion of multi-locational organizations. The paucity of local control over financial institutions is illustrated by the fact that even the Commercial Bank of Wales is owned by the Bank of Scotland (*Euromoney*, 1988). Nevertheless, as property prices in Bristol continue to spiral, there is at least the chance that Cardiff may benefit from short-distance relocation across the Bristol Channel.

This chapter has illustrated that the common depiction of the north-south divide as an exclusively prosperous 'south' and permanently depressed 'north' is over simplistic, given that in some sectors at least northern localities have been centres of rapid employment growth and have enjoyed economic benefits such expansion brings with it. Nevertheless, as spatial centralization among northern centres proceeds, those pockets of relative economic wealth in the north will become even more concentrated around only a few, key, metropolitan areas. Moreover, it would seem likely that the future growth of financial and producer service employment will be largely concentrated within the south. This is because of the continued reluctance of decentralizing firms to move their operations out of the south and also because the most buoyant areas of new economic growth also tend to be confined to the south. In particular, the growth of new firms in 'Silicon Fen' is encouraging financial and producer services firms to move into Cambridge, especially in order to establish early client links with 'up and coming' companies, while the same motivation underlies the dramatic influx of financial and producer service firms into Swindon (Bassett, 1988; Hodson, 1988).

The continued viability of provincial financial centres throughout Britain is ultimately related to the demand for their services from their principal clients, i.e. the corporate sector. There is a clear symbiotic relationship between the level of corporate sector decision-making activity and the level of financial and producer service employment within an area, since the latter functions are in essence an extended form of the management division of labour (Gillespie and Green, 1987). As such the rate at which the processes of capital concentration and centralization are depleting northern regions of key decision-making functions would seem to be of fundamental importance for the future viability of many northern centres. Hence the enthusiasm of local financiers and professionals for local sources of venture capital. However, the prospect that new northern firms will come through at sufficient speed to counterbalance the rate at which existing firms are being absorbed by large organizations is not a hopeful one. This will inevitably cast doubt upon the ultimate long-term functional importance of the northern financial centre.

Acknowledgements

Andrew Leyshon gratefully acknowledges the bridging finance provided by Bristol University, which enabled him to remain in his post while this paper was written and researched.

Notes

1. There are necessary caveats to be attached to any analysis of the occupational data of the Census of Population. First, employees are classified purely by occupation, and cross-analysis by industry is possible only at high levels of spatial aggregation. It is important, therefore, to appreciate that what we have defined as financial and producer service occupations may not necessarily be located within financial and producer service firms. For example, certified accountants are predominantly employed within industry while chartered accountants may also be employed in industry and in public practices. 'Taxation experts', meanwhile, include not only those engaged in private practice but also civil servants employed by the Board of Inland Revenue.

2. Although other studies of financial-service employment limit the sector to banking and bill discounting, insurance and other financial institutions (for example, Draper *et al.*, 1988), we have also classified accountancy services as a 'pure' financial service since the mainstay of accountancy practice remains the adjudication of financial exchange (Leyshon, Daniels and Thrift, 1987).

3. Throughout this chapter Department of Employment data is analysed at the Amalgamated Office Employment Area (AOA) level. The exception to this rule was London. The metropolitan area was analysed in its entirety given the difficulty of separating out functionally-independent sub-areas of the city.

4. There are two main problems with the variable used to represent 'consumer demand'. First, the number of employees within the relevant TTWA may, in fact, understate the number of people using the centre for financial and producer services. A further problem arises in the use of employees in employment only. This excludes people who may in fact exercise a demand for financial services but be outside employment – for example, pensioners with investment income. The use of the 'business demand' variable is also problematic. First, the use of county-based data means that for some centres – Leeds and Bradford, Birmingham and Coventry – the values are replicated. Moreover, the county GDP figures are calculated from nation-level data and reduced geographically on a pro rata basis related to industrial structure, incomes and earnings. Even beyond this there are problems, as, for

example, in the exclusion of the demand generated by the incomes of commuters in their places of residence. These are instead apportioned to their places of work (for full details, see CSO, 1988).

6

NON-FINANCIAL HEAD OFFICES: A VIEW FROM THE NORTH

H.D. Watts

'300 jobs go as city firm shuts'
    The Star, Sheffield, 18 November 1987, p.1
'Council slams company move'
    The Star, Sheffield, 19 November 1987, p.1
'Furious MP challenges company's move south'
    The Star, Sheffield, 3 December 1987, p.11

Three headlines from the local newspaper of a northern city dramatically illustrate northern concern over the loss of head-office activities to the south. Only weeks later, central government and Scottish interests were embroiled in debates over the future role of Britoil's head office in Glasgow as a consequence of the acquisition of the firm by southern based BP. Despite government assurances that BP would retain many of the Glasgow-based office activities, it was seen by the opposition as 'a betrayal of public interest, exemplified by an increase in monopoly power,... [and] a move of decision taking power to London' (*The Independent*, 24 February 1988, p.6). In 1988, when the Swiss firm, Nestle, acquired the old-established Rowntree–Mackintosh, with headquarters in York, one of the grounds of public opposition lay in the probable withdrawal of head-office functions from the north of England. These events set the scene for considering the role of head offices in contributing to north-south contrasts.

This chapter examines the head offices of large non-financial firms in the north at both a regional and a local scale, and complements the previous chapter with its focus on the financial sector. The limited knowledge of the role and character of head offices in the north means that environmental planners, and local economic-development units making recommendations to their county and district councils, are unable to set their areas' offices in the context of the north as a whole. At the more local scale, developments concerning head offices in northern cities raise a number of interesting questions. Some companies are unhappy with their existing facilities, while local economic-development units are seeking to retain or expand employment in major decision-making units like head offices; environmental planners have to attempt to resolve the conflicts that exist between office activities and competing land-uses.

An examination of head-office location falls at the interface of two contemporary research areas. Head offices are clearly part of the office sector (Alexander, 1979; Daniels, 1979; Bateman, 1985), although most office-location literature ignores offices that are on the same site as other activities. They are also arguably part of the service sector (Daniels, 1985) and especially the producer-services sub-sector (Watts, 1987). Indeed, this chapter is a contribution to the 'disaggregated analysis of producer services' deemed necessary by Marshall, Damesick and Wood (1987, p.585). The importance of head offices is seen by combining Marshall's (1985b, p.8) claim that 'producer services are the main contribution to spatial variations in service employment' with the later view that 'the location of corporate headquarters... have a critical bearing on the location of producer services' (Marshall, Damesick and Wood, 1987, p.590).

In assessing head-office activities it is sometimes forgotten that 'a head-office is not just a building, it is a group of people who are called the head office-staff in the administrative structure of the corporation' (Crum and Gudgin, 1977, p.100). It can include, for example, directors, senior managers, corporate planners, financial advisers, accountants, lawyers and specialists in marketing, computing, personnel and public relations. All are highly qualified, they often have professional qualifications and tend to be on high salaries. In terms of social class, virtually all would be categorized as Social Class I (professsional occupations) while in terms of 'socio-economic groups' most would fall in SEG 1 (employers and managers in large establishments in industry and commerce) or SEG 4 (professional workers and employees). Head-office staff bring to a region a number of high-income households; conversely, of course, an absence of such staff can contribute to an unbalanced social mix that leads to a truncated social structure. This, in turn, can result in reduced local demand for services, for example private education and health; (see Chapters 7 and 8) and a relative lack of those vociferous middle-class groups who can often argue loudly (and effectively?) for more resources for their town and region.

Studies of the location of head offices were fashionable in the early 1970s (Parsons, 1972; Watts, 1972; Evans, 1973; Westaway, 1974) although these analyses placed emphasis on activities in the South East. This arose, in part, from the fact that from 1964 to 1979 attempts were made to control office development in that region through Office Development Permits (ODP) and that the dispersal of offices was encouraged through the Location of Offices Bureau (LOB) from 1963 to 1980 (Daniels, 1982, pp.82–7). At the same time, central government was encouraging the dispersal of government offices from London, and the 1970s saw a number of government offices located in northern towns (Daniels, 1985, pp.238–40).

Not surprisingly, the late 1970s saw a greater interest both in the changing geography of head offices and the patterns of head-office activity outside the South East (Goddard and Smith, 1978). Detailed analysis of office location in provincial cities, which dates fom the pioneering study of Leeds by Facey and Smith (1968), now encompasses studies of other northern cities such as Manchester (Damesick, 1979; Law, 1985, 1986), but they make few references to head-offices activities within the office sector. While to some extent this chapter provides an updating of the 1970s material, it does, at the same time, make two new contributions to the head-office literature. First, it provides a distinctly northern perspective to counterbalance the southern bias of earlier studies. Second, and perhaps most importantly, it illustrates the particular impact of head offices on a specific locality – the city of Sheffield. Although larger provincial centres can contain twenty or more head offices, there has been little discussion of how they are located within the urban fabric, nor indeed of patterns of change or the pressures imposed by their needs.

The main section of this chapter falls into six parts. The first outlines the problems presented by the spatial distribution of head-office activities, while the second considers the methodology employed in the study. The third compares the characteristics of head offices in the north and south, emphasizing similarities and contrasts. The fourth describes the distribution of head offices within the north, examining their interrelationships with the urban system. The fifth begins the examination of a specific locality by analysing the processes of change in head-office activities in Sheffield, while the final part continues the focus on a locality and considers some of the implications of the changing geography of head offices for local-office policies. In many ways this chapter is essentially descriptive, but exploring the head-office characteristics of the north is a first step towards explaining their key features.

The problem

A concern about the uneven distribution of head offices arises from its contribution to the unbalanced nature of regional development in the UK. Local communities react strongly to a loss of local control, a concern that is even more marked in Scotland and Wales, which form national minority groups within the UK as a whole. The main concern is usually with a loss of economic power, typified by the dramatic southern concentration of control in the UK's major non-financial companies. Only 10 per cent of the 100 largest non-financial firms have their head offices in the north, despite the fact it is an area that contains 59 per cent of the UK population (Healey and Watts, 1987; Watts, forthcoming). This is not the place to consider all the implications of this distribution but three are worth emphasizing.

The most straightforward implication of an uneven spread of head-office activities is the loss of jobs and the removal of high-level orientation decisions and high-level decision-makers from certain areas. Instead of the pattern shown in Figure 6.1Ai, the spatial pattern shown in Figure 6.1Aii emerges. Not only does this affect the social mix of the population, it also has political repercussions where communities recognize that they are controlled by absentee decision-makers.

A second consequence of an uneven spread of head offices appears to be an uneven spread of other producer services. A uniform spread of head offices would strengthen the demand for producer services (such as market research and financial activities) in all regions as shown in Figure 6.1Bi; concentration reduces the demand in some regions as shown in Figure 6.1Bii. There is a reasonable amount of evidence to support this pattern at least for the manufacturing sector. Externally-owned

A. Occupational mix

B. Linkages to producer services

C. Investment / Disinvestment

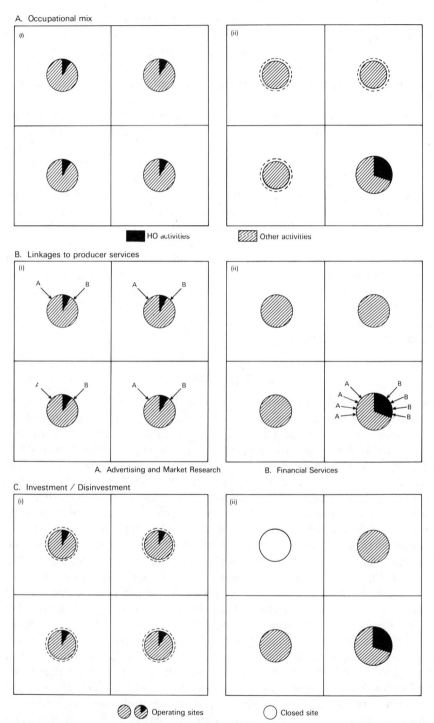

Figure 6.1 Regional consequences of head-office concentration

plants are more likely than indigenous plants to seek services outside the region in which they are located.

The final consequence is rather more problematic. There is a suspicion that activities distant from head office receive less-favourable treatment than those located closest to head office; in particular, there is a belief that activities distant from head offices are less likely to receive new investment and are more likely to be closed or sold as part of a disinvestment strategy. With dispersed head-office activities in a number of single plant firms, employment contraction may be spread evenly through all regions, as shown in Figure 6.1Ci whereas concentration of head office might result in the complete withdrawal from one region as in Figure 6.1Cii. The evidence for these beliefs is rather contradictory and whereas some studies have confirmed the expected pattern, others have refuted it.

The wider consequences arising from a lack of head offices in certain regions were summarized, for the manufacturing sectors, in Watts' (1981) discussion of branch plant economies. However, the three scenarios described in Figure 6.1 indicate that a lack of head offices in a particular area could give cause for concern. Whether the advantages gained by the economy as a whole from the concentration of head offices in a particular region are sufficient to offset the disadvantages experienced by regions lacking head offices is still open to debate.

Methodology

Previous studies of head offices examined the location of non-financial head offices at a number of scales, but the spatial divisions they use are not necessarily appropriate for the late 1980s. This is partly because of changes in administrative and functional boundaries, and partly because of the southward movement of the north-south divide over the last decade. The divide used here is that line approximately running from the Severn to the Wash, which separates the South West, South East and East Anglia (the south) from the rest of the UK (the north). (It may be difficult to accept that Stratford-upon-Avon and Leamington Spa are in the north and that Camborne-Redruth is part of the south, but the line represents a boundary in a system of regions for which published data are readily available.)

Within the north the data are analysed in terms of regions, local-authority districts and Local Labour Market Areas (LLMAs). Although LLMAs are perhaps most appropriate, policy-oriented research must, of necessity, use the district units the policy makers employ. Similarly, at intra-urban scale, the inner area of a city can be defined by the area recognized by the local authority and Department of the Environment for implementing inner-area initiatives.

Since the particular interest of this chapter is the nature of non-financial head offices in the north, there is no discussion of the distribution of offices within the south. The roles of Greater London and outer South East in the corporate hierarchy are not considered. In part this serves to redress an imbalance found in earlier studies, which dissect the patterns in the south but which tend to give only brief analyses of the main features of the north. It might be argued that this fails to deal with the fundamental concentration in London itself, but head offices are dispersed up to 60 to 80 miles (100 to 125 km) from London, and the long distance commuting of professional staff means that the white-collar employees of these offices live throughout much of the south. In a more technical sense, the indirect effects may impinge on an area of 60 to 80 miles (100 to 125 km) from London while the induced effects are spread further still.

Use is made of three data sets:

1. *Southern data* This is based on the top 100 non-financial companies with head offices in the south as listed in *The Times 1000 1986-7*, the latest edition available when this project was begun (the NOSO data set).
2. *Northern data* A data set relating to the 100 largest northern non-financial firms, again as listed in *The Times 1000 1986-7*. Head offices are here classified by their position on the urban-to-rural size continuum (the AHON data set).
3. *Sheffield data* A listing of all the head offices of non-financial firms in Sheffield recorded in *The Times 1000 1976-7* and *The Times 1000 1986-7*, sub-divided geographically into offices located in inner and outer Sheffield (the SHEFF data set).

The *Times 1000* data has at least three major limitations for this analysis. The registered head office may not be the main centre for administration; this was recognized in earlier studies and might have more force in the late 1980s as technological developments permit the dispersal of a wider range of operations than in the past. However, it is the only comprehensive national data set to provide an indication of the location of head offices.

The second difficulty it presents is rather more fundamental. Many activities are controlled through the head offices of subsidiary firms and these head offices are not listed by *The Times 1000*. Survey work can establish readily the location of such offices within individual cities, but a comprehensive listing of all such offices of non-financial firms within the UK is not available. It is recognized that many changes have taken place within these sub-corporate head offices but, in the absence of a readily-available national data set, these changes had to remain outside the scope of this enquiry.

A final, but relatively small, difficulty is that *The Times 1000* listing excludes the head offices of employers associations, unions, charities and similar organizations.

Head offices in the north

A general picture of the nature of northern head offices can be derived from an examination of the features of the 100 largest northern firms, with a turnover in excess of £153 million. Table 6.1 presents a series of four profiles based on size, financial, organizational and sectoral characteristics.

The top 100 northern firms are by no means small-scale operations. They have a median turnover of £305 million, with a range from £2,200 million (GKN) to £154 million (Bulmer). In terms of total employment (that is UK and overseas) they have a median employment of 5,861 and a range from 67,643 (Boots the Chemist, based in Nottingham) to 617 (Batleys, cash and carry wholesalers based

Table 6.1 Northern head offices, 1986–7

Profiles	Median
Size profile	
Turnover	£305 million
Employment	5,861
Financial profile	
Profit as % turnover	7
Profit as % capital employed	17

	% of northern firms
Organization profile	
UK quoted	74
Overseas ownership	13
UK unquoted	9
UK public sector	4
Sectoral profile	
Manufacturing	64
Services	36
Regional market	17
(retail, motor distribution)	
Resources	15
(drink, food, mining, oil and gas)	
High-tech	11
(chemicals, electrical)	

(*Source*: AHON data.)

in Huddersfield). The median net profit before interest and tax represents some 7 per cent of turnover and 17 per cent of the capital employed. Not surprisingly, over 74 per cent of the firms were UK quoted companies and 13 per cent were either public-sector organizations (4 per cent) or unquoted companies (9 per cent). A further 13 per cent were overseas owned, almost half of these firms from the USA. A broad grouping of the sectors shows a predominance of manufacturing firms, a limited number of firms based on resources or local markets and just over 10 per cent in a very crudely-defined high-tech category.

A more detailed analysis of sectoral mix can be provided by examining the distribution of the firms in relation to the twenty categories identified in *The Independent*'s share-price listings. Fifty per cent of the northern firms are listed under three heads (engineering, industrials and retailing), and the remaining firms are spread over virtually all the other categories. Perhaps particularly interesting are two major absences; there are no firms whose activities are classified to leisure or property. Analysing the sectoral structure of northern firms by divisions of the Standard Industrial Classification shows that three represented no less than 75 per cent of the firms. These were 'metal goods, engineering and vehicles', 'other manufacturing industries' and 'distribution, hotels and catering, repairs'.

This cameo of northern firms, while interesting in itself, takes on more meaning if the 100 largest northern firms are compared with the 100 largest southern firms. Northern firms differ significantly from southern firms on only three of the thirteen parameters listed in Table 6.1. First, they are significantly smaller than the southern firms; whereas 90 per cent of southern firms are above the 'all-firms' median turnover, 90 per cent of northern firms are below it. Second, the differences in employment are smaller but nevertheless marked; 78 per cent of the southern firms are above the all-firms median employment, whereas 78 per cent of the northern firms are below this median. Third, these firms show a distinct bias away from resource utilization. If the firms listed by *The Independent*'s financial page under oil and gas, food, drink and mining, are isolated, then whereas 15 per cent of northern firms fall in this category as many as 31 per cent of the southern firms are classed in this group. Analysis using the two-digit SIC categories produced a similar result.

On most other parameters, the northern and southern firms show only *small* differences. The northern firms show a slightly-greater emphasis on manufacturing (64 per cent compared with 56 per cent) and on services geared specifically to the local markets (17 per cent compared with 12 per cent), but have slightly under-representation of 'high-tech' activities (only 11 per cent compared with the south's 13 per cent). Profit as a percentage of turnover shows an almost identical pattern in north and south when compared in terms of the number of firms above and below the median; although when profits are measured as a percentage of capital employed, 55 per cent of northern firms are below the median compared with only 48 per cent of the southern firms. The differences between northern and southern firms are small when the proportion that are foreign-owned is examined, although the north has a smaller proportion of such firms than the south (13 per cent, compared with 18 per cent).

The most striking features of these northern firms is, then, that – apart from the differences in size – they do not differ markedly from their southern counterparts, except that southern firms show a greater dependence on the utilization of resources. On all the other parameters measured here the differences were small. One obvious omission from the measured characteristics is the degree to which industrial firms are linked into international production and marketing systems. It is suspected that southern firms may be more strongly linked into those systems than their northern counterparts.

Head offices and the northern urban system

In the previous part of the chapter, the characteristics of northern head offices as a whole were considered to provide a context for a discussion of their geographical distribution within the north. The broad framework of this geography can be appreciated at regional scale as shown in Figure 6.2. Perhaps the most striking feature of this distribution is the marked under-representation of head offices in Northern Ireland, Wales and the Northern region, which make up a major part of the 'industrial periphery' as defined by Martin in Chapter 2. These areas account for only 8 per cent of the head offices although they have almost 22 per cent of the population; 75 per cent of all northern head offices are in the 'industrial core' of the north (West Midlands, East Midlands, North West and Yorkshire & Humberside), which has only 62 per cent of the

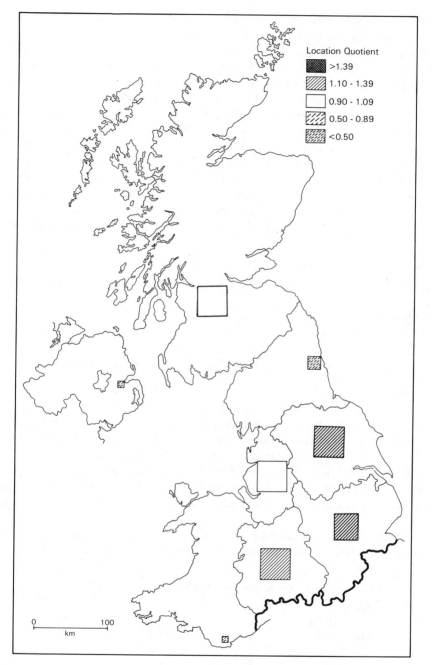

Figure 6.2 Head offices of 100 largest firms in the North, 1986-7 (Source: based on The Times 1000 1986-7)

population. Scotland forms a separate part of this pattern and it has just over its expected share of head offices (within the north). It has 17 per cent of the northern head offices compared with 16 per cent of the population. There are hints here of a separate organizational system. A more-detailed geography of the head offices in the north shows that distinct clusters of activity are obvious in some of the major urban centres, but in no way do any of these centres ever equal the major southern concentration in London. There are no signs of strong and prosperous head-office centres in the north. An analysis based on groupings of towns, cities and conurbation/provincial 'dominants' (as in Chapter 3) provides an insight into the detailed geography of northern head offices.

Overall, 40 per cent of the head offices were in the major conurbations, 36 per cent in cities and 24 per cent in towns and rural areas (Table 6.2). This compares with 29 per cent of the population in major conurbations, 36 per cent in cities and 35 per cent in towns and rural areas. Head offices are not characteristic of

Table 6.2   Head offices and the northern urban system, 1986–7

Urban category	Northern population[1] %	Northern head offices[2] %
Conurbations	29	40
Cities	36	36
Towns and rural areas	35	24

(*Sources*: 1. Champion *et al.,* 1987, Table 1.5. This source uses a slightly different definition of the north.
2. AHON data set.)

rural LLMAs. Only three firms had head offices in rural areas: Geest Holdings in Spalding (Lincs.), Croda Chemicals at Snaith, near Goole (Humberside) and the Irish Dairy Board has the head office of its UK operations at Uttoxeter (Staffs.). All other head offices lie within LLMAs with 'urban' status and there is an over-representation of the head offices in conurbations, a fair representation in the cities and an under-representation in the towns and rural areas.

The more detailed conurbation pattern is shown in Table 6.3. In Scotland, Glasgow and Edinburgh account for 75 per cent of the Scottish head offices, and

Table 6.3   Head offices of largest 100 northern firms, major LLMAs, 1986–7

Glasgow	8	Newcastle	4
Birmingham	6	Leeds	3
Manchester	6	Sheffield	2
Edinburgh	5	Nottingham	2
Liverpool	4		

(*Source*: AHON data.)

similarly in the Northern region, Newcastle holds four of the five head offices in the region, while the only head offices from the top 100 in Wales and Northern

Ireland are in Cardiff and Belfast. In other areas the head offices are spread more widely – for example, only 20 per cent of the head offices in Yorkshire & Humberside are in the principal LLMAs of Leeds and Sheffield, while in the East Midlands the proportion of East Midland firms in Nottingham is only 13 per cent.

The allocation of firms across more detailed (two-digit) groupings of the 1981 Standard Industrial Classification showed no major differences between conurbations, cities and towns. However, construction showed a bias towards conurbation head offices, the manufacture of both mineral products and chemicals showed a bias towards cities, while towns had an over-representation of head offices associated with both manufacturing and retailing/distribution. Ownership and profitability patterns did not differ between the three categories of urban place, but size of firm did differ when conurbations and cities were compared. Perhaps not surprisingly, the conurbations were significantly associated with the head offices of the larger northern firms whether measured by turnover or number of employees. These patterns were replicated when the data were analysed in terms of large (>400,000) and smaller local-authority districts. What became more evident here was the absence of foreign-based firms from the very largest northern centres. Thus Michelin is in Stoke-on-Trent, Goodyear in Wolverhampton and Cummins in Huddersfield.

This geography of northern head offices presents a static picture. Although it would be interesting to explain the location and characteristics of head offices in the north, the essentially descriptive nature of the analysis provides a setting for the more detailed study of a particular urban area. It has, none the less, to be stressed that the pattern is constantly changing. Over 10 per cent of the firms have changed ownership over the last year in a process that removed the last head office in the top 100 from Wales! These processes of change in one large city (Sheffield) form the starting-point for a consideration of the impacts of head offices on a specific locality.

Head offices in a northern city: Sheffield

Sheffield is the fourth largest city in England outside London and has a population of half-a-million inhabitants. The city is the largest urban area in South Yorkshire and is adjacent to the M1 motorway, some three hours north of London. It lies approximately equidistant from the other northern cities of Manchester, Leeds and Nottingham. Like most cities, the majority of its employment is in the service sector, manufacturing accounting for only 32 per cent of employees in employment. A diversity of activities within the service sector is contrasted with the specialized manufacturing sector, where metals-related industries account for 70 per cent of the manufacturing workforce. Overall, manufacturing employment in the city has dropped by around 50 per cent over the last decade.

Sheffield has also witnessed a dramatic fall in the number of head offices within its boundaries. Since the mid-1970s when the Sheffield City boundary encompassed some 22 head offices, the number has almost halved to 13 and, as was seen in Table 6.3, only two of the north's top 100 firms have had a Sheffield head office. A fall in the number of offices is probably typical of other northern cities; in the case of Manchester, Law (1986, p.32) notes a weakening of its role as a head-office centre, while from 1971 to 1981 the major conurbations experienced a 'sharp decline' in employment in 'central offices not elsewhere classified' (Gillespie and Green, 1987, p.408).

The processes by which the number of head offices of large firms in a provincial centre can change are six. There are firms rising above and falling below the critical turnover for inclusion in the top 1000, firms moving head offices in and out of the area, the disappearance of old firms by acquisition, and the emergence of new ones from management buyouts. Of course, the relative importance of these different processes will vary in time and space, and what has happened in Sheffield between 1976 and 1988 is not necessarily typical of all northern cities, nor a reliable indicator of what will occur in Sheffield in the future. Nevertheless, it does provide an indication of the dynamics of head-office location in a major northern city.

Examination of Table 6.4 reveals the importance of the different processes in the Sheffield area. Gains were few (three), with two arising from growth and one

Table 6.4   Sheffield head offices, 1976–88

Category		Number
Total head offices 1977		22
Survivors		10
New entries		3
Entries into top 1000	2	
Moved in	1	
Losses		12
Fall below top 1000	1	
Moved out	2	
Acquired	9	
Inside Sheffield	3	
Outside Sheffield	6	
Total head offices 1988		13

Note
This table summarizes some complex organizational changes affecting Sheffield firms and thus is indicative only of broad patterns of change over the twelve-year time period.

(*Source*: SHEFF data, updated to early 1988 from press reports.)

from a move to the city. There have been no sufficiently large management buyouts in Sheffield for new head offices in the top 1000 to be created in this way. Losses arose predominantly from acquisition activity (nine), two firms moved out and a third fell below the critical turnover figure.

The gains are perhaps the most interesting. One (Tinsley Wire) arises from a statistical quirk due to accidental movement around the critical turnover for inclusion in the data set. The other firm (Sheffield Insulations) is a strong and growing element in the Sheffield economy. Throughout the 1970s and 1980s it was gradually extending its markets through the UK. For example, in 1985 it purchased a Scottish manufacturer of insulated panels and moved the work to Sheffield, while in 1986 new outlets were being opened in Newcastle, London and Bristol, with one scheduled for Plymouth later in the year. The in-mover, the UK head office of a US multinational (Union Carbide), moved to Sheffield from a head office in Grafton Street in London, W1. Sheffield was attractive to the firm because of the presence in the city of its major UK manufacturing facility, plus the availability of suitable modern office space. Although the firm has had a number of difficulties after its disaster in Bhopal, India, it does show that provincial cities can attract the office facilities of foreign multinationals. Perhaps significant and important parallels are the move of Hoover's UK administration to Merthyr Tydfil, Wales, from London, and the presence of the UK head office of another US multinational (Stanley Tools) in Sheffield itself.

The acquisition-related changes have predominated over the last decade, half of them reflecting the classic acquisition of a locally-based operation by an external firm. For example, both Wigfalls (TV rentals and sales) and Weston Pharmaceuticals were acquired by Dixons, Sheffield Smelting was acquired by Engelhard Industries (a US firm), T.W. Ward (engineering) was acquired by RTZ and Hadfields (steel and forging) was acquired by Lonrho. Loss of white-collar employment, as distinct from the head office itself, may not be immediate. Daniel Doncaster was acquired by Inco Alloys, the Canadian multinational, in the mid-1970s, but the dramatic local effects were not felt until Doncaster's Sheffield work was integrated into Inco's UK operations in March 1982. Cuts amounted to 137 jobs and activities were transferred to the firm's central headquarters and laboratory facilities in Birmingham.

While external acquisitions lead to a loss of head offices, local restructuring can maintain some head-office activity in the locality. Restructuring in Sheffield not only involved the traditional re-organization of private-sector local firms, but also incorporated a number of changes arising from the re-organization of the public-sector–private-sector interface of the steel and steel-using sectors.

Local restructuring in the private sector saw the amalgamation of four locally-based steel-making firms into one, a reflection of the fall in demand for engineering steel and the foundry and forging work based upon it. Edgar Allen Balfour, Balfour Darwin and Samuel Osborn all became part of the Aurora group. Head-office functions at several sites were replaced by a single headquarters unit. Restructuring at the public/private interface affected firms in the heavy-forging industry. In this industry the setting up of a new subsidiary firm (Sheffield Forgemasters), made up of Johnson, Firth Brown's and British Steel's heavy-forging plants, led to the closure of the Johnson, Firth Brown Sheffield head office. They were left with few Sheffield-based operations and transferred their head office to the North West, which is now their manufacturing base. (Sheffield Forgemasters does not appear in Table 6.4 as its head office was both set up and moved out within the period covered by the table.) A further loss arose from a local firm (Neepsend) that, during the period 1982–7 embarked on a five-year programme of rationalization, including a complete withdrawal from the special-steels sector. The loss of turnover resulting from this strategy took the firm out of the top 1000 listing.

Head offices and local-office policy

The surviving firms in Sheffield show both the expected proportion of foreign-owned operations (two out of thirteen, both controlled from the USA) and an industrial structure that, as a whole, is a reflection of Sheffield's industrial specialization in metal-based industries and refractories. Almost 60 per cent of the firms fall in this category, and the others were based originally on northern markets as in retailing, motor distribution, building materials and construction.

In examining the local distribution of these firms it is important to distinguish between the head office on the same site as major manufacturing/retailing/warehouse facilities and the detached head office located at some distance from a firm's other activities. Similarly, three types of office location can be identified: the central business district; the industrial/warehouse zone; and other out-of-centre sites. By combining the head-office types and the urban zones, head-office location policy in a major urban area can recognize the existence of three distinct intra-urban locational patterns:

1. The on-site head office set within a manufacturing/warehouse area.
2. The detached head office set in a predominantly residential suburban area.
3. The detached head office set in a central-area office complex.

This categorization excludes the rural/small-town head office outside the urban administrative area and perhaps neglects the role of significant groupings of office activities in out-of-centre (suburban) areas.

The distribution of head offices within Sheffield at the end of 1987 is shown in Figure 6.3. This distribution in part reflects the extent to which head offices are tied to warehousing/manufacturing sites. In fact, seven head offices are tied in this way while six are detached. Five out of the six detached offices occupy locations outside Sheffield's inner area, while the sixth, within the inner area, occupies a prestigious office development on the edge of the central shopping zone. The attached offices are all within Sheffield's industrial zone with one exception, located at a former extractive site on the edge of the city. In reality, much of the administration of this firm is undertaken through a subsidiary operating from a detached office in a suburban area.

Certainly, on-site head offices in old-established industrial areas present problems. Sheffield Forgemaster's view of their 1907 granite-faced and marble-lined Brightside head office was that it presented 'an image of the past. If you bring overseas visitors here, the street outside is filthy and full of refuse. It simply is not suitable for a company in the 1990s' (*The Star*, 31 March 1987, p.7). In part its move from Sheffield was stimulated by the restructuring of the firm into a number of separate manufacturing units, each with its own management staff, thus reducing the size of the overall headquarters unit. Although a search was undertaken for a site within the city, the firm's management team opted for a headquarters location at the Old Rectory at Whiston some 5 miles (8 km) from the Sheffield manufacturing sites. In addition to achieving a more impressive office site, the head office was also closer to Doncaster with its fast rail service to London. The old office building was subsequently listed as being of

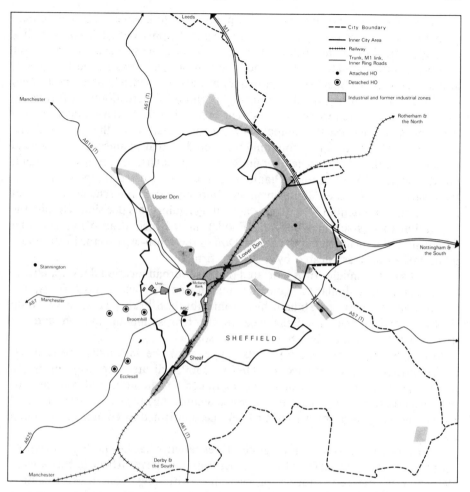

Figure 6.3   Head offices of 1000 largest firms based in Sheffield, 1988 (Source: based on The Times 1000 1986-7, Press reports and fieldwork)

architectural and historical interest, thus restricting the uses to which the site can be put.

However, not all firms view the inner area in this way and steel-makers Arthur Lee have built striking new premises in the lower Don Valley. Perhaps significantly a site was readily available upon which a new office could be constructed, and while the firm recognized that it could have chosen to move out of the zone, it felt that it had a commitment to Sheffield and that it would be wrong to contribute to the further decline of the once-thriving east end of the city.

While a suburban site may be more attractive to customers than one in an old industrial area, it can present difficulties to a firm where residential sites surround the office site. The Henry Boot head office in the early 19th-century Banner Cross Hall (a Grade II listed building) illustrates this point. Surrounded by one of Sheffield's wealthier suburbs, plans to build a three-storey office were described by a local residents' representative as 'totally out of keeping with a residential area' (*The Star*, 6 April 1987, p.3). Again, the stimulus to change was a re-organization of Henry Boot's activities by which it was hoped to transfer around 250 staff to Sheffield from offices in nearby Dronfield and Chesterfield (Derby.). What is more, the developments promised the creation of a further 80 jobs. Local objectors tended to stress their opposition to the development on the basis of increased traffic, damage to the appearance of the hall and the destruction of wildlife in surrounding woodland. Local planners recommended acceptance of the scheme to help retain Boot's national headquarters in Sheffield, but the Sheffield City Council Planning Committee rejected the plan, much to the amazement of some Labour members who supported the scheme because of its job-creation potential. The firm is appealing against this decision. Despite the opposition to this scheme, Bassetts (Foods) moved their head office activities from a manufacturing site in the Upper Don to the south-west sector in late 1987, taking over premises vacated by a smaller firm.

The loss of the smaller firm indicated that a suburban location does not always ensure survival. A similar loss, but this time of one Sheffield's major firms, was the move of Burnett and Hallamshire from suburban Psalter Lane to Worksop (Notts.). Offices were available next to the firm's mining division and the detached office in suburban Sheffield was sold.

Although suburban environments appear to be attractive head-office environments, the experience of Henry Boot indicates the way in which developments in those areas may be constrained. In the industrial zone at least one firm (Sheffield Forgemasters) has voted against the image created by the local environment, while another (Arthur Lee), has confirmed its commitment to that zone.

In turning finally to the central zone, the experience has been rather mixed. At least two of the firms affected by restructuring had head offices in this area in 1976 and in the restructuring process they withdrew from these facilities. However, Sheffield's one major in-mover selected a central-area site and is now the only major non-financial head office in the central part of the city. While the reasons for the move to Sheffield were set out earlier, its specific location within the city was influenced by the availability of a speculative office development on a prime city-centre site. This latter point emphasizes that the availability of office space may be important in local policies for head offices.

Attracting new head offices is worth considering as a first line of policy by northern authorities not because it has been successful in the past, but because the overheating of the southern economy may encourage southern firms to disperse their head-office facilities. If one 'blue-chip' firm could be persuaded to adopt a northern city it could be of great mutual value, with the firm acting as a high-profile caring concern in its adopted home. Perhaps local administrations should seek out such potential partners, targeting their earliest efforts on firms with some of their activities already in the urban area. Indeed, this could form part of the increasingly-popular strategies to develop producer (business) services in northern cities.

In developing such services, it is vital that modern office space be readily available for letting. Much depends on local administrations levering new developments out of the private sector. Yet developers, not unexpectedly, are reluctant to construct major office buildings in advance of demand. For example, for a number of years prior to 1979–80, Sheffield City Council dealt with around 125 planning applications for office development each year, but in the first half of the 1980s applications fell below 100 per annum, and for most of the 1980s 'change of use' rather than 'new developments' made up most of the permitted space. The absence of permissions for new developments reflects the absence of demand from developers rather than an unwillingness to grant planning permission by the City Council.

Available new office space may help in a policy to monitor and to have a dialogue with rapidly-growing local firms. It is vitally important that such firms, their head offices and associated local employment are not lost. Such monitoring should include the smaller firms that are outside the top 1000 at present but that seem likely to be major organizations in the future. Every effort should be made to ensure the future needs can be met within the local area.

Policies for the offices of firms undergoing restructuring are more difficult to suggest. Certainly attempts should be made to advise on and to anticipate their office needs. Local restructuring usually results in concentration of office activities on a more limited number of local sites, but national acquisition and restructuring can result in local-office employment loss. This loss may occur some time after the acquisition, suggesting that here is a breathing space offering administrations time to 'sell' their local communities.

Both the attraction and retention of offices may be further enhanced by actively recognizing and strengthening any naturally-emerging office zones. Although it is politically difficult to encourage commercial development in predominantly-residential areas occupied by social classes AB it does need serious consideration. Both external and local firms would appreciate both a clear statement on office policies and the identification of intra-urban areas where such developments would be welcomed.

Conclusion

Clearly, the north has a marked under-representation of non-financial head offices. Within the north, head offices are especially absent from the Northern and Welsh areas, while in Scotland they are markedly polarized on the two main cities. In other regions they show a dispersion across cities of various sizes. In aggregate, northern head offices are over-represented in the large cities like Sheffield. Analysis of change in Sheffield shows the key role of company acquisitions in reducing head-office activity. The identification of transfers in and out of Sheffield suggests that there is scope for a policy to retain or attract head-office activities. However, the limited representation of head offices in the north not only limits their impact on northern localities but also severely constrains the relevant policy options open to local administrations. Nevertheless, a head-office policy for a northern city might include the attraction of head offices engaged in dispersal from sites in the south, the maintenance of a dialogue with, and anticipation of, the head-office needs of rapidly-growing local firms, the selling of the area to the new management of local firms taken over by external organizations and a promotion of clearly-defined zones in which office development would be welcomed.

7

THE GEOGRAPHY OF ILL HEALTH AND HEALTH CARE

Sarah Curtis and John Mohan

This chapter reviews some of the evidence for a north-south divide in the health status of the British population, and considers how the health service has reacted to this difference. It asks why the disparities have proved so persistent in spite of forty years of a National Health Service (NHS). Much of the present-day debate surrounding health and health care is in fact focused on illness and death and the reactive treatment of illness. This is reflected in the title of this chapter, which, in the absence of information about more positive aspects of health, is forced to concentrate mainly on mortality and morbidity (levels of sickness) as indicators of the health status of the population. The first part of the following considers a range of evidence concerning the north-south dimension of what has been called 'the Health Divide' (Whitehead, 1987).

The emphasis in health care on treating illness may help to explain why the historical north-south divide in health status has persisted. Pro-active policies to prevent illness and promote health are still relatively under-developed in the British health service, and the factors that influence health, such as housing, diet and occupational health hazards, remain largely intractable problems in health and welfare policy. Indeed, some of the aspects of the north-south divide discussed in other chapters, relating to housing, economic prosperity and education, may be as important to health differences as are health-service differences. The second section examines the distribution of health-service resources, and argues that many aspects of health-service policy have been essentially regressive in the 1980s.

The north-south divide in patterns of death

Mortality data remain the most comprehensive source of information about the health status of the British population. Death rates reveal broad disparities between the north and south of the country that have been persistent over time and are partly, but not entirely, explained by socio-economic characteristics of the population. There is evidence for this pattern from both aggregate mortality statistics for populations of geographical areas, and from studies of the mortality rates of individuals living in different parts of the country.

The Registrar General's decennial supplement on area mortality (OPCS, 1981) provides an indication of the pattern of mortality in standard regions of England and Wales in periods close to *Census of Population* dates. The standardized mortality ratios (SMRs) show how regional death rates, when standardized by age and sex, compare with the average mortality rate in the country as a whole, which is represented by a value of 100. The pattern of standardized mortality ratios in 1969–73 showed a regional gradient from the highest level of 116 (16 per cent above the average), in the North West region, to a minimum SMR of 84 in East Anglia. Regions with relatively-high SMRs above 100 are generally those in the north west, and those with relatively low mortality, below 100, are in the south and east of the country. Fox and Adelstein (1978) showed that this gradient was still evident even after controlling for the social-class composition of the regions (Table 7.1).

Table 7.1 Standardized mortality ratios for standard regions of England and Wales

	Age-adjusted SMR 1969–73	Age- and class-adjusted SMR 1969–73	SMR in 1983	SMR in 1986
Northern	113	113		111	111
Yorkshire	106	105		105	105
North West	116	116		111	111
East Midlands	96	94		100	100
West Midlands	105	105		104	105
East Anglia	84	83		90	91
South East	90	90		93	94
South West	93	93		92	93
Wales I	114	117			
Wales II	110	113	Wales	106	103
England and Wales	100	100		100	100

(*Sources*: Fox and Adelstein, 1978; OPCS, 1987a.)

The information for 1983 and 1986 shows a similar pattern. Mortality rates (Figure 7.1) had by then declined slightly in absolute terms, but the differences between regions in the SMRs had not been much reduced. Townsend, Davidson and Whitehead (1988) showed that, for men of working age, the disparity between manual and non-manual workers was variable between regions. Manual workers always had higher SMRs, but the greatest differentials were in Scotland and the north of England, and the smallest differences in East Anglia (Table 7.2). Manual workers in East Anglia have SMRs that are lower even than non-manual workers in some parts of the north.

Standard regions are rather large zones for analysis, and within them quite marked variations in mortality rates are to be observed. In particular, highly-urban areas have higher rates on average than do rural and semi-rural areas. At the scale

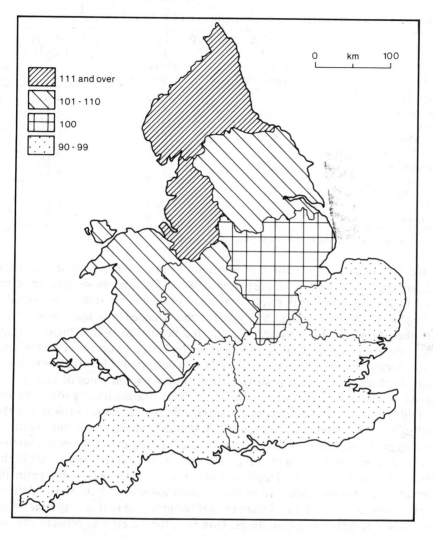

Figure 7.1   Standardized mortality ratios, 1986

of local authorities, the highest mortality rates (over 20 per cent above average) occur in inner-city authorities in the north of the country. Even in the most deprived parts of inner London (e.g. Tower Hamlets' SMR of 106 in 1986) the mortality rates are lower than in urban areas of the north of England (e.g. 124 in Hartlepool and 117 in Bolton, Bury, Manchester and Oldham).

The pattern differs somewhat according to cause of death. For some specific causes, the north west–south east divide is clear (heart diseases, stomach cancer, bronchitis) but other causes (e.g. some neoplasms) are more variable in pattern. The *Atlas of Cancer Mortality in England and Wales* (Gardner *et al.*, 1983)

Table 7.2   Male class differentials in mortality at 1979–80 and 1982–3

	SMR of men 20–64 in:		Ratio of (2)/(1)
	(1) Non-manual occupations	(2) Manual occupations	
Northern	88.5	131.5	1.48
Yorkshire	85.3	117.1	1.37
North West	89.8	131.8	1.47
East Midlands	80.0	104.8	1.31
West Midlands	79.6	118.0	1.48
East Anglia	68.9	85.8	1.25
South East	72.7	103.4	1.42
South West	73.3	99.5	1.36
Wales	84.4	120.2	1.42
Scotland	93.3	145.8	1.56

(*Source*: Townsend, Davidson and Whitehead, 1988, Table 2.4.)

enables us to examine the pattern of mortality from cancer in areas smaller than standard regions or counties for the period 1968–78. The atlas shows the complexity of the local variation in death rates at this scale. In general, mortality due to cancer of the pharynx, rectum, cervix, kidney and stomach tended to be lower in the south than the north, but the reverse was true for neoplasms of the breast, brain, melanoma and ovary, and for non-Hodgkins lymphoma. Lung cancer deaths were most common in urban areas (Gardner, 1984). The authors identified seven areas where death rates were significantly high for at least seven types of cancer. All but one (Barking, London) were in the north. Twelve areas had significantly low mortality rates for five or six types of cancer. Of these, five were in Wales or the north west of England, two were in the Midlands and the rest in the south.

Infant mortality and perinatal mortality rates are somewhat lower in regional health authorities (RHAs) in the south and east of the country, and higher in the north and west (Table 7.3). Disparities also exist between RHAs for perinatal mortality, which is considered to be more closely associated with the standard of hospital maternity care than is infant mortality during the first year of life, which more closely reflects living conditions. However, the differences between regions are much less striking in infant and perinatal mortality than the social-class differentials.

Information on mortality rates among individuals also reflects a north-south divide in the likelihood of death. The best source of such information for the country as a whole comes from the longitudinal study, a one per cent sample of the population enumerated in the 1971 census. This study shows mortality rates for those living in the north west of Britain in 1971 to be higher as compared with mortality among people from the south east of England.

The longitudinal study has been used to study, at the local scale of electoral wards, mortality in different types of geographical area, according to the Webber and Craig classification (Webber and Craig, 1978). For most area types, wards in the north west had a higher male mortality rate than those in the south east

Table 7.3   Infant mortality rates, 1986

Regional health authority	Deaths under 1 year /1,000 live births	Perinatal mortality rate per 1,000 total births
Northern	9.8	10.1
Yorkshire	10.6	10.3
Trent	9.9	10.2
W. Midlands	10.0	11.0
Mersey	9.4	9.2
North Western	10.7	10.4
East Anglian	8.1	7.7
N.W. Thames	8.6	8.6
N.E. Thames	9.3	9.6
S.E. Thames	8.6	8.5
S.W. Thames	8.8	8.2
Wessex	9.1	8.8
Oxford	9.0	8.9
South Western	9.5	9.5
Wales	9.5	10.3

(*Sources*: OPCS, 1987b)

of the country. Thus regional variations cannot be statistically explained by differences in the type of area as defined by Webber and Craig.

Although there is an urban–rural mortality gradient, the urban residents in the longitudinal sample showed higher mortality rates if they were from the north west than from the south east (Fox and Goldblatt, 1982, Table 8.7). Similarly, in an analysis of the socio-economic type of area of residence, based on Webber and Craig's classification, the longitudinal study revealed that residents of wards with similar socio-economic characteristics generally appeared to have higher mortality rates in the north west than in the south east (Fox *et al.*, 1985). Other factors associated with mortality also show a regional gradient. For example, Moser *et al.* (1987) report that while the longitudinal study reveals higher mortality among unemployed men than among those in work, the effect was strongest in areas where unemployment rates were highest. The longitudinal study also shows how the mortality rate for migrants varies according to the direction of movement and may accentuate regional differences in mortality rates slightly, since those moving out of high-mortality areas had lower mortality than those moving in. Males and females migrating from the south and east to the north and west had SMRs of 103 and 113 respectively, while those moving in the opposite direction had SMRs of 83 and 89.

Fox and Goldblatt (1982), in their report of the longitudinal study, point out that the north-south differential is not a new phenomenon, but has been in evidence since the last century. There is no clear evidence that it has increased over recent years, but it does seem stubbornly persistent in spite of efforts discussed below to shift health-care resources to those areas where mortality is high. The geographical pattern of 'avoidable mortality' (untimely premature death due to diseases that should be amenable to medical intervention to affect the outcome of the disease) shows some evidence of a north-south divide, although there is much variability within regions at the scale of area health authorities analysed by Charlton *et al.* (1983).

While mortality is a good proxy indicator for health during life, it is of limited value as a direct measure of need for health care. Some chronic but not life-threatening diseases have significant resource requirements in terms of health and welfare services (for example, arthritic and rheumatic diseases). When mortality due to diseases such as cancer and heart disease is avoided, there may, nevertheless, be considerable need for nursing and rehabilitative care. Furthermore, mortality rates reflect circumstances throughout the whole of life, and may reflect past conditions as much as the present. If we are looking for measures of current health status and need for health care in the British population, we should also take account of illness and, in so far as the limited data allow, positive aspects of health in the population.

North-south differences in illness and health

Our information on illness in the population is very limited by comparison with mortality data. In particular, there is a lack of information for small areas across the country as a whole. Our range of data source is further limited because we cannot rely on health-service activity data to indicate reliably the prevalence of illness in the population, since the use of health care is partly affected by the geographical variations in the accessibility of care itself.

Nevertheless, there are some national and regional data on the prevalence of illness and other aspects of the health status of the population. The main source of data on trends in illness is the *General Household Survey (GHS)*, an annual national survey of a representative sample of households in Great Britain. Since 1972, this survey has included general questions on self-reported health status (the respondent's own assessment of his or her health, rather than their clinically-diagnosed condition). One question in the survey asks whether the respondent has any 'long-standing illness, disability or infirmity'. About a third of the population nationally report some long-standing illness in response to this question, the proportion varying considerably with age and sex of the respondent. Presence of this type of illness is not necessarily evidence of a medically-recognized illness, so that it does not automatically imply need for health care. The cause and severity of the illness reported may vary considerably, and the responses are probably subject to some degree of bias or error at the level of the individual. However, when analysed by types of people in the survey they provide some indication of the experience of illness by the population. Since these data were first collected, they have shown a greater prevalence of long-standing illness reported among those in manual occupational groups than among non-manual workers and their families (OPCS, 1986). The responses also show a regional pattern since, when age and sex effects are taken into account, respondents from more northern regions are more likely to report illness than those in the south.

The Health and Lifestyle Survey (Cox *et al.*, 1987) is another national survey that suggests that self-reported illness is more common in the north of England. It covered 9,003 individuals over the age of 18 living in 12,254 households in 1985. This collected a much wider range of health information than the *GHS*, and it also permits an analysis of standard regions. The survey demonstrates social-class differentials in health, with manual (especially unskilled) groups reporting poorer health than non-manual (particularly professional) groups. There are also geographical variations in the proportion reporting various illnesses.

Generally speaking, chronic illness is more often reported by people from standard regions in the north and west, and less often by people from the south and east. This is the case, for example, for heart disease, arthritis/rheumatism and bronchitis. However, for other diseases (migraine, asthma, diabetes) some of the highest rates of prevalence were reported by people from the south east of England. As a result, the pattern of illness reporting between regions does not show a completely clear-cut north-south division (Table 7.4). The proportion of people who report at least one chronic disease is highest in the West Midlands (for men) and in Yorkshire &

Table 7.4   Results from *The Health and Lifestyle Survey*, 1985

Region	Age-adjusted % reporting some chronic disease		Percentage with good or excellent respiratory function		%Normotensive (age-adjusted)	
	Males	Females	Males	Females	Males	Females
Northern	36.4	30.9	84	92	70.2	77.5
Yorkshire	32.1	37.9	93	92	63.2	75.9
North West	32.3	30.5	84	89	70.3	77.5
East Midlands	35.2	31.5	91	94	72.9	78.1
West Midlands	38.3	37.3	91	92	68.0	75.1
East Anglia	28.4	25.4	94	94	81.3	81.1
South East	32.0	28.9	92	91	73.5	78.1
(Greater London)	33.6	35.4	82	83	76.6	81.4
South West	33.0	25.8	89	91	71.9	81.0
Wales	29.0	28.4	92	83	69.0	82.8
Scotland	34.3	28.0	90	89	74.8	77.9

(*Source*: Cox *et al.*, 1987.)

Humberside (for women) and the lowest proportions with illness are found in East Anglia. However, Table 7.4 shows that while illness is generally less-commonly reported in the South East than in many other regions, rates of reported illness were high in Greater London.

The Health and Lifestyle Survey also collected information from physical measurements of health such as respiratory function, blood pressure and body-mass index. Table 7.4 shows the proportion of respondents who had good or excellent respiratory function (the remainder had poor respiratory function). Although the proportion is relatively high in East Anglia and rather low in the North West, there is no obvious regional pattern. It should be noted that these figures make no allowance for differences between smokers and non-smokers. The proportion of respondents with normal blood pressure is also given in Table 7.4. While the proportion is less variable for women, there is some evidence of greater hypertension in the north. For men the proportion with normal blood pressure was more variable, but a broad geographical pattern is more difficult to detect. Patterns of hypertension and heart disease among men are discussed in more detail later.

Patterns of health-related behaviour, especially diet, have received a good deal of publicity, and reduction of smoking and encouragement of healthy eating are major health-education targets in Britain. Variation in health-related behaviour is closely related to socio-occupational group, and within standard regions, respondents in different social groups showed differences in behaviour. Nevertheless, broad regional patterns are discernible.

Regular smoking by men and women was more often reported in Wales, Scotland and the north of England. In southern England, especially among women, smoking was less common. The Royal College of Physicians have estimated that a significant proportion of deaths due to ishaemic heart disease, lung cancer and bronchitis and emphysema are directly attributable to smoking, and Roberts and Graveling (1985) reported that death rates from these smoking-related diseases were highest in the regional health authorities in the north and west of the country, and generally lower in the south. The death rate attributed to smoking ranged from 242 per 100,000 in the Northern RHA to 155 in Oxford RHA (Figure 7.2 and Table 7.5).

Table 7.5   Death rates due to disease induced by smoking

Regional health authorities	Death rates attributed to smoking per 100,000 population
Northern	242
Yorkshire	227
Trent	209
East Anglia	193
N.W. Thames	188
N.E. Thames	203
S.E. Thames	207
S.W. Thames	207
Wessex	193
Oxford	155
South Western	200
W. Midlands	185
Mersey	216
North Western	237
Wales	213
England and Wales	208

(*Source:* Roberts and Graveling, 1985)

The Health and Lifestyle Survey shows that those in the southern regions of England were more likely to eat predominantly brown bread, fruit and salad than those in regions of northern England, Wales and Scotland. The proportion of obese people was highest in Wales and Scotland, and the proportion with an acceptable weight was highest in the South East region. Data for women are shown in Table 7.6.

While the results from these national surveys give some impression of regional variations in health and health behaviour at the individual level, they have not yet been analysed in sufficient depth to allow us to tease out the complex relationships between socio-economic group, living conditions and area of residence. Although there is some evidence of regional differences, the north-south divide in health and illness is often indistinct, especially by comparison with contrasts between

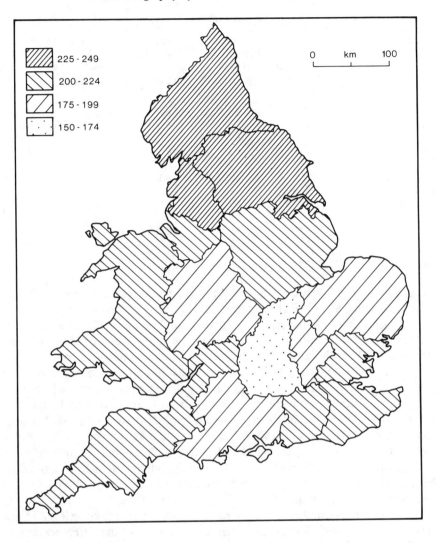

Figure 7.2   Smoking disease death rates, 1981

occupational and social groups. In order to elucidate the regional aspects of ill health, a more elaborate strategy of data collection and analysis is required, which enables a longitudinal investigation of individuals, and can disentangle socio-economic class effects from other aspects of the social and physical environment.

An example of a study that was designed to test regional variations in morbidity is the Regional Heart Study (Shaper *et al.*, 1981). This study of 24 British towns was primarily concerned with regional variations in cardiovascular disease and the possible relationship with variations in water quality (hardness). The researchers selected 24 towns representing the range of geographic conditions (and all standard regions). Medium-sized towns, generally of 50,000 to 100,000 population in 1971,

Table 7.6   Results from *The Health and Lifestyle Survey*, 1985

Region	% of women respondents eating			% of women	
	Mainly brown bread (18–49 group)	Fruit daily (18–39 age group)	Salad most days in summer	Under weight	Over weight/obese
Northern	40	60	65	2	13
Yorkshire	45	54	68	5	16
North West	51	60	70	3	15
East Midlands	46	62	72	5	13
West Midlands	35	62	68	4	18
East Anglia	39	62	80	2	13
South East	54	69	71	5	11
(Greater London)	54	66	71	9	14
South West	55	68	66	3	16
Wales	42	61	62	6	21
Scotland	39	50	63	5	20

(*Source*: Cox *et al.*, 1987.)

were selected. Towns were chosen to reflect socio-economic conditions in the region as far as possible, as well as the range of associations between water hardness and heart disease. Although the selection of towns could be criticized and does not fully represent conditions within standard regions, the study does give us some insights into patterns of cardiovascular morbidity and a whole range of factors that might relate to heart disease. Heart disease is of particular importance because it is a major killer, causing over half of all deaths in Britain. Data was collected about the aggregated population of the towns, but also about a sample of middle-aged men, who were particularly susceptible to premature death due to heart disease. The results show a clear increasing gradient in both cardiovascular mortality and average blood pressure from towns such as Guildford (Surrey), Shrewsbury, Exeter (Devon), Harrogate (N. Yorks.), Ipswich (Suffolk) (mainly, but not exclusively in the south) and towns in the north of England and Scotland, e.g. Dewsbury (W. Yorks.), Ayr (Strathclyde), Dunfermline (Fife), Merthyr Tydfil (Mid Glam.), Wigan (Gtr Manchester). The researchers tried to find an explanation for varying levels of heart disease between towns, and were able to account for some of the differences in terms of social factors, water hardness and climatic effects. The power of this study is its capacity to examine the effects of social and behavioural factors at the level of the individual as well as for aggregated populations of particular areas. Individual differences in blood pressure were partly related to variation in class, drinking and smoking behaviour, body mass and marital status, but these factors did not fully explain differences between men from different towns. The regional heart study does seem to underline the influence of geographical as well as socio-economic effects on morbidity.

Dimensions of the health divide

The material reviewed here shows that there are clear differentials in patterns of health, illness and death between different population groups in Britain. There seem to be at least two dimensions to these disparities: differences between social classes and differences between geographical areas. Within regions, and smaller geographical areas, there are clear social-class differences in death rates, illness and health behaviour. However, we also observe considerable geographical variations in health within social classes, according to their residential location. The north-south divide typifies this geographical dimension at the broad scale, but there are also interesting disparities between different types of area, especially categories reflecting different levels of urbanization. These geographical variations in health raise interesting questions about their underlying causes. We have noted individual health-related behaviour as a factor, but other factors such as environmental risks to health, health and welfare policies and provision of health care are also likely to play a role. We therefore move on to consider how geographical aspects of the health-care system and current health policy may relate to the north-south divide in health.

Health-care provision

The previous section described spatial aspects of inequalities in health and evaluated the notion of a north-south divide in health status. This section considers current policies to alter the distribution of resources, examines the extent to which private-sector growth will contribute to equalizing access to health care and discusses the spatial implications of employment change in health care.

Redistributing health-care resources

The notion of a north-south divide does not accurately capture geographical variations in NHS provision. For a start, both Scotland and Northern Ireland have levels of expenditure that, on a per-capita basis, are far higher than in England – some 20 per cent higher in the case of Scotland. Furthermore, there remains a commitment to eliminating geographical disparities in health-care provision within England via the Resource Allocation Working Party (RAWP) formula and separately within Scotland, Wales and Northern Ireland, each of which have their own resource-allocation formulae.

Considering simply hospital provision, the NHS is still trying to eliminate the last traces of a pattern of service provision that was uneven both between and within regions prior to the setting up of the NHS. Aptly summarized by Abel-Smith (1964) as being a result of the 'donations of the living and the legacies of the dead' (p. 405), inter-regional disparities were substantial. England and Wales were divided into ten areas by the wartime hospital surveyors who found that the ratio of hospital beds per 1,000 population ranged from 4.8 in south Wales to 7.7 in Berkshire, Buckinghamshire and Oxfordshire. This pattern of inequalities was effectively frozen by 15 years of minimal capital investment in the NHS (Webster, 1988, pp. 292–8) and by an incremental system of revenue budgeting; so substantial inequalities remained both between and within regions (Mays and Bevan, 1987). The principal divide was between London and the South East, where per-capita bed provision and expenditure were high, and relatively underprovided areas such as the East Midlands and East Anglia.

The most important attempt to deal with these inequalities has been the policy introduced following the RAWP report (DHSS, 1976). This identified the relative 'needs' of the 14 regional health authorities (RHAs) in England using a combination of demographic data and Standardized Mortality Ratios (SMRs), compared the RHAs' existing levels of resource with their supposed 'targets', and found that the Thames RHAs (including London) were 'overprovided' relative to their needs. It therefore proposed a net transfer of resources away from these RHAs towards the north and west of England.

In the abstract terms of reference of the RAWP formula, there has indeed been progress towards ironing out regional disparities within England. The gap between the most over-funded and the most under-funded regions has narrowed from some 25 per cent in the mid-1970s to 13 per cent in 1986-7. The reduction in the rate of growth in NHS expenditure since 1979 and particularly since 1983 has, however, meant that redistribution has taken place effectively through differential cuts rather than through differential growth. It is generally recognized that health-care expenditures need to rise by some 1-2 per cent above the rate of inflation annually, in order to cope with demographic change, higher rates of inflation applicable to medical costs and rising public expectations. Prior to 1983 the RAWP formula was implemented in such a way that all RHAs received growth in resources, over and above inflation, but some received more than others in recognition of their greater relative needs. Since 1983, resource allocation has in effect been a zero-sum game. It has been widely questioned whether NHS expenditure has increased sufficiently to cope with the additional pressures on the service (House of Commons Social Services Committee, 1988) and regional redistribution has involved growth in below-target RHAs taking place only at the expense of revenue reductions, of some 0.3-0.5 per cent per annum, in the above-target RHAs. For individual district health authorities (DHAs), this has involved rapid reductions in budgets, with some London authorities facing reductions in financial allocations of some 10-20 per cent in real terms over a ten-year period (See Mohan, 1988a).

The effects of this have been felt in three ways: reductions in hospital capacity; increases in waiting lists; and reductions in the rate of growth of health-care employment. Considering only provision of non-psychiatric acute hospital beds, between 1983 and 1986, 159 out of 191 district health authorities in England reduced bed provision; within London, virtually all DHAs lost between 10 and 30 per cent of their acute hospital capacity and in total 3,700 beds were lost in the capital. This has had knock-on effects on waiting times for treatment. Although these are unreliable as guides to the difficulties of obtaining hospital care, 20 of the 30 DHAs in London experienced increases in waiting lists between 1982 and 1986 and in several cases there were substantial increases. In consequence it has become very difficult, if not impossible, to admit for non-urgent surgery (Beech, Challah and Ingram, 1987; Langman, 1987). Changes in health-care employment are dealt with later.

There is another sense in which the widening north-south divide interacts with the NHS's ability to provide services. The NHS pays low wages and, apart from the (small) London allowance, has no regional variations built into its wage structure. The combined effect of this, plus the rise in house prices and the scarcity of rented accommodation in the South East (Chapter 4), has meant that recruitment difficulties are severe. In addition, the large private-sector presence in the South East provides a substantial competitor for skilled nursing staff, especially theatre nurses. While this problem has become best publicized as a result of shortages of nurses at teaching hospitals, it also includes secretarial and technical staff in certain buoyant local labour markets where there are numerous competing opportunities in services or in high-technology industry.

One effect is that DHAs are spending much higher proportions of their budgets on agency staff. In several London DHAs, over 5 per cent of the authorities' budget is spent in this way and this can divert resources from priority areas such as community services. Because of agency fees and overheads, buying agency staff is an expensive way to purchase a given quantity of nursing. There have been a number of initiatives designed to attract staff back to nursing (e.g. through flexible working hours). There are also schemes to make it easier for NHS staff to purchase housing (e.g. through equity-sharing schemes under which building societies subsidize mortgages on the understanding that they receive a share in the profits when the property is sold). To the extent that such schemes expand demand for a limited quantity of property, however, they will have the effect of fuelling the flames of the very problem they are designed to ameliorate.

Even with these initiatives, the ability of the NHS – and indeed the public services more generally – to recruit staff is heavily constrained by low pay. Unless this is tackled, or unless suitable low-cost rented accommodation is made available, it would seem that the process of 'overheating' within the South East will make it extremely difficult for the public sector to recruit sufficient staff to maintain essential services over the next decade. In this respect declining public-sector services may prove to be the other side of the growth coin as far as the South East is concerned.

Private-sector growth

It is sometimes claimed that the recent growth in private health care reflects the free play of market forces. In fact, this growth results in part from the unintended and intended effects of State policies: the Labour government's attempts to abolish private practice in NHS hospitals created a climate in which private hospital developers were forced to invest in new hospital capacity while, since 1979, successive Conservative governments have encouraged the expansion of private care in several ways. Some would interpret the latter as part of a systematic politics of inequality (e.g. Jessop *et al.*, 1984), whereby the 'productive' members of society are rewarded for their contribution to production via high levels of personal consumption, often subsidized by employers, while the 'unproductive', 'second nation' remains dependent upon declining public services.

The motor behind the growth of private hospital provision is the insurance market, since over 80 per cent of private treatment is paid for in this way. Insurance coverage varies greatly by socio-economic group (SEG), with 23 per cent of the professional and managerial SEGs benefiting from it, while only 2 per cent of semi- and unskilled manual SEGs are covered; in the 45–64 age group, over 31 per cent of the professional and managerial SEGs are covered. Much of the insurance market consists of company-paid schemes under which employers pay all or part of insurance premiums for their employees. The extent of coverage obviously relates to position within a firm as well as type of employer. Without relying on simple stereotypes it should be obvious that executives working in financial services or in 'sunrise industries' are most likely to be the beneficiaries of the warm glow of corporate capitalism, while those engaged in routine production functions are most unlikely so to benefit. Given the spatial distribution of the type of employers likely to reward their staff in this way (Incomes Data Services, 1984), one could argue that, just as 'spatial divisions of labour' may be identified in the allocation of work, for instance, between a firm's southern headquarters and northern branch, so too there is emerging a spatial division of welfare: overlying the State's attempts to equalize service availability is a new pattern of inequality in access to facilities.

This can be portrayed by examining insurance coverage by standard regions in Figure 7.3, which shows 1983 *General Household Survey* estimates of insurance

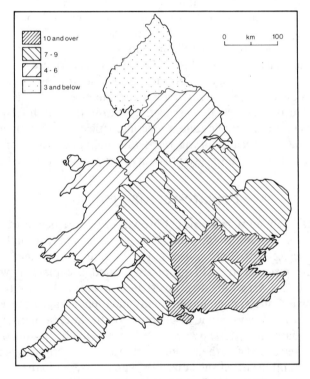

Figure 7.3   Private health insurance, 1983

coverage. In the Outer Metropolitan Areas (OMA), even in 1983, 14 per cent of the population had insurance coverage and it was estimated that this proportion rose to some 18 per cent in certain counties such as Berkshire and Buckinghamshire (Mohan, 1984). The contrasts with Scotland, Wales and the North are evident. Nationally, some 10 per cent are now insured (around 5.1 million people), so even if coverage has only risen pro rata since 1983, around 20 per cent of the OMA's population will now be insured. One should not underestimate the potential ideological significance of this, for a substantial number of people have built up a 'mixed bundle' of welfare provision in which they depend on the NHS for serious conditions while relying on the private sector to bypass the NHS waiting list for non-urgent treatment, 'without seeing any great ideological implications in so doing' (Crouch, 1985, p.13).

This growth in insurance coverage has been accompanied by expansion in acute hospital provision: some 200 private hospitals exist, providing over 10,000 beds, and there are few urban areas of any size without a local private hospital. While the private acute sector is numerically small in relation to the NHS, in some RHAs over 20 per cent of the non-urgent case-load in certain specialities – such as orthopaedic surgery – was carried out privately in 1981 (Williams *et al.*, 1984 – more recent estimates are not available), and this proportion will have risen in recent years as reductions in hospital capacity have reduced the NHS's ability to undertake elective surgery (Beech, Challah and Ingram, 1987).

Private-sector expansion has also occurred with the direct financial encouragement of the government, in the form of social security payments for nursing home care for the elderly; if no suitable accommodation is available in public-sector facilities, the DHSS will now pay for private care. This has led to extremely rapid expansion in private nursing homes for the elderly: total bedspaces in this sector are now over 50,000 compared to some 25,000 in 1982 (DHSS, 1987). If one examines the ratio of private hospital and nursing homes to NHS non-psychiatric bed numbers for English DHAs only, there are several health authorities where private-sector capacity exceeds total NHS bed provision. Much of this capacity is located within RHAs from which the RAWP process is seeking to redistribute resources and so, perversely, one branch of the DHSS is removing funds from RHAs such as S.W. and S.E. Thames while another is channelling other funds back into these regions. Not surprisingly, this has fuelled speculation about the existence of a 'two-tier' health-care system (Hunter, 1983; Day and Klein, 1985).

Employment change in health care

The developments described herein have effects other than those on access to health services for health care is also a major employer. Some one million people are employed in 'medical and dental services', but spatial aspects of health-care employment have by and large been ignored.

The creation of the NHS meant a commitment to evening out disparities in health-care provision between and within regions and this implied a parallel expansion in employment opportunities. Until 1981 health care was generating substantial numbers of new jobs in all regions and, to the extent that regional redistribution of resources was taking place in the NHS, this growth was faster in several peripheral regions (Mohan, 1988b, Tables 1–4). Between 1952 and 1975, employment in health care more than doubled in the South West, East Midlands, the Northern region and Wales and it nearly trebled in Northern Ireland; between 1971 and 1978, total employment in health care grew by 30 per cent or more in the

South East, East Anglia and the East Midlands and in all regions except London (14 per cent) it grew by over 20 per cent. Thus, health care's expansion had a broadly beneficial spatial policy effect, providing a stable source of new job opportunities everywhere and creating opportunities for women to enter the labour market in large numbers. Since 1981, however, health-care employment has increased in Great Britain by only 6, 000, and in Greater London (21,800), the South West (8,600), Wales (2,570) and Scotland (1,400), there have been reductions. Elsewhere increases have been small, of the order of 1–2 per cent per annum. This is partly a statistical artefact: with the growth in subcontracting of NHS ancillary services, many people who were formerly classified as employed in health care will now be classed as working in cleaning, catering, and so on. Reductions in the rate of growth of health-care employment result from three processes: an *overall* slow-down in the rate of growth of public expenditure on the NHS; the uneven spatial impact of resource-allocation policies; and the introduction of new labour processes, notably subcontracting of ancillary services and a general drive towards greater 'productivity' in the NHS (see Mohan, 1988b and c).

In spatial policy terms there are two notable points about these changes. First, jobs have been lost in health care mainly in inner-urban health authorities from which NHS resource-allocation policies are transferring resources. London has been hardest hit but health authorities in Birmingham, Manchester, Liverpool and Nottingham have not been unaffected. The social impact of this will be further to reduce the employment opportunities available to many people who are effectively 'trapped' in inner-city areas by housing-market constraints (see also Chapter 4). Second, to the extent that health care has had a beneficial spatial policy effect in peripheral regions in the past, this is no longer the case. The limited expansion of jobs in this sector is reducing the extent to which the public sector has cushioned the effects of unemployment in recent years.

Conclusions

The basic question posed by the evidence of health inequalities presented here is not so much that a 'health divide' exists, and that it has a clear geographical expression, as how one explains this divide, since this will constrain what one does about it. Few would dispute Townsend, Phillimore and Beattie's (1988) analysis that attributes inequalities in health to material deprivation. In terms of policy responses, preventive health care is seen, broadly, as a desirable solution, but this is cast by government spokespersons such as Edwina Currie as being a matter of individual choice. A large-scale attack on the social origins and causes of ill-health – poor housing, poverty, pollution, smoking – seems a remote possibility for so long as the present government remain committed to an ideology of individualism and to the rigid control of public expenditure. Health policy arguably ought to be much more concerned with the elimination of health hazards and the removal of constraints on people's ability to lead healthy lives than with minor adjustments to the distribution of health services, yet it is the latter that has dominated debate about the NHS in recent years.

In terms of the spatial impact of present health-care policies, those areas hardest hit by reductions in finance have been inner-urban health authorities, especially in London, and this, rather than a crude contrast between north and south, is the key divide. This reflects a deliberate political decision to reduce the rate of growth of NHS expenditure and to develop services in some locations only at the expense of reductions in budgets elsewhere. One aspect of the other side of the growth 'coin' in the south may thus prove to be declining public health services, caused in part by rapid net transfers of resources from the Thames RHAs, and in part by the difficulties of adjusting the distribution of resources to cope with rapidly-increasing populations and the problems of recruiting staff due to high house prices. Despite the limited growth in NHS finance, convergence between RHAs has taken place and considerable progress has been made since 1976 in redistributing resources to where they are needed. In addition, the expansion of private health care is superimposing a new layer of service provision onto that provided by the NHS. This is leading to rapid shifts in the balance between public and private provision, especially in southern England, and this has already reached the point where the private sector is as large as the NHS for certain types of service. The present government are known to have considered the possibility of a much greater role for the private sector, and if this comes about it will lead to much greater differentiation between communities in the availability of health services. This could begin to reproduce the spatial inequalities in the availability of health services that were characteristic of pre-NHS days.

Acknowledgement

John Mohan would like to acknowledge the financial support of an Economic and Social Research Council Post-doctoral Research Fellowship, grant no.: A23320076.

8

PRIVATIZATION, EDUCATION AND THE NORTH-SOUTH DIVIDE

Michael Bradford and Frank Burdett

A north-south divide in private education was recognized nearly twenty years ago by Coates and Rawstron (1971). Since then there have been major changes in the structure of the British educational system as a whole. The State-funded system, which accounted for 93 per cent of all pupils in England and Wales in 1987, has been reshaped by the spread of comprehensive, co-educational, schooling. Many of the schools that had been in the direct-grant category joined the private sector when that category was abolished. Private schools are growing in number and experiencing an upsurge in demand for places during the 1980s. Furthermore, there are possibly bigger shifts yet to come with the implementation of the Education Reform Act 1988.

Such changes have profound geographical consequences and form an important element in the emerging north-south divide within Britain. This chapter explores the changes taking place in private education by first examining the general implications of the privatization of education and then identifying regional trends in school attendance in England and Wales.

The New Right and privatization

In many western countries, since the economic recession precipitated by the 1973 oil crisis, there has been a resurgence of right-wing thought – the 'New Right' as it is commonly called (Levitas, 1986; King, 1987). This has led to a re-evaluation of the balance between public and private in the control and provision of many goods or services. It has meant a cultural change in the way that public sectors are run, with the introduction of commercial ideals and practices, which has been described as a switch from 'public administration' to 'public management' (Kooiman and Eliasson, 1987). Kooiman and Eliasson suggest that this has involved a change in emphasis from an interest in equity and fairness to a concern for efficiency and cost-benefit. This change within the public sector has been triggered by the perceived need to reduce public expenditure, a major plank of the 'New

Right'. State-funded education in Britain experienced a reduction from 1976, and since that time has felt pressures to 'manage' rather than 'administer' pressures that are intensified by the Education Reform Act 1988. It has also experienced a change in emphasis from a concern for equality of opportunity and outcome to a major interest in careers and parental choice, reflecting the general trends towards economic rather than social goals and towards market mechanisms rather than bureaucratic, allocative ones (Bradford, 1989). The political and economic climates have, then, begun to change both the goals of the public sector of education in Britain and the way in which it is run.

The New Right's influence has not only been felt within the operation and policies of the public sector. It has also advocated the diminution of State provision and the expansion of that by the private sector and by the family, reflecting both its liberal and conservative strands (King, 1987). The trend away from State provision, which has resulted from the emerging dominance of this ideology, is usually summarized in the ill-defined term, privatization. This is popularly used to describe the transfer of nationalized industries or utilities into the private sector. It also includes moves to introduce the market into the provision of public goods and services, with the introduction of commercial ideals and practices and with greater emphasis on choice and competition – one example of which would be the use of vouchers in education (Blaug, 1984). Privatization may also refer to the contracting out of provision to private companies, while a political body still retains overall responsibility for the particular good. The provision of school meals by a private company is an obvious example. This chapter concentrates on yet another aspect of privatization, the substitution of pure public provision by private provision with State subsidies in the case of education.

In order to situate the trend toward private education and allow a clearer debate over its relative advantages, it is useful to review definitions of privatization. Savas (1982) identifies three dimensions that can illuminate the public–private continuum: the arranger, producer and financer (Table 8.1). In a pure market system, it is

Table 8.1   A characterizaton of the private-public continuum

Dimensions	Public or State	Contracting out	Vouchers	Assisted places	Market
Arranger	Political body	Political body	Consumer	Consumer	Consumer
Producer	Public institution	Private companies	Private companies	Private companies	Private companies
Financer	Political body	Political body	Political body	State subsidy	Consumer

suggested that consumers arrange the system through consumer sovereignty – private companies produce, while the consumers finance. At first sight, this might be thought to be an adequate description of private education, but various subsidies, as will be shown, complicate the picture. At the other extreme, a public service has a political body arranging and financing, and a public institution producing.

Although we would debate the suggested role of the consumers as arrangers in any real private system, since it under-estimates the effect of producers and distributors in influencing demand, the dimensions are useful in examining the continuum and showing how privatization can involve a change on any one of the dimensions. Contracting out, for example, changes the public-service producer without affecting the arranger or financer. The Assisted Places Scheme (Fitz, Edwards and Whitty, 1986), by which very able pupils, once educated in the State system, can be wholly or partly subsidized by the State to permit their entry into some private schools, involves changes on two dimensions and an amendment on the other (Table 8.1).

Such discussions raise other important dimensions connected to the public-private continuum, which are particularly relevant to our discussion of education. A major one is access. This includes spatial access, which involves the differential availability of alternatives from one area to another, as well as the varying distances that people live away from the alternatives in any one area. It also concerns social access, the ability of different genders, social classes and ethnic groups to enter the institutions. For education, it also includes access according to ability. All of these aspects of access are relevant to the debate about private education (Fox, 1985; Griggs, 1985). They may themselves be closely interrelated. For example, particular types of schools may be few in number in one area and distant from certain classes or ethnic groups, who may be noted for their relatively poor performance in selection tests (which have been designed implicitly for other classes or groups).

Spatial, social and intellectual access may be correlated with access to finance. This highlights one of the major differences between public and private systems, their consequences for social justice. In a private system of education, where the consumer or parent pays, access can be based on 'ability to pay', unlike a public system where the political body pays from taxes, implying some redistribution of income. Even where there is a selection test for private schools, those who have been trained for the test in a private preparatory school usually have an advantage. It is this differential access based on finance that can arguably sustain the privileged position of a dominant social class over generations.

While Savas's characterization of the private–public continuum is a helpful start, at least one further dimension may be added. Peston (1984) and Leat (1986) also suggest three dimensions but they replace the economistic 'arranger' category with a more public-oriented 'control' or 'regulator' one. In so doing, they ignore any consideration of consumer choice. Deregulation, as has occurred in public transport, is to them another form of privatization. In education, the State controls the operation of the Assisted Places Scheme and recognizes certain schools as being good enough to participate in the scheme. This may in part replace the process of recognition by Her Majesty's Inspectors of some private schools as efficient – a process that had been withdrawn by the 1974–9 Labour government. Although this was done to thwart private schools, it may actually have helped them to recover from their loss of pupils, by allowing them to use the reputation of the best. Just as the abolition of direct-grant schools strengthened the private sector, so too may have this similarly anti-private schools policy. The Conservative government immediately on its return to office in 1979 established the Assisted Places Scheme rather than restore the direct-grant system. With the current reforms it is seeking to introduce a national curriculum for the State sector but not for the private one. This will increase its control over State schools and possibly reinforce differences between the sectors. Thus changes in the degree of regulation can affect the differences between the sectors and the relative attraction of the sectors to parents.

State subsidy

The financial dimension of the public–private continuum is more complex than at first seems. The State can subsidize what is apparently a market system. This raises questions of social justice as well as doubts about any simple comparison of the benefits of the private and the public systems. There is a parallel argument in housing provision over the degree to which the State subsidizes private consumption. In Britain there is no equivalent to mortgage interest tax-relief for private schooling, such as there is in Minnesota through a tax deduction (Darling-Hammond and Kirby, 1988). State subsidization does occur through the Assisted Places Scheme but, unlike mortgage interest tax-relief, it is progressive. It operates on a means-test principle with the State paying all the fees for about 40 per cent of the 5,000 pupils who take up places, and part of the fees of the rest. This subsidized scheme has been criticized as being based on a false premiss: that a private school was automatically a better place to educate a bright child (Rae, 1981). Rae, a private-school headmaster, further argues (*ibid.* p.179) that 'to help parents move a child in circumstances where the state sector is perfectly capable, would be a waste of public money and an insult to the maintained [State] sector'. Doubt is then cast over the efficiency of the use of public resources that, in this case, support the private system.

There are numerous other forms of subsidy, the most contentious of which is that received in tax and rate relief by the schools because of their charitable status. The Public School Commission, set up by the Labour government in the mid-1960s, found that of the '1500 independent recognised efficient schools in England and Wales, nearly 900 were charities – including... all public schools' (Newsom 1968, p. 157). Less than an eighth of the non-recognized schools were charities. It has been estimated that about a quarter of direct subsidies to private schools comes through charitable status (Pring, 1983). The Labour Party continues to promise to remove charitable status, even though it did not do so in the 1960s and 1970s when elected with similar intentions. It would also stop the Assisted Places Scheme as part of its attack on private schooling. When in power in the 1970s, it effectively reduced the number of places in private schools being bought by local education authorities, another form of subsidy that continues. There is yet another major element of direct subsidy, through that given to government personnel (such as those in the armed services and diplomatic service) for their children to attend private schools.

There are more indirect subsidies through the use of local authority in-service training facilities, advisory services and school medical services, and the training of their teachers at the taxpayers' expense (Griggs, 1985). Set against this, parents will argue that they are paying twice for education, once through their taxes and rates, and again through their school fees. The sting of this argument is removed when it is applied to childless couples who similarly pay for other people's children to be educated. Until the 1988 budget, tax concessions on covenanting have also been available. School fees, then, have thus also been subsidized directly, as well as indirectly through the tax and rate relief to schools.

A review of the arguments for and against private or State education should recognize that the former has effectively mixed funding rather than purely private, so that it is not a pure market system that is being compared.

Arguments for and against State and private provision

The major arguments advanced over the public and private sectors concern their relative efficiency and responsiveness to consumers' needs, their effect on equality, the degree of consumer choice available and their effect on creating communal and self-interest (Le Grand and Robinson, 1984).

Efficiency and responsiveness to consumer needs

Efficiency arguments revolve around the use of resources and 'value for money', with opponents of public expenditure objecting to increases due to vote-catching, the expansion of 'needs' characteristic of a bureaucracy and even trade-union monopoly of the supply of labour (Dennison, 1984). Proponents of these views suggest that employees of State organizations pursue their own ends at the expense of their clients or consumers, because they cannot be taken over or go out of business if they use resources inefficiently. To this extent they are supposed to be less receptive to client or consumer needs. Often such arguments reveal an idealized view of the private sector, since it has also been argued that large corporations have developed their goals of growth through the individual, empire building, ambitions of their executives, with scant attention being paid to consumer demand. Resources may be inefficiently used in both systems, to the extent that consumers' needs and wants are not fully met.

It is difficult, if not impossible, to assess the efficiency of schools. So much of education cannot be measured (Smith, 1988). Efficiency can be reduced to an equation between inputs and outputs (Flynn, 1986), but it is difficult to agree on what constitute inputs and outputs. Any decision would be value laden. Economic and financial arguments, rather than social and educational ones, have tended to dominate the last decade of contraction in the British State sector. Public expenditure cuts, together with falling school rolls, have resulted in school closure and amalgamation. This demonstrates that the State system can respond to efficiency arguments, even when there were strong educational arguments for reducing class sizes rather than closing schools. Ironically, at the same time as national government was reducing resources for State education, from 1981 onwards it was subsidizing able students to enter private schools through the Assisted Places Scheme. For some private schools this now accounts for 20–40 per cent of their places and is an important source of income. The cost of these places has risen faster than inflation, so while educational expenditure has been reduced in the State sector, State subsidy of the private sector has increased. It can be argued that attempts to control government expenditure and make its use more efficient in the State sector have not been paralleled in its use in the private sector.

The private system obviously has to be aware of its market and the effect of rising costs. One way in which it responded to inflation in boarding costs, particularly in the 1970s, was to increase day places. Boys' schools also began to see advantages in widening their market to include girls, first in their sixth form and later throughout the school. This increased their market at a time of demographic contraction and simultaneously improved their academic standards, on which they were increasingly being judged. Both strategies required increased marketing, as did the response of the girls' schools, which reacted to this inroad into their market. The point to emphasize is not so much that marketing increases costs, which will be reflected in fees, but that the response to a need to reduce costs was less one of increased efficiency and more one of attracting new market segments and changing the nature of the school. It could be argued that these were responses to consumer demand. If that were the case, then the State system had responded much faster to co-education and had led the way.

In short, it is difficult to see any basis for concluding that for education the private system is more efficient or responsive than the State one. The argument in this section is particularly significant to the empirical analysis of this chapter, as it shows the degree to which changes in the private system may have been supply rather than demand led. Public provision is also supposed to be indirectly inefficient since, it is argued, the Welfare State removes the incentive to work and to save. It is difficult to see how this might be applied to State education. It could, however, be argued that the fees for private education act as an incentive to work and perhaps to encourage a second income for the household, if the local labour market is sufficiently buoyant. It might also orient parents to savings plans and introduce them to the financial sector, through school fees schemes.

Equality

Le Grand (1982) argues that many public services do not lead, as intended, to increased equality, however defined. This is largely due to their universal provision, such as education, mortgage interest tax-relief and the National Health Service, much of which the rich use more than the poor. This argued failure to achieve equality does not necessarily imply that a private system would produce greater equality (Le Grand and Robinson, 1984). It might well be argued that in education, if access is by ability to pay, it would lead to:

1. inequality of opportunity (or input);
2. inequality of the education process (or through-put); and
3. inequality of educational or occupational outputs and outcomes.

For the 190 parents of public-school boys interviewed by Fox (1985, p.187), 'social inquality is inevitable; what is important to them is the equality of opportunity to become unequal'. Yet there is not even equality of opportunity. Griggs (1985), while clearly a critic of the private system, observes that many private schools are socially selective because of their high fees, which cannot be equated with holidays abroad forgone or some other similarly-substitutable private consumption deferred. Examination of fees and the distribution of family incomes do not support the notion of equality of opportunity. Neither does the longitudinal work on origins and destinations (Halsey, Heath and Ridge, 1980). This refers to a much earlier era when the tripartite system dominated the State sector and direct-grant schools straddled the two sectors. Even then the conclusion was that 'the private schools represent a bastion of class privilege compared with the relatively egalitarian state sector' (*ibid*. p.203).

As for inequalities in the educational process, many private schools use their small classes as part of their promotion and, while there are debates over the effects of class size, there is evidence (Glass *et al.*, 1982) to suggest that once a class goes below twenty pupils, there are dramatic improvements in attainment. The educational process in many private schools may, in this sense, be better that that in the State sector.

Whether the qualifications received and the positions obtained by private-school educated pupils are better than they would have achieved through the State system is debatable. Halsey, Heath and Ridge's (1980, p.212) evidence for the brighter pupils is that for boys of the same social background (remembering that private and State schools had very different social compositions), there was relatively little difference between O-level records at Headmasters Conference schools (public schools), direct–grant and grammar. There were indications, however, that for the less able there was a difference in performance, as measured by length of time in education, between the somewhat better, lesser private schools and secondary-modern schools. Perhaps as important as any objective evaluation of this is the belief of parents sending their children to the schools that they are better, that the schools promote themselves as better and socialize their pupils to think that they have been to better schools.

Interestingly, Fox (1985, p.182) found that it was parents in the smaller day-schools who expected most from private education. They saw them as helping their sons get on in life, not only through qualifications and the development of self-discipline but also through making useful social contacts and developing desirable personality traits. This corresponds to the critics' view of private schools in general that they sustain élites that operate through 'the old-school tie' and shared values. They would argue that it is not so much in examination results that pupils gain advantage but through social contacts that enable them to obtain senior positions (Giddens, 1979, quotes over 80 per cent of all judges, QCs, bishops and directors as being privately educated). Some of Fox's parents recognized the social divisiveness of private education in that they feared their sons would carry feelings of superiority into the world of work or that they would be regarded as acquiring their qualifications by illegitimate means (Fox, 1985, p.164).

While allowing for the heterogeneity within each sector, there still seems to be considerable evidence of all three kinds of inequality. Certainly those using private education perceive it as a positional good.

Consumer choice and liberty

Advocates of the private system advance the argument of greater consumer choice. As the Education Reform Act 1988 demonstrates, this can be provided within the State system although, in its case, it is accompanied by a national curriculum that may standardize schools and limit the variety of choice that is made available by other clauses in the bill (Bradford, 1989). Choice, instead of allocation, may prove a costly use of resources, as either schools expand or contract rapidly in response to the vagaries of the market, or there is sufficient over-supply to accommodate the choice process (10–15 per cent more costly than the conventional system as suggested by voucher experiments). Recently, such an over-supply has been available because of a decline in the birth rate, so a greater degree of choice between sectors, for example, has been possible. Consumption changes between State and private have, therefore, been able to occur without too many supply constraints. Alternatively, instead of over-supply, popular schools can institute some form of selection, as private schools already do, which raises the question of differential access, as discussed earlier. In this case, the power to choose is not equal.

The argument for greater consumer choice is based on the underlying assumption of consumer sovereignty. Any changes in the relative importance of the private and State systems of education would, under that assumption, be interpreted as changes in consumer preferences. In many systems, however, consumer preferences can be affected by the suppliers and by the context within which decisions are made; so interpretations of change should not ignore suppliers' activities.

In education, consumer choice usually means parental choice, an area where the New Rights' liberal views of the market coincide with their conservative ones of the family. The prudent/disciplinarian family constitutes an alternative caring/control agent to that of the State and as such, it is argued, represents a 'saving' of public monies (Fitzgerald, 1983). Although the family may be a cheaper 'arranger' than the State, the system in which it operates, as argued above, may not be. It has also been pointed out that in many other instances the State intervenes to protect the individual from other members of the family. Such an argument could be advanced for education, where the future of the child should not be left, in the extreme cases, to parents who are either totally apathetic to education, and lacking in 'cultural capital', or dangerously over-ambitious for their child.

Communal and self-interest

Le Grand and Robinson (1984) defend the Welfare State and criticize privatization on the basis of the former's encouragement of communal interest and the latter's of self-interest. They quote Titmuss' view (1962) that privatization would restrict individuals' rights to act altruistically, actions that he regards as ethically superior to the market pursuit of self-interest. Since education is collectively consumed, it is possible to claim that pupils at private schools may obtain as great a sense of community as those in State schools. Indeed, the traditional values of the British 'public schools' are service to the community, leadership, initiative and self-reliance (Newsom, 1968). The State system may not then be able to claim a monopoly on communal interest, as acquired at school.

Critics of the private system may argue that it is based on claiming to enhance the individuals' ability to compete and obtain access to 'positions within the haute bourgeoisie or the upper echelons of the service class – the professionals, senior managers and successful entrepreneurs' (Fox, 1985, p.186). These are the positions that Fox's parents value and seek for their 'public-school' sons. Many see private schools as providing a better chance of their children obtaining academic qualifications, and note the increasing emphasis on credentials as a means of access to key positions within the division of labour. Smith (1976) observes that in State schools new methods of learning have been introduced with new norms that are not meritocratic. Those who can afford to exit to the private system, where there are norms they can recognize and endorse, contribute to the continuation of its goals and maximize their children's chances of economic success. At the same time, they are helping to sustain the meritocratic ideals of the post-war era into which many parents were socialized and thereby retard potential change in the State system. The private system, then, is helping to preserve a particular form of education that some parts of the State sector are trying to replace.

Any exit to the private system may be caused by what is perceived to be happening in the State system as much as any attraction of the private system. 'Rightly or wrongly, the majority of... [those interviewed by Fox] believe... [State] schools to have been sacrificed to new educational and moral standards where cooperation and levelling down to a notional average rather than competition and individual achievement are seen as the order of the day' (Fox, 1985, p.187). Paradoxically, Barnett (1972) has laid the responsibility for the decline of Britain as a colonial and industrial power at the door of the 'public schools' and their principle of hierarchy, with its call for obedience to authority that has crushed the competitive spirit. Perhaps the schools put less emphasis now on playing rather than winning the game!

Whether or not self-interest is promoted more by one sector than the other, it has been argued more generally that consumption cleavages, between those who see themselves as dependent on State services and those who use the private sector, feed into political consciousness as a major division in conceptions of self-interest (Dunleavy and Husbands, 1985). The users of State and private education would then have different self-interests, which, it is argued, then affect voting patterns. Given the threats of the Labour Party to abolish private schools this would not be altogether surprising. That threat has been well publicized by the Independent Schools Information Service (ISIS) and the Independent Schools Joint Council (ISJC), set up in 1972 and 1974 respectively. A national network of local groups was established by an action committee of ISJC for the 1983 and 1987 elections, which detailed the threat of both Labour and the Alliance to private schools. It is difficult to tell whether this overt campaign has had as much effect on voting as having a child in a private school or, indeed, whether those who vote Tory are more likely to send their children to private school in the first place. The campaign, behaviour and attitudes are likely to be reinforcing, particularly in areas where there are a number of private schools.

The link between private education and voting patterns becomes a more interesting question when applied to those who have exited from State education. Initially, Hirschman (1970) argued that exit and voice were alternative strategies, so those who exited seem very unlikely to use their influence to improve the system they have left. Others (Birch, 1975) countered that in some situations, exit permitted a use of voice that could not have occurred while the people were in the system. Parents would tend not to criticize a school, for example, while their child was there, as it might put the child in a difficult position.

Thus some have argued that those who have left the State system may well participate in trying to improve it. This is partly used to justify the exit strategy and the availability of the private option. Some may be altruistic or want to return if improvements are made. For many, one might expect limited support for improvement because they will share the tax burden without directly benefiting. More crucially though, by supporting improvement to the State system, they would be making private education less attractive as a positional good. While it is regarded as such, it is to the benefit of parents choosing private education to downgrade State education, but not to such an extent that the demand for private schools becomes too great. If too many have access to private education, it loses its attraction as a positional good. It should not have been such a surprise, therefore, to Taylor-Gooby (1987) to discover that the cleavage in welfare support, which included education, was not between those who were pro- and anti- the Welfare State, but between those who supported the Welfare State, pure and simple, and those who wanted a mixed economy. As Peston (1984) observed, virtually nobody advocates wholly private provision and finance for education.

At this point it is worth highlighting some of the major aspects of the discussion that are crystallized in the name by which private schools are now commonly and officially known – 'independent schools'. As Rae (1981, p.15–16) argues, it is a title 'which suggested – as it was intended to do – liberty and individual enterprise'. Both fit present New-Right thinking. Independence can be more easily defended than the old cachet, public schools. The title also suggests, as it is supposed to, independence from the State, with the State system being termed the 'maintained sector'. Yet, as the subsidy discussion indicates, this is misleading. The private schools have marketed themselves very well.

Geographical consequences of education change

Any spatial differentiation in the rate of growth of private education may reflect and reinforce cleavages in public opinion on the issue of individualism versus collectivism. This can arise from the operation of various processes that produce contextual effects. As has been shown, there is a class bias to the adoption of private education. Spatial differences in adoption may then simply reflect the class composition of areas. In areas where there are more than expected in private education, given the social composition, contextual effects may be occurring; that is, people from a given social class may have a greater probability of entering private education than they have in other areas. This greater predisposition can be acquired through social interaction, or the neighbourhood effect (Warde, 1986). It may result from imitating the behaviour of the local reference group, or it may be acquired over time through socialization (Johnston, 1985).

Such behaviour may also be influenced by the supply side, which is too often omitted in the literature. Greater private-school provision in certain areas is obviously likely to attract more people; so, too, may greater or better marketing of the provision or of the financial packages that make it affordable. Equally it may be State education in that area becoming less attractive relative to other areas, rather than private education becoming relatively more attractive. A move towards private education may then be a push rather than a pull. The two can even be interlinked: in Manchester at the time of the teachers' dispute, private schools advertised 'the more peaceful academic groves of the private school sector, where industrial action is rarer than rain in the Sahara' (*Manchester Evening News*, 1984, p.8).

Any geographical variation in private education has consequences for the spatial distribution of State subsidy. If private education is unevenly distributed relative to the population and/or growing at a faster rate in certain areas of the country, then this is a further way in which some regions will be indirectly gaining more State funds than others. Paradoxically, this may be achieved by greater exit from the State system.

If private education leads to, or sustains, inequality, an argument for which there is considerable support, then a greater incidence and/or expansion of private education in one part of the country would lead to greater potential social mobility or retention of social position for people from that part of the country. If this is the case, it would also have been achieved with the aid of more State subsidy. If the relative growth of private education in such a region is accompanied by a reduction in the per-capita national-government contribution to pupils in State schools, as is possible in the Inner London Education Authority, or by a reduction in the Rate Support Grant, which may have a similar effect in other local authorities, then this would also exacerbate inequalities between private and State pupils within the region.

There is a further inequality that should be noted before examining the changing geography of education: private education has a gender bias towards boys. Much of the research on private education focuses on boys, partly because of the impact of the 'public schools'. The analysis here examines changes by gender, in order to understand the processes producing geographical change and to probe New-Right thought, which shows an antipathy towards feminism, and, through its advocacy of the family, re-affirms woman's place in the home.

Education and the north-south divide

The regional divide in the use of public and private education that was noted by Coates and Rawstron in 1971 was still apparent in 1981 (Figure 8.1(a)). These differences are not simply the reflection of the social-class compositions of the regions, as Figure 8.1(b) makes allowance for this. It is based on an approximation of the expected numbers attending private schools given the social-class structure, reported in the *General Household Survey* and 1981 population census[1]. All northern regions have at least 20 per cent fewer pupils in private schools than would be expected on this basis, while three of the southern regions are over-represented by over 20 per cent. Only in East Anglia is attendance like that predicted by class composition. The north and the south have different attitudes to private education.

Furthermore, Figure 8.1(a) shows that the division grew between 1981 and 1986. There was a more-rapid relative growth of private education in all the regions south of the Severn–Wash line except the South West. The South West has a greater proportion of boarding pupils than other regions and this is a segment of private education that declined in this period. In the rest of the south, private-sector expansion was greatest in Greater London. There and in East Anglia, growth was both absolute and relative.

The relative growth of the private schools has occurred at a time of declining numbers of schoolchildren and a general contraction in the number of schools. Hence, the regional differences are not simply due to a differential increase in the supply of schools. In general, the number of private schoolchildren has contracted less rapidly than that for State schools. The decline in the birth rate may not have affected private schools as much as State ones, because of the less-rapid decline in rate for social classes one and two, the dominant classes in private schools. There is, however, little evidence that regional differences in the birth rates of these classes may have accounted for the differential relative rates of increase in attendance at private schools. Although there may be some contribution from changes in the social-class composition of regions between 1981 and 1986, through differential rates of social mobility and even net migration, these may not be sufficient to explain the increasing polarization. The social-class compositon of regions in 1981 certainly does not account for the changes (Bradford and Burdett, 1989). There seem to be different processes operating in the southern and northern regions, or similar processes operating at different rates, which account for the initial and increasing spatial polarization of private education.

It is difficult to understand the changing predisposition to private education and its geography by analysing 2–15-year-olds. Pre-school, primary and secondary stages are combined and the overall picture represents decisions taken at very different times. The examination of a single cohort at the age of usual entry into the secondary stage, 11-year-olds, is more sensitive to change. It does have one major limitation though, in that class compositional effects cannot be adequately estimated. By using 1977 as the base year, the complication of the category of direct-grant schools is avoided as their status was abolished in 1975.

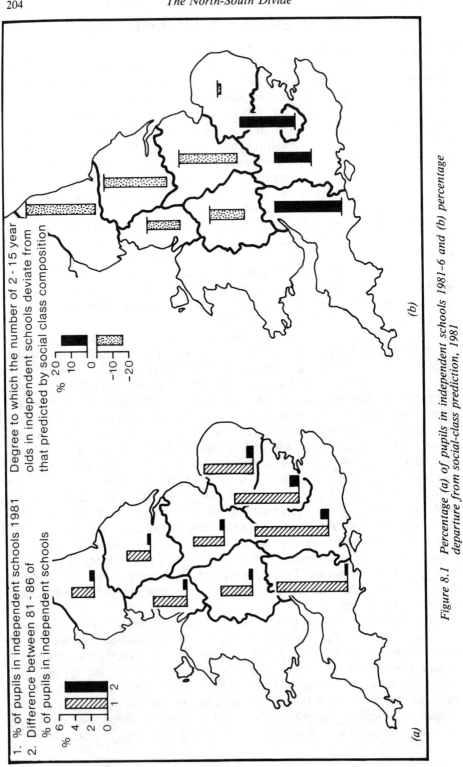

Figure 8.1   Percentage (a) of pupils in independent schools 1981-6 and (b) percentage departure from social-class prediction, 1981

The year 1977 is also the demographic peak of 11-year-olds, so from then on, the system as a whole is contracting. From 1981 the introduction of the Assisted Places Scheme complicates the picture, and the geographical distribution of its places will have to be considered in the analysis.

The data from the Department of Education is available only by school and not by home address. Cross-boundary flows of day pupils from homes on one side of boundaries to schools on the other side may be considerable at the local-authority scale but much reduced at the standard region level, the scale used predominantly in this analysis. The cross-boundary flows of boarding pupils, who account for about a fifth of all private-school pupils, will be more significant at the regional level. The differential spatial incidence of boarding, which can be estimated from ISIS censuses, will then also have to be borne in mind in the analysis. Although the data do not establish the location of households making the decisions, some indication of the consumption cleavage between private and State education can be presented at the regional scale.

Table 8.2   North-south differences in the private education of 11-year-olds, 1977–86

	a 77	b 86	c 77–86	d	e 77	f 86	g 77	h 86
England	6.20	7.83	−2.80		5.05	6.37	6.23	7.88
North	4.22	5.07	−9.24	−25.07	3.50	4.28	4.24	5.16
South	8.36	10.72	0.75	−23.46	7.70	10.40	5.68	6.87
Difference	4.14	5.65			4.20	6.12	1.44	1.71

(a) Independent pupils as % of all pupils, 1977.
(b) Independent pupils as % of all pupils, 1986.
(c) % change in absolute no. of independent pupils, 1977–86.
(d) % change in absolute no. of maintained pupils, 1977–86.
(e) Median of % independent pupils for constituent LEAs, 1977.
(f) Median of % independent pupils for constituent LEAs, 1986.
(g) Inter-quartile range of % independent pupils for constituent LEAs, 1977.
(h) Inter-quartile range of % independent pupils for constituent LEAs, 1986.

Table 8.2 confirms the increasing polarization between the north and the south for this cohort. The proportion of pupils in private schools has risen for both parts of the country but more so for the south than the north. The widening gap could have been produced in a number of ways, so the components of change are separately examined. Both the north and the south have experienced rapid demographic declines for this cohort, as can be seen for the State sector (Table 8.2, column d). The private sector in the south has managed to retain its numbers, while in the north it has suffered a much less dramatic decline than the State sector. The changes in the proportions of private pupils (Table 8.2, columns a and b) are therefore mostly due to the differential retention of private numbers rather than differential demographic change.

This difference in retention is not due to a marked change in the supply of schools, since the net closure rates are very similar, being 5.8 per cent in the north and 5.1 per cent in the south. It is then mainly the expansion and contraction of existing schools that account for the differences.

The Assisted Places Scheme represents another component of change. The gap between the north and the south, however, was already widening between 1977 and 1981, and after its introduction in 1981 the scheme, in fact, acts to offset the increasing polarization – because there are disproportionately more available places for 11-year-olds in the north (45.2 per cent) than in the south (54.9 per cent), given their respective shares of the private sector as a whole (33.1 per cent and 66.8 per cent). This scheme, therefore, is operating relatively, if not absolutely, to decrease inter-regional inequalities, even though it may be increasing intra-regional ones. So this element of public subsidy is slightly offsetting the other elements that are directed more towards the south.

While still retaining the focus at the north-south scale, it is possible to observe the changes at the scales of their constituent standard regions and local authorities. All the southern regions are above the national percentage (Figure 8.2) for all years from 1977 to 1986 and, with the exception of the South West, deviate increasingly further from it. On the other hand, all the northern regions lie below the national percentage and consistently deviate further from it throughout the period. The increasing polarization observed at the aggregate level is then mirrored in all the constituent standard regions, except the South West, where the high proportion (40 per cent) of boarders has dampened the increase.

Increasing polarization can also be observed at the level of constituent local authorities, which have more meaning as spatial units for the delivery of State education than do standard regions, but of course are more prone to cross-boundary flows. The differences between the northern and southern medians increase over time, as do their deviations from the national medians (Table 8.2, columns e and f). Greater understanding of this widening gap can be gained from examining the inter-quartile ranges of the northern and southern local authorities (Table 8.2, columns g and h), both of which are increasing over time. This suggests that, although there are increasing differences both within the north and the south, the high extreme of the southern distribution and low extreme of the northern are moving further apart. So at both the levels of the standard regions and the local authorities, the divide is growing.

Regional differences

An analysis focused on the standard regions rather than the north and south suggests a rather different location of the dividing line between north and south, at least for this phenomenon.

The most marked change at this scale is the absolute and relative growth of pupils in Greater London's private sector (Figure 8.3). This is despite having the greatest demographic decline of all regions for this cohort. Its expansion is partly due to the proportionally greater availability of assisted places (21.8 per cent to a 16.8 per cent share of private pupils). East Anglia has an even greater absolute rate of growth than Greater London, but the least demographic decline of all regions, reflecting its recent position as lead region in overall population growth.

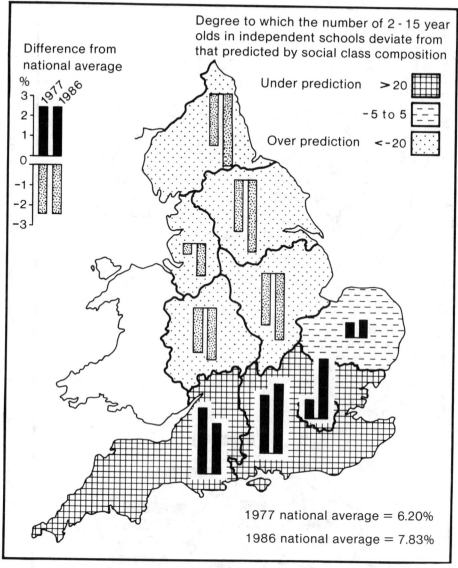

Figure 8.2 *Change in 11 year olds in independent schools, 1977–86*

So its relative rate of growth in private education is not as great as that of Greater London.

The rest of the South East and the Midlands share some similar characteristics. The absolute numbers of their private pupils slightly increases while they experience similar rates of demographic decline to that of England as a whole. The rather unexpectedly low increase in private education in the Outer South East is partly due to it receiving only half of its predicted share of assisted places (15.4 per cent rather than 32.6 per cent).

The Midlands seem much more part of the south than does the South West,

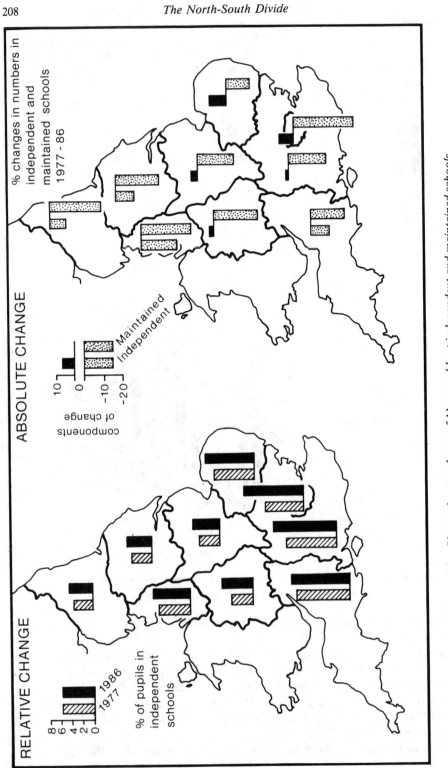

Figure 8.3   Change in attendance of 11 year olds at independent and maintained schools, 1977–86

which – despite a relatively small demographic decline – has lost over 10 per cent of its private pupils. This has been associated with the closure of 13 per cent of its schools. Its high boarding component may account for much of this loss, and given the greater degree of cross-boundary flows for boarders, the decline in private education should not necessarily be taken in this case as a change in orientation to State and private education of people in the region.

From these figures, though, the South West has more in common with the three other northern regions. All four have declining shares of England's private pupils (Table 8.3). For the North West the numbers of both private pupils and schools decline at similar rates, but nearly twice those of the South West. If it

Table 8.3   Inter- and intra-regional differences in private education of 11-year-olds, 1977–86

	a 77	b 86	c	d 77	e 86	f 86–77	g 77	h 86	i 86–77
Greater London	15.18	16.81	21	6.72	9.42	2.70	7.68	13.37	5.69
Outer South East	31.45	32.70	12	9.12	11.28	2.16	4.67	7.54	2.87
South West	13.65	12.56	7	9.60	10.58	0.78	4.39	5.49	1.10
East Anglia	4.25	4.81	3	6.31	8.36	2.05	2.52	2.99	0.47
West Midlands	7.43	7.80	11	3.08	4.59	1.51	5.28	6.60	1.32
East Midlands	4.79	5.08	5	3.60	4.70	1.10	1.11	2.25	1.14
North West	13.24	10.91	17	5.31	5.38	0.07	6.21	8.91	2.70
North	3.65	3.45	9	2.51	2.67	0.16	2.32	2.73	0.41
Yorkshire & Humberside	6.37	5.88	11	1.90	3.39	1.49	4.15	3.58	−0.57
England	100.00	100.00	96						

(a) % of England's independent pupils, 1977.
(b) % of England's independent pupils, 1986.
(c) Number of LEAs.
(d) Median of % independent of all pupils in constituent LEAs, 1977.
(e) Median of % independent of all pupils in constituent LEAs, 1986.
(f) Difference between (e) and (d).
(g) Inter-quartile range of % independent of all pupils in constituent LEAs, 1977.
(h) Inter-quartile range of % independent of all pupils in constituent LEAs, 1986.
(i) Difference between (h) and (g).

were not for the Assisted Places Scheme the decline would have been more marked. The North West receives nearly twice as many places as expected (21.3 per cent to 10.9 per cent). This is partly because the region had a large share of the old direct-grant schools and all those that became private after abolition in 1975 received assisted places in 1981. The two remaining northern regions both declined in absolute numbers of private pupils at a faster rate than their decline in numbers of schools. They have similar percentages of private schools to those of the West and East Midlands for 1977 but, because they experience a decrease rather than an increase in absolute numbers of private pupils, their increase in relative numbers of private pupils is much more like that of the North West.

From this analysis, it seems that in terms of change, if not from starting levels, the South West has more in common with the peripheral regions of the north, while the two Midland regions have more in common with the rest of the south.

There is also considerable change occurring within regions (Table 8.3 columns g, h and i), particularly Greater London (Bradford and Burdett, 1989). This scale of analysis bears further attention when there is greater information available on cross-boundary flows. The increasing inter-quartile ranges for all but one region serve as a reminder that greater polarization between places is occurring at a number of scales, not just between north and south, however defined.

The gender shift

One possible explanation of the contextual effects that have been observed in this analysis is associated with increased marketing by private schools. ISIS has been promoting them generally, especially as a reaction to threats to their survival by the Labour Party. As mentioned previously, boarding schools have been advertising for day pupils and boys' schools have been trying to attract girls, in response to inflation, declining birth rates and the need for high academic success. The increased marketing, it is suggested, has had a multiplicative effect, whereby the overall impact is greater than the sum of the marketing of the individual schools. It is further suggested that this overall impact is more than proportionately greater in areas where there are already a considerable number of private schools.

The success of the search for girls is summarized in Table 8.4, which displays both the initial gender bias in private education, its overall increase during the period, and the greater spatial polarization of girls. The peripheral northern regions and the South West again declined in absolute numbers while the rest increased. This amended definition of the divide describes the changes better, while the standard definition summarizes more effectively the percentage of girls in private as against State education, both at the beginning of the period and, despite the changes, also at the end of the period. The most interesting trend, though, is seen in the changing percentage of private-school pupils of this cohort who are female (Table 8.4, columns f, g and h). The peripheral northern regions have a declining proportion of girls in private education. So their decline in absolute numbers is greater for girls than for boys. This contrasts sharply with the expanding West Midlands, Outer South East and East Anglia, where there have been marked gains in both the absolute numbers of girls and the proportion of pupils in private schools who are female. In these six regions there has been a significant gender shift.

In the East Midlands there has been no gender bias to the changes. Greater London, like the peripheral northern regions, has also experienced a declining proportion of girls but, in contrast, it is an expanding system, with the growth in absolute numbers of boys exceeding that for girls. Unlike the Outer South East it has not replaced boys with girls. The sector has expanded for both sexes. In the South West, in contrast to Greater London, the proportion of girls has increased while their absolute numbers have declined.

In summary, in the southern regions and the Midlands there has been either

Table 8.4 The gender shift for 11-year-olds in private education, 1977–86

	a	b	c	d	e	f	g	h
North	3.3	4.1	0.8	−10.3	−6.0	50.1	48.9	−1.2
Yorkshire & Humberside	3.4	3.7	0.3	−17.1	−4.7	45.0	41.6	−3.4
North West	5.6	5.6	0.0	−26.7	−13.4	48.9	44.7	−4.1
East Midlands	3.3	4.2	0.9	3.4	3.2	44.4	44.4	0.0
West Midlands	3.5	5.0	1.5	7.8	−2.4	43.8	46.3	2.5
East Anglia	6.1	7.8	1.7	14.0	6.8	42.4	44.0	1.6
Outer South East	8.4	10.7	2.3	3.0	−0.6	45.2	46.1	0.9
Greater London	7.0	10.5	3.5	4.9	10.5	49.3	48.0	−1.3
South West	9.2	10.2	1.0	−9.0	−12.0	47.8	48.7	0.9
North	4.0	4.7	0.7	−12.6	−6.3	46.6	44.9	−1.7
South	8.0	10.3	2.3	1.5	0.1	46.6	46.9	0.3
England	5.9	7.4	1.5	−3.5	−2.2	46.6	46.3	−0.3

(a) Independent girl pupils as % of all girl pupils, 1977.
(b) Independent girl pupils as % of all girl pupils, 1986.
(c) Difference in % between 1986 and 1977, (b) − (a).
(d) % change in absolute numbers of independent girl pupils, 1977–86.
(e) % change in absolute numbers of independent boy pupils, 1977–86.
(f) Independent girl pupils as % of all independent pupils, 1977.
(g) Independent girl pupils as % of all independent pupils, 1986.
(h) Difference in % between 1986 and 1977, (g) − (f).

an absolute growth in the numbers of girls receiving private education or a greater increase in the proportion of girls in private education. In most of these regions both have occurred. In contrast, in the peripheral northern regions, the absolute number of girls has declined and declined faster than that for boys. The spatial polarization is, therefore, more marked for girls than it is for boys.

This is a curious paradox. Increased private education is associated with the New Right; yet it sees a woman's place as in the home. This might not be associated with sending girls to private schools, especially if it is to gain better qualifications and access to higher education. Many authors writing on consumption cleavages and growing privatization would emphasize people's changing orientations and the exercising of choice. These results indicate that the marketing efforts and dynamics of the supply side should not be ignored.

Conclusions

This analysis shows that for private and State education a north-south divide existed at the beginning of the period in 1977, with all its spatial consequences for the unequal distribution of State subsidy, life chances and social mobility. The divide widened over the next nine years, particularly for girls, though the changes were more marked between the peripheral northern regions and the South West on one hand, and the Midlands and the rest of the south on the other. The resulting geographical inequalities have then generally increased. The more prosperous south has received even more direct and indirect subsidies, while more of its children have acquired what is viewed as a positional good.

The faster rate of privatization in the south could be due to demand-side processes: a more rapid acceptance of individualistic ideals, associated with similar growth of private medicine and privatized shares; and/or the greater socialization effects that are possible in areas of already-higher provision. This analysis, though, suggests that the 'arranger' role of consumers may be over-estimated. Consumer choice has been much influenced by the increased marketing of the private sector to protect itself and to attract day pupils and, in this period particularly, girls. This has undoubtedly raised the profile of private education that, where supply has permitted, has led in some areas to its absolute as well as relative expansion for both girls and boys.

This may have been reinforced in the South East by the attack of politicians, the media and some educationalists on the State system as a whole that, although general in nature, has focused particularly on Greater London. Exit to the private system in the south is made more possible by the more buoyant economy that sustains higher salaries and allows greater possibility for two-income households. This might be a particularly important difference between the north and the south, in addition to any variation in cultural attitudes to women's education, in deciding whether families can afford to educate girls privately. The south's initially greater involvement with the private sector will also have led to it being targeted in the marketing of school-fees packages by the financial sector, a further influence of the supply side (Bradford and Burdett, 1989).

There may be further privatization and greater spatial polarization in the future, since many of the present decisions on State education are being made by people educated privately, and they are being made in London where privatization is most rapid and State education is under the greatest attack. The forced reduction in the spending of the Inner London Education Authority and its intended abolition suggest that intra-regional inequalities in education will increase, at least in the most privatized area, at the same time as inter-regional inequalities magnify through the reinforcement of the north-south divide.

Note

1. The expectation is based on the socio-economic composition of the 0–15 age group from the 1981 census and the national participation rates of different socio-economic groups from the *General Household Survey* (1977). This is an approximation because of sampling errors in the survey (a sample of 11,644 pupils) and the census (10 per cent sample), and the slight difference in timing and age groups.

9

VOTING IN BRITAIN SINCE 1979: A GROWING NORTH-SOUTH DIVIDE?

R.J. Johnston and Charles Pattie

The results of the 1987 General Election in Great Britain produced a number of journalistic analyses suggesting the existence of an ever-widening north-south divide in the country's electoral geography. For some academic analysts, such a divide has been present for at least thirty years, and the trends across the three elections won by the Conservative Party in 1979, 1983 and 1987 have merely been an accentuation of an already-existing polarization. The difference between the two sets of authors reflects the focus of their empirical analyses. For the academic psephologists, the major concern has been with the percentage of the votes won by each of the political parties, whereas for their journalistic counterparts attention has centred on seats won. Because of the way in which the British electoral system transforms votes into seats, the trends in vote percentages could be concealed from the journalists until a major shift in the pattern of seats won eventuated. Thus, 1979–87 may be no more than a continuation of general trends, brought to public attention because they have resulted in greater polarization in seats won during the 1980s.

The polarization received particular attention in 1987 because of a growing realization that the country was becoming increasingly divided on a range of economic and social criteria, as shown by other chapters in this book. The north-south divide identified in the election results was seen as further evidence of that division: the economic and social cleavage of the country into a relatively-deprived north and an increasingly-affluent south was paralleled by an electoral cleavage. People were no longer voting according to their class position, it seemed, but rather according to their spatial location.

The aim of this chapter is to present a brief academic analysis of that interpretation of the country's electoral geography. In the first part, we set the recent trends in context by looking at the regional distribution of votes and seats won since the Second World War. From that, we analyse the 1979, 1983 and 1987 General Elections, to show the extent of the spatial polarization. Finally, we investigate the reasons for the changing electoral geography, and discuss several implications to be drawn from the observed trends.

The changing regional electoral geography of Great Britain

The classical analyses of British voting behaviour typically portray the country as dominated by a class cleavage, in which people from white-collar households have been mobilized as Conservative voters, whereas those from blue-collar households have habitually voted Labour (see, for example, Butler and Stokes, 1969, 1974; Johnston, 1985 and 1986a, reviews this literature). During the 1970s and 1980s, this cleavage has declined according to some analysts (e.g. Franklin, 1985; Dunleavy, 1987; though see Heath, Jowell and Curtice, 1985, 1987). The nature of its replacement is a subject of considerable debate: Sarlvik and Crewe (1983; see also Crewe and Denver, 1985; and Crewe, 1986) suggest a process of de-alignment whereby voters' choices are the function of ideological attitudes and evaluations of parties, policies and leaders, but those evaluations are neither closely linked to class positions (as they were in the past) nor permanent over several elections (even though attitudes may be – Curtice, 1986), producing a more volatile electorate. Rose and McAllister (1986) propose that the link between attitudes and voting is as weak as that between class and voting, producing an unpredictable outcome (though see Johnston and Pattie, 1988). Dunleavy (1979; see also Dunleavy and Husbands, 1985) suggests a new cleavage around consumption issues, whereby the Conservative Party is linked to people who obtain major consumption items (housing, transport, etc.) from the private sector, and the Labour Party increasingly represents those who obtain such goods and services from the public sector. Finally, both Curtice and Steed (1982) and Miller (1984) suggest that there is a growing spatial cleavage within the electorate, only partly linked to class and other cleavages.

Evaluating these four theses is a major task for electoral analysts. Available data suggests some support for all four (though that associated with Rose and McAllister, 1986, finds least confirmation in other studies: Johnston and Pattie, 1988; Whiteley, 1983, 1986). Our concern here is mainly with the fourth: has there been an increased spatial divergence in the pattern of support for the parties, and why?

The data in Table 9.1 suggest that the thesis is valid. Over the four decades since the Second World War, there has indeed been an increased concentration of, for example, Labour MPs in the northern regions and Conservative MPs in the south. The growing Conservative dominance of the south (coupled with the substantial fall in the number of Labour MPs for Inner London Constituencies and the Midlands) means the present government virtually has a majority in the House of Commons in the south and Midlands alone. It has also eaten into Labour's strength in the north of England and in Wales, though Labour remains the largest party there and Scotland's delegation to the House of Commons has increasingly been dominated by Labour MPs. There is, then, a prima-facie case for arguing, as Denver (1987) did after the 1987 election, that the most obvious variations in the pattern of voting are now regional, as the different parts of Great Britain increasingly diverge in the composition of their parliamentary delegations.

Extending the analysis

The patterns displayed in Table 9.1 present a very gross picture of Britain's changing electoral geography, for two reasons. First, the regions are large, so that they do not provide fine detail. Second, and most importantly, those regions are internally very heterogeneous, because they contain very different types of social milieux. Much information is lost, and for this reason our analysis of the 1979, 1983 and 1987 elections focuses on two more-detailed sets of regions.

The first of these sets of regions – *the geographical regions* – is based on a division of the country devised by Steed (and used in *The Economist* for several years) that incorporates the two components of the spatial polarization of the vote identified by Curtice and Steed (1982): inter-regional polarization and urban-rural polarization. Thus the 22 regions used (and named in Table 9.2) sub-divide the standard regions into their major urban and rural components, though still presenting a relatively gross picture (e.g. free-standing cities outside the major conurbations, such as Bristol, are not separately identified). Second, there is a set of 31 *functional regions* based on a cluster analysis of 1981 census data for the 633 constituencies and published by Crewe and Fox (1984). This classifies constituencies by common socio-economic characteristics, irrespective of geographical location; the short titles in Table 9.3 indicate the nature of those functional regions.

Tables 9.2 and 9.3 show the changes in voting in those two sets of regions between the 1979 and 1987 elections (in these tables and all of the analyses, the percentages refer to the total electorate and not just to those who voted). As will be seen, there were quite substantial variations around the national averages. With the Labour Party, for example, the average rate of increase of its vote between 1983 and 1987 was more than twice the national figure in some regions, and the decline in the Alliance vote between the same two elections was three times the national figure in some parts of the country. There is little doubt that, at both scales, there were substantial differences between the regions in party fortunes.

The nature of the variation by geographical region is shown in Figure 9.1, which maps the 'percentage-point change' in each party's percentage of the electorate between 1979 and 1987 (percentage share of the total vote in first years minus the second). There is clearly a north-south divide in each map, with the Conservative vote declining in most regions to the north and west of the West Midlands conurbation but increasing in south and east England; with the Labour vote falling more rapidly in the latter than in the former; and with the Alliance increase generally greater in southern than in northern England. But there are variations around that divide. The Conservative vote fell in Devon and Cornwall and in Inner London, for example, and increased in the Rural North, in Rural Wales and in West Yorkshire. Labour's percentage of the electorate increased in five regions (three of them in Scotland), and the Alliance's largest increases also included two Scottish regions.

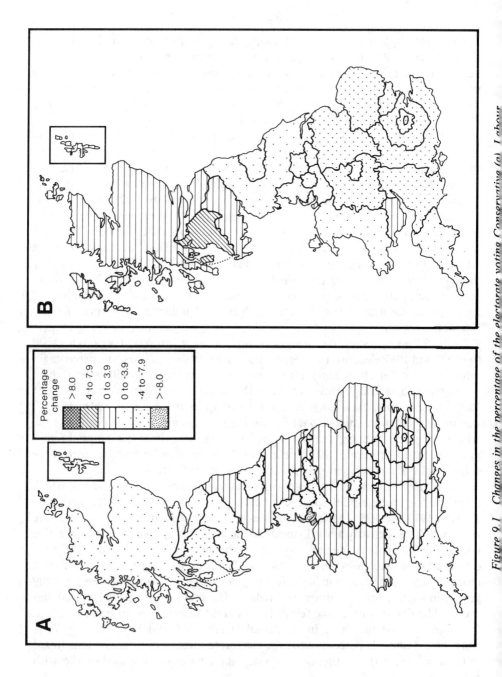

Figure 9.1 Changes in the percentage of the electorate voting Conservative (a) Labour

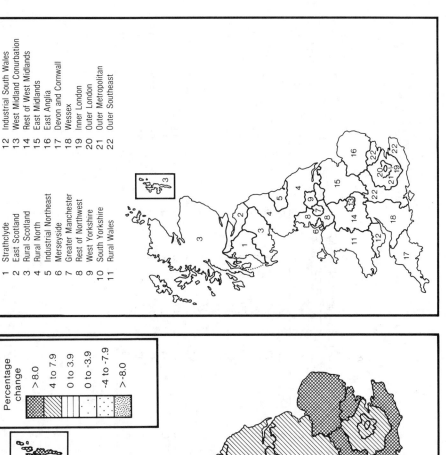

1 Strathclyde
2 East Scotland
3 Rural Scotland
4 Rural North
5 Industrial Northeast
6 Merseyside
7 Greater Manchester
8 Rest of Northwest
9 West Yorkshire
10 South Yorkshire
11 Rural Wales

12 Industrial South Wales
13 West Midland Conurbation
14 Rest of West Midlands
15 East Midlands
16 East Anglia
17 Devon and Cornwall
18 Wessex
19 Inner London
20 Outer London
21 Outer Metropolitan
22 Outer Southeast

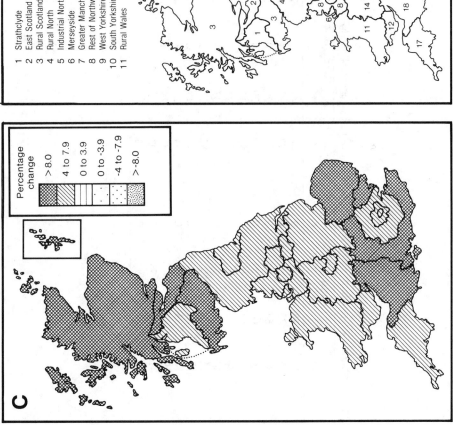

C

Percentage change

>8.0
4 to 7.9
0 to 3.9
0 to -3.9
-4 to -7.9
> -8.0

Figure 9.1 (cont.) (c) Alliance

Table 9.1 The distribution of parliamentary seats in Great Britain, by region, 1945–87[1]

	London				Rest of South				Midlands			
	C	L	B	O	C	L	B	O	C	L	B	O
1945	19	77	0	3	48	49	2	2	27	71	0	2
1950	28	72	0	0	72	27	1	0	37	63	0	0
1951	33	67	0	0	77	23	0	0	37	63	0	0
1955	36	64	0	0	79	20	0	1	41	59	0	0
1959	43	57	0	0	83	17	1	0	51	49	0	0
1964	24	76	0	0	76	23	1	0	44	56	0	0
1966	14	86	0	0	65	33	2	1	36	64	0	0
1970	21	79	0	0	82	17	1	1	53	47	0	0
1974(F)	17	83	0	0	79	19	2	0	44	56	0	0
1974(O)	17	83	0	0	74	23	3	0	41	59	0	0
1979	29	71	0	0	85	14	1	0	58	42	0	0
1983	41	52	7	0	92	6	2	0	73	26	1	0
1987	41	50	9	0	93	4	3	0	67	33	0	0

Table 9.1 (cont.)

	North of England				Wales				Scotland			
	C	L	B	O	C	L	B	O	C	L	B	O
1945	25	74	1	0	11	71	18	0	48	44	0	8
1950	36	63	1	0	11	75	14	0	45	52	3	0
1951	41	58	1	0	17	75	8	0	49	49	1	0
1955	45	54	1	0	17	75	8	0	51	48	3	0
1959	46	53	1	0	17	78	5	0	44	53	3	0
1964	32	68	0	0	17	78	5	0	32	61	7	0
1966	26	72	2	0	8	89	3	0	28	65	7	0
1970	38	62	0	0	14	75	3	3	32	62	4	2
1974(F)	29	68	2	1	22	67	6	6	30	56	4	10
1974(O)	27	71	2	0	22	64	6	8	22	58	4	16
1979	32	65	3	0	31	61	3	5	31	62	4	3
1983	42	55	2	0	37	53	5	5	29	57	11	3
1987	39	59	2	0	21	63	8	8	14	70	13	3

1. Data for 1945–79 derived from Butler and Sloman (1980, p. 213). London refers to the old London County, now the Inner London Education Authority boroughs.

C = Conservative; L = Labour; B = Liberal; O = Others. Number of Seats is expressed as a per cent of the regional total.

Table 9.2 Inter-election changes in percentage of the electorate voting for each party, 1979–87, by geographical region

	Conservative			Labour			Alliance		
	79–83	83–7	79–87	79–83	83–7	79–87	79–83	83–7	79–87
Strathclyde	−3.3	−2.4	−5.7	−3.9	10.5	6.6	11.2	−4.0	7.2
East Scotland	−0.9	−0.9	−1.8	−4.6	7.9	3.3	11.0	−3.3	8.6
Rural Scotland	−0.3	−0.3	−0.6	−4.0	5.2	1.3	8.1	1.0	9.1
Rural North	−0.2	0.4	0.1	−7.1	3.7	−3.4	6.2	−0.9	5.2
Industrial Northeast	−2.3	−1.2	−3.6	−8.6	7.3	−1.3	9.6	−2.4	7.2
Merseyside	−5.0	−3.5	−8.5	−4.5	7.7	3.1	6.8	0.7	7.5
Greater Manchester	−4.0	0.8	−3.1	−6.3	4.6	−1.7	6.9	−1.8	5.1
Rest of Northwest	−2.5	0.4	−2.1	−5.7	4.9	−0.8	7.4	−2.1	5.3
West Yorkshire	−1.4	1.8	0.4	−8.2	5.6	−2.6	7.8	−2.8	5.0
South Yorkshire	−2.7	−1.4	−4.1	−7.9	7.8	−0.1	7.9	−2.5	5.4
Rural Wales	−0.1	0.7	0.6	−6.8	6.1	−0.7	6.1	−0.2	5.9
Industrial South Wales	−2.6	0.7	−1.9	−8.4	10.2	1.8	10.1	−4.2	5.9
W. Midlands conurbation	−3.4	1.4	−2.0	−6.2	2.9	−3.3	8.7	−1.9	6.7
Rest of West Midlands	0.3	1.2	1.5	−7.4	2.3	−5.1	8.3	−0.8	7.5
East Midlands	−0.3	2.8	2.5	−8.0	2.7	−5.3	7.6	−1.6	6.0
East Anglia	0.4	2.1	2.5	−8.8	1.5	−7.3	9.3	−1.2	8.0
Devon and Cornwall	−0.9	−1.1	−2.0	−6.8	4.3	−2.5	8.4	−2.0	6.4
Wessex	−0.1	1.8	1.7	−7.8	1.2	−6.6	7.9	0.9	8.8
Inner London	−3.8	2.6	−1.2	−7.4	3.2	−4.1	7.8	−0.1	7.7
Outer London	−3.2	3.7	0.5	−9.0	1.6	−7.3	8.3	−2.3	6.0
Outer Metropolitan	−0.5	2.9	2.4	−8.4	1.1	−7.3	8.5	−1.2	7.2
Outer Southeast	−0.4	1.8	1.4	−7.7	1.3	−6.4	8.1	0.4	8.5
National	−1.7	1.1	−0.6	−7.2	4.1	−3.1	8.3	−1.4	6.9

Accounting for polarization

The changes described in the last part of the preceding section suggest that Curtice and Steed (1982) and Miller (1984) were right in arguing that the topography of the British electoral map was becoming more pronounced. But why should this have occurred? Miller's view is that people are increasingly influenced more by their spatial than by their social location – where you are is more important than who you are. Thus whereas in the 1950s it might have been the case, as Pulzer (1967), Bogdanor (1983) and others have expressed it, that people in the same class position voted the same way, wherever they lived, that is not true in the 1980s.

To test Miller's hypothesis we need data on the voting behaviour of similar people in different places. Survey data, because they are based on relatively small samples, cannot be disaggregated sufficiently for the purpose (though Butler and Stokes, 1974, produced graphs that are based on aggregating data from a large number of comparable surveys). However, recent work applying the entropy-maximizing techniques introduced to geography by Wilson (1970) for estimating traffic flows has provided a way of combining survey, electoral and census data to provide maximum likelihood estimates of voting by particular social groups in different places. (The methods were first applied in this way in Johnston and Hay, 1982, and used extensively in Johnston's, 1985, study of the 1983 election.) Data limitations constrain such estimations to patterns of voting by occupational groups, but allow substantial insights to the detailed electoral geography of the country.[1]

These procedures have been applied to data for the 1979, 1983 and 1987 General Elections, to provide estimates of voting, by occupational class, in each of the 633 constituencies at each election.[2] (Johnston and Pattie, 1987, discuss general aspects of these estimates; Johnston, Pattie and Allsopp, 1988, provide extensive analyses that complement those presented here.) Here we focus on three occupational classes only:

1. the *Administrative and Managerial* occupational class, which provides the core of support for the Conservative Party;
2. the *Unskilled Manual* occupational class, which provides core support for Labour; and
3. the *Professional* occupational class, which provides more votes proportionately to the Alliance than does any other class.

In the analyses, we look at the geography of voting for both Conservative and Labour by the first two classes and at the geography of voting Alliance by the third. Brief summary data for each, to show the range of voting, is given in Table 9.4; Figure 9.2 illustrates that variation.

The tabulated data show a substantial range in the estimated percentage voting for a particular party (as a percentage of the electorate, not of the votes cast), but demonstrate that the range did not increase over the three elections. (For example, the range for the percentage of Unskilled Manual workers voting Labour was 62 points in 1979, 53 points in 1983 and 54 points in 1987.) What did increase, however, was the coefficient of variation (CV), which is the standard deviation as a percentage of the mean. The larger the CV value, the greater the spread in

Table 9.3 Inter-election change in the percentage of the electorate voting for each party, 1979–87, by functional type of place

	Conservative			Labour			Alliance		
	79–83	83–7	79–87	79–83	83–7	79–87	79–83	83–7	79–87
Inner-City Immigrant	−3.2	3.0	−0.2	−6.9	2.6	−4.3	7.5	−1.4	6.2
Industrial Immigrant	−2.6	1.3	−1.3	−6.7	4.4	−2.3	7.3	−2.2	5.1
Poorest Immigrant	−3.5	1.5	−2.0	−4.6	4.7	0.1	6.9	−4.8	2.1
Intermediate Industrial	−1.8	0.9	−0.9	−8.1	4.5	−3.6	8.5	−1.8	6.7
Old Industrial/Mining	−2.4	1.3	−1.1	−8.1	7.1	−1.0	7.5	−3.2	4.4
Textile	−1.8	1.3	−0.5	−6.6	4.7	−1.9	6.6	−2.6	4.0
Poorest Domestic	−2.6	0.4	−2.2	−8.4	10.6	2.2	8.2	−0.7	7.5
Conurban Local Authority	−3.3	−0.4	−3.7	−7.8	6.2	−1.6	8.2	−2.5	5.8
Black Country	−2.2	2.6	0.5	−6.4	2.2	−4.1	9.1	−2.2	6.9
Maritime Industrial	−3.4	−1.0	−4.4	−8.6	7.4	−1.2	10.0	−2.7	7.4
Poor Inner-City	−2.3	0.9	−1.4	−6.6	4.4	−2.2	7.8	−0.5	7.3
Clydeside	−4.1	−1.9	−5.0	−5.1	11.5	6.4	9.2	−3.7	5.6
Scottish Industrial	−1.2	−2.1	−3.4	−3.4	9.7	6.3	12.8	−4.0	8.8
Scottish Rural	−0.3	0.1	−0.2	−4.0	3.4	0.6	8.4	0.7	9.1
Inner Metropolitan (I.M.)	−4.4	2.0	−2.4	−6.6	4.1	−2.6	7.4	−0.7	6.7
High Status I.M.	−5.4	2.3	−3.1	−5.6	3.4	−2.2	6.5	−1.7	4.7
Outer London	−3.3	3.4	0.2	−8.2	2.0	−6.2	8.3	−1.8	6.5

Very High Status	-2.0	1.9	-0.1	-7.3	1.7	-5.6	7.3	-0.7	6.6
Conurban White Collar	-4.0	1.0	-3.0	-7.3	3.4	-3.9	8.3	-0.6	7.7
City Service	-3.3	0.1	-3.3	-7.7	4.5	-3.9	8.5	0.4	8.9
Resort/Retirement	-1.0	1.2	0.2	-6.3	2.1	-4.3	6.1	0.6	6.7
Recent Growth	0.9	1.2	2.1	-6.7	3.7	-3.1	11.1	-1.4	9.6
Stable Industrial	-1.0	1.7	0.7	-8.0	3.6	-4.4	9.8	-2.5	7.4
Small Towns	-0.4	1.2	0.8	-8.0	2.6	-5.4	7.7	-0.2	7.5
Southern Urban	0.4	2.3	2.6	-8.4	0.9	-7.5	9.4	-0.2	9.2
Modest Affluent	-1.5	0.9	-0.6	-8.5	3.2	-5.3	9.2	-1.1	8.1
Metropolitan Industrial	-1.1	3.4	2.4	-9.8	2.9	-6.9	0.7	-3.2	6.5
Modest Affluent Scotland	-1.8	-0.4	-2.2	-4.3	8.4	4.2	10.7	-3.7	7.0
Rapid Growth	1.7	2.7	4.4	-7.7	1.9	-5.9	8.0	-1.6	6.4
Prosperous/No Industry	-0.3	0.6	0.3	-7.1	2.5	-4.6	6.6	0.6	7.2
Agricultural	0.6	0.9	1.5	-6.5	2.2	-4.2	6.4	-0.3	6.1
National	-1.7	1.1	-0.6	-7.2	4.1	-3.1	8.3	-1.4	6.9

Table 9.4 Summary statistics for the five voting variables

Occupational class and vote	1979 Range	1979 Mean	CV[1]	1983 Range	1983 Mean	CV	1987 Range	1987 Mean	CV
Administrative and Managerial									
Conservative	10–65	47.7	20	11–61	45.8	22	12–62	46.5	24
Labour	1–33	14.8	38	1–34	11.7	53	2–38	12.5	59
Unskilled Manual									
Conservative	3–31	18.8	31	3–29	17.7	34	3–32	19.4	37
Labour	4–66	41.6	27	4–57	28.9	40	6–60	29.8	42
Professional									
Alliance	0–54	15.6	53	4–48	21.4	27	7–56	25.9	33

Note
1. Coefficient of Variation.

the distribution – i.e. the larger is the average distance between an individual constituency percentage and the national percentage. For each of the first four voting patterns in Table 9.4, the CV increased over the period, indicative of a greater spatial polarization in voting for both the Conservative and Labour Parties. The increases were particularly large for Labour voting, suggesting that, relative to the national average, it did much better in some places than others. For voting Alliance within the Professional occupational class, the CV declined between 1979 and 1983, and the new grouping picked up votes in areas where the Liberal Party was traditionally weak. Between 1983 and 1987 support for the Alliance became more polarized again, however, indicating that the Alliance vote held up much better in some constituencies than it did in others.

The spread of values for the three occupational classes is illustrated by the triangular graphs in Figure 9.2, in which the numbers voting Conservative, Labour and Alliance in each constituency are expressed as percentages of the totals voting for those three alone. If the percentages voting for the three parties were virtually the same in every constituency, all the dots would be clustered around one point on each graph. Instead they are widely scattered, and increasingly so. In 1979, for example, the Conservative Party won a majority of the votes cast by the Administrative and Managerial occupational class in nearly every constituency, but by 1987 not only had its average percentage declined (the swarm of points had moved to the left in the graph) but it had also lost its majority – mainly to the Alliance – in a substantial number of constituencies. Similarly, the swarms of points for the Unskilled Manual and Professional occupational classes became much less concentrated over the three elections, creating much greater inter-constituency heterogeneity in the pattern of voting by the members of each class.

Two theses regarding spatial polarization

The data just presented provide clear evidence of an increase of spatial polarization in British voting behaviour over the period 1979–87. To understand how people

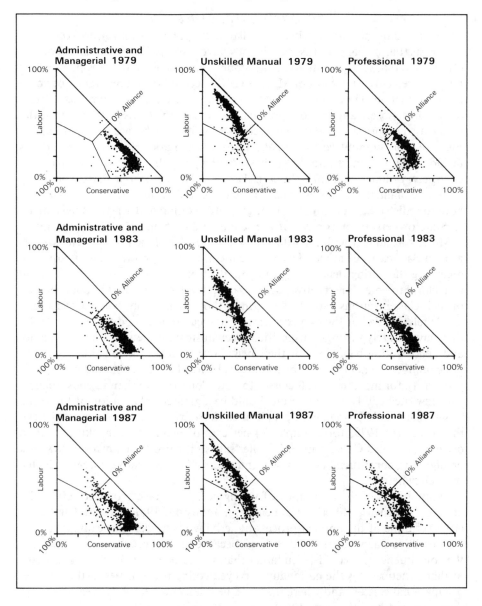

Figure 9.2   The percentage voting Conservative, Labour and Alliance, by occupational class, at each of the three elections

in similar social locations (occupational classes) vote, it is necessary to know where they are voting. Thus to advance that understanding we turn to analyses of the geography of voting by the three groups identified above. In these, we look at two possible accounts for the polarization.

The party-strength effect

The first of those accounts – which we will term the *party-strength effect explanation* – suggests that voting patterns traditionally have displayed an accentuation of class effects, and that such accentuation has simply been magnified over the period under review here. This is the basis of Miller's (1977) account of the geography of voting in Great Britain. He argues that within society there are two *core classes*, each of which is closely aligned to a political party. For the Conservative Party, that core class comprises those in managerial occupations who are owner-occupiers; they are more committed to the concept of a free market in goods and services, including labour, and so traditionally vote for a party that promotes such a model of society. Countering them is the core class linked to the Labour Party, comprising unionized manual workers, who have been mobilized to support a party committed both to redistribution of wealth through State taxation and service provision and to State ownership or control of the 'commanding heights of the economy'.

Miller's argument with regard to these core classes alone is consistent with the general class-cleavage model. His particular contribution, however, is his argument regarding the voting behaviour of members of other classes. Some of these will be inclined to vote Conservative, whereas others will lean towards Labour, because of their class positions. But the strength of those inclinations will vary according to the relative size of the two core classes in local milieux and the influence that they have (largely through unspecified mechanisms) on the political socialization and hence voting behaviour of their neighbours. Thus in a constituency with a large number of members of the Managerial core class, there should be a greater propensity for members of all classes to vote Conservative than in constituencies with few such catalysts. The result should be a greater polarization of the voting results than would be the case if people in all classes voted in the same way wherever they lived. (In 1979, for example, 24 per cent of people in semi-skilled manual occupations voted Conservative. If Miller's thesis is correct, that percentage should be higher in constituencies with large numbers of Conservative core-class voters than elsewhere.)

Many studies of the geography of voting in Britain have produced results that are consistent with Miller's argument (e.g. Johnston, 1981), despite Dunleavy's (1979) critique of the implicit process underlying his model. Basically, where the Conservative Party vote should be large because of the occupational structure of the constituency, its vote is even larger than would be predicted from knowledge of that structure plus the nationally-surveyed voting propensities of the different occupational classes, and where it should be relatively weak it is even weaker (as demonstrated by Johnston, 1985).

There are other geographical influences, however, that follow the same process. Miller (1977) showed that the greater the proportion of a constituency's workforce employed in agriculture, the greater the Conservative vote – holding the general party-strength effect constant (Johnston, 1987a) – whereas the greater the proportion employed in coal-mining, the greater the Labour vote, other things being equal (see also Crewe and Payne, 1976). Others have identified further influences. Johnston's (1985) analysis of the 1983 General Election, for example, showed a greater Labour vote among all occupational classes, the greater the level of unemployment in a constituency, whereas analyses of the Alliance vote in 1983 (e.g. Steed and Curtice, 1983) suggest that the greater the percentage of a constituency's electorate who were highly educated, the greater the overall support for the Liberal or SDP candidate. Finally, it has been shown that Labour tends to do better in a constituency the larger the percentage of its households that are headed by coloured immigrants, and also the larger the percentage of households living in council tenancies. Council estates have been major centres of Labour organization and support (Johnston, 1987b).

The 'party-strength effect' thesis can readily be evaluated by regressing the percentage of members in each occupational class estimated to vote for a party against indicators of the social and economic structure of a constituency's population. For the present analyses, seven such indicators have been selected:

1. The percentage of a constituency's workforce who are employed in Managerial and Administrative occupations (Miller's Conservative core-class) - CORE.
2. The percentage of a constituency's workforce who are employed in Agriculture - AGRI.
3. The percentage of a constituency's workforce who are employed in Energy Industries (the best available indicator of employment in Mining) - MINING.
4. The percentage of a constituency's adult population who have a Degree or equivalent qualification - DEGREE.
5. The percentage of households that are council tenants - CT.
6. The percentage of households headed by people born in the New Commonwealth (with Pakistan) - NCWP.
7. The percentage of a constituency's workforce who are Unemployed - UNEMP.

The first six of these are taken from the 1981 census data. For unemployment, the 1979 and 1983 voting patterns are regressed against 1981 unemployment data extracted from the census. For 1987, the unemployment data refer to December 1986 and are taken from the constituency tabulations published in the *Employment Gazette* (Table 2.10, monthly).

If the 'party-strength effect' thesis is valid as an account of the voting patterns in 1979, 1983 and 1987, each of the regressions should have significant slope terms. If, in addition, the thesis that the importance of the effect increased over the period is valid, then those slopes should become steeper over time. The evidence against which to test this hypothesis is given in Figures 9.3–9.7 that show the simple linear regressions between the dependent variables and six of the seven independents. Placing the regression lines for all three elections on the same graph allows a clear comparison of the relative strength of the effect over the period. (No graphs are provided for NCWP, because only three of the fifteen regressions produced statistically-significant results, indicating that voting patterns were not substantially related to the ethnic composition of a constituency's population.)

For the pattern of Conservative voting by members of the Administrative and Managerial class, Figure 9.3 shows only small changes in the slope of the relationship in most cases, indicating just minor shifts in the degree of

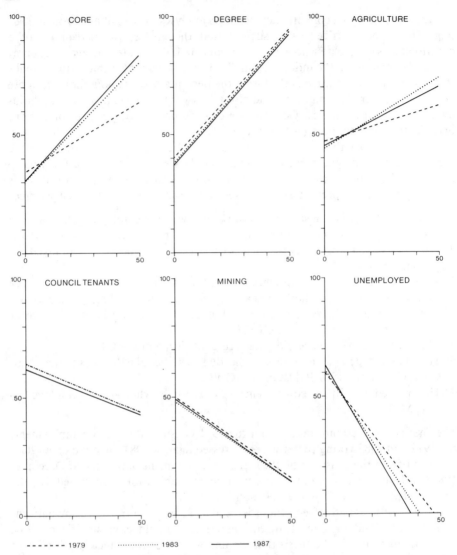

Figure 9.3   Slopes of the simple regression relationships for Conservative voting by the Administrative and Managerial occupational class

polarization. The biggest change is with regard to unemployment: the greater the level of unemployment in a constituency, the greater the loss of Conservative votes from the party's core class of supporters over the period, clearly indicating a shift away from the party in those parts of the country suffering from the worst of the recession. This is matched by the steeper slopes for Labour voting against unemployment within that class (Figure 9.4). Over the period 1979–87, the greater the extent of job loss in an area, the greater the probability that a member of the Administrative and Managerial class would vote Labour.

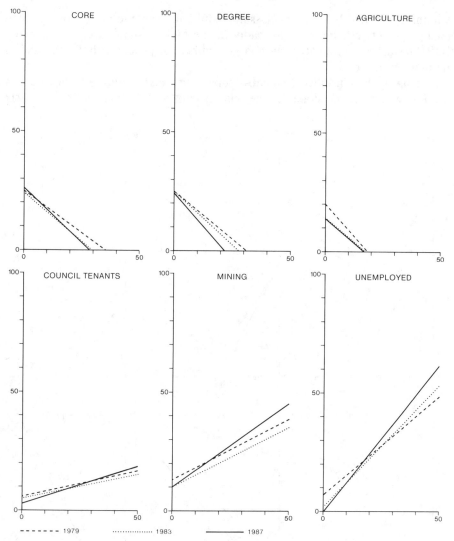

Figure 9.4 *Slopes of the simple regression relationships for Labour voting by the Administrative and Managerial occupational class*

Among the other five variables representing constituency characteristics (Figure 9.3) there is virtually no change in the pattern relative to the percentage with degrees, the percentage living in council housing or the percentage employed in mining. With regard to the percentage employed in agriculture, there is a very slight increase in the slope of the relationship, indicating a small shift towards the Conservatives in the rural areas among that party's core supporters. The same was the case with the variable CORE, indicating a relative swing to the Tories among Administrators and Managers in the constituencies where they were most numerous. The patterns of voting Labour by that class not surprisingly show the mirror image (Figure 9.4). Labour performed increasingly well among the

Administrative and Managerial class in the mining areas and in the areas of high unemployment, but increasingly badly in the highest status areas (with many CORE residents), in the areas with large numbers of people with degrees and in the more rural areas.

Turning to the Unskilled Manual occupational class, Figure 9.5 shows shifts in the steepness of the slopes of the relationships with Labour voting in all six

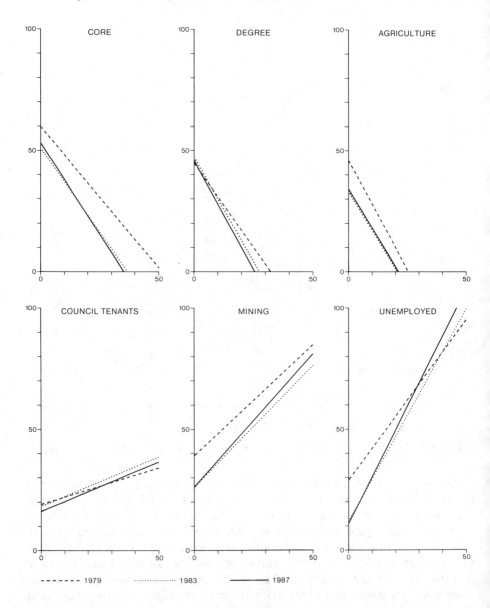

Figure 9.5   Slopes of the simple regression relationships for Labour voting by the Unskilled Manual occupational class

cases. In each one, the shift is in the expected direction – the Labour vote increased relatively in the constituencies with high unemployment, with large percentages employed in mining, and with large percentages living in council housing. Its performance declined (relatively, and probably absolutely too) in the agricultural areas, in the constituencies with many graduates and in the areas where the Conservative core class was concentrated. Among its major supporters, therefore, Labour maintained its hold much better in some areas (those where the party has traditionally been relatively strong) than in others, producing a greater spatial polarization to its support. This was matched by the trends in voting Conservative by members of the Unskilled Manual grouping: the lower the unemployment, and the greater the percentage of Conservative core supporters, in the local milieu, the greater the probability of those people voting Conservative (Figure 9.6). (For example, in 1979 a constituency with 30 per cent in the CORE class would have 12 percentage points less Unskilled Manual workers voting Labour than one with 20 per cent in that class. In 1987, the difference would have been 15 points, on average.)

Turning to the pattern of Alliance voting by members of the Professional occupational class (Figure 9.7), all six graphs show a steeper slope in 1979 than in 1983. Compared to the Liberal performance in 1979, the Alliance support was less polarized into certain types of constituency (those with high unemployment and large percentages employed in agriculture, for example) in 1983. Over the next four years, Alliance support became more polarized again, however. In two cases, the degree of polarization was greater in 1987 than in 1979, to the Alliance's benefit in the constituencies with large percentages of graduates but to its disadvantage in the mining areas. In the other four, the shift was towards the pattern of polarization in place for the Liberals in 1979, but not as extreme.

The regional effect

The second of the accounts – the *regional effect explanation* – suggests that an increasing influence on how people vote comprises not the characteristics of the constituency itself in which they live, but rather the wider context of which that constituency is just a part. As indicated earlier, two types of wider area can be identified in this context – geographical and functional – and each can provide the wider milieu within which voting decisions are influenced.

With regard to geographical regions, the case is that voters are aware of the general economic and social changes in their wider locales, and link these to political actions. Thus, for example, there are very wide intra-regional differences in unemployment rates, and although voters may live in a constituency with a relatively low rate (Sheffield Hallam, for example), they are aware of much higher rates nearby (e.g. Sheffield Central) and that wider regional context influences their evaluation of the political parties. Further, in some regions it is possible to identify political actions specifically targeted at them, and which will influence voters. Scotland is an excellent case of this with, for example, the revaluation of properties in 1984 that substantially affected many voters' rate payments, and hence their attitudes to the government. With regard to functional

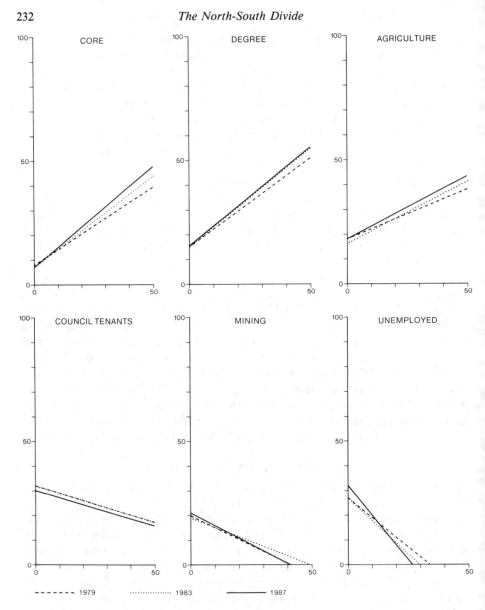

Figure 9.6   Slopes of the simple regression relationships for Conservative voting by the Unskilled Manual occupational class

areas it is argued that many government policies affect particular types of place, irrespective of where they are. The quotas on dairy-farm production introduced as a result of EEC decisions generated substantial economic problems, which apparently led dairy farmers to shift their electoral support away from the Conservatives. Again, therefore, one could expect trends in voting behaviour by functional type of place, as a consequence of the differential impact of government policies and party programmes on different types of local economy.

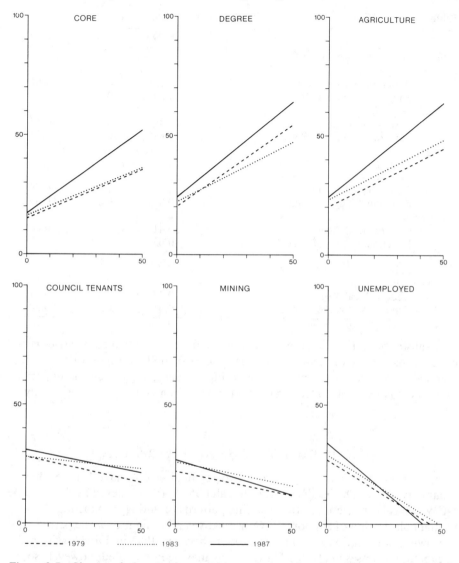

Figure 9.7 Slopes of the simple regression relationships for Alliance voting by the Professional occupational class

The existence of regional effects can be tested for by analyses of variance, and the multiple correlation coefficients are presented in Table 9.5. They indicate trends very similar to those reported in Table 9.4. Over the three elections, the regional structuring of voting patterns has become increasingly marked. For the first two occupational classes shown in the table, the functional type classification provides a better statistical account than do the geographical regions, although the margin between the two declined over time as the R^2 increased for the latter but declined between 1983 and 1987 for the functional regions. The type of place and the region that people lived in apparently had a

Table 9.5 The R^2 values associated with the analyses of variance

	1979	1983	1987
Administrative/Managerial			
Conservative			
Geographical Region	0.53	0.59	0.61
Functional Type of Place	0.59	0.66	0.61
Labour			
Geographical Region	0.46	0.52	0.62
Functional Type of Place	0.68	0.74	0.72
Unskilled Manual			
Conservative			
Geographical Region	0.54	0.61	0.66
Functional Type of Place	0.85	0.71	0.69
Labour			
Geographical Region	0.41	0.48	0.56
Functional Type of Place	0.65	0.72	0.70
Professional			
Alliance			
Geographical Region	0.27	0.18	0.21
Functional Type of Place	0.41	0.23	0.30

very substantial influence on whether the members of the two core classes voted either Conservative or Labour. For the Professional class, there was much less regional patterning to the percentage voting Alliance, suggesting the impact of more local issues, with intra-regional variability as a consequence, especially in 1983.

Constituency: region interactions

The seven party-strength effects and two regional effects have been evaluated separately above. The results suggest that all but one (that indexed by the variable NCWP) has been related to the changing patterns of voting, producing a greater spatial polarization of support for Conservative and Labour over the period, and a growing polarization of Alliance support between 1983 and 1987, within the occupational classes analysed. Those effects may be interrelated, however, so, to evaluate their relative strengths when all other influences are held constant, a series of multiple regressions was run. These had seven independent variables to represent the party-strength effects and two sets of dummy variables to represent the two regionalizations. The full technical details are reported elsewhere (Johnston and Pattie, 1988b); our attention here focuses on an interpretation of the regional variations, given that the polarization effects associated with the seven other independent variables operate too.

Looking first at the *geographical regions*, there is clear evidence of a widening gap between the Outer South East (which was the baseline region against which voting in all others was contrasted) and most of the regions in northern Britain. Figure 9.8 shows the average differences between constituencies in the Outer

South East and constituencies in the other regions in voting Conservative and Labour among the Administrative and Managerial and Unskilled Manual occupational classes respectively. (Regions that were not significantly different from the Outer South East in the multiple regression equations are left blank.) They show very clear north-south differences, with most northern regions providing less votes for the Conservative Party and more for the Labour Party than did the Outer South East (even after the influence of constituency characteristics, as represented by the seven independent variables, has been taken into account). No map is provided for the Professional occupational class voting Alliance, since there were virtually no statistically significant inter-regional differences.

Figures 9.9 and 9.10 show trends in those inter-regional differences over time, and indicate the degree to which divergence has taken place, especially with regard to Labour voting. Thus in the Administrative and Managerial occupational class (Figure 9.9) several of the northern regions – especially the three in Scotland – have percentages voting Conservative up to 20 points lower than that in the Outer South East, but only in Strathclyde, Merseyside and South Yorkshire was there a clear increase in the difference over time. For Labour voting, on the other hand, such a trend was clearly evident in 11 regions, with a major increase in the difference between those regions and the Outer South East between 1979 and 1987.

Among the Unskilled Manual occupational class, the same trend of greater differences between most northern regions and the Outer South East in the percentage voting Labour is very evident, again with marked increases between 1979 and 1987. Thus in most of the regions in northern England, as well as all of Wales, for example, the difference between Labour voting in the average constituency and Labour voting in the average constituency in the Outer South East at least doubled. The percentage of the Unskilled Manual occupational class voting Conservative also fell in those regions relative to the Outer South East, although in most the shift away from the Tories was not as large as that towards Labour (because of differentials in voting Alliance and non-voting also).

Figure 9.9, therefore, provides clear evidence of increased polarization among the geographical regions of Great Britain in the support given to the Conservative and Labour Parties, which is clearly in line with the thesis of a widening north-south divide. With the *functional types of place* the evidence is of considerable variation, but of relatively little increase in the degree of variation, in the average percentages voting Labour and Alliance, but not Conservative. In these analyses, the baseline was the Agricultural region, so the average pattern of voting there is contrasted for each of the 30 others. With regard to Conservative voting, only six regions recorded significant differences from the Agricultural areas in all three years among the members of the Administrative and Managerial occupational class: it was about 10 percentage points less in the constituencies with the Poorest Domestic Conditions and between 3 and 12 percentage points more in Scottish Rural, Outer London, Small Towns, Modestly Affluent and Modestly Affluent Scotland. Only in the last of these was there a substantial increase in the difference, from 7 to 13 percentage points, showing that while most of Scotland

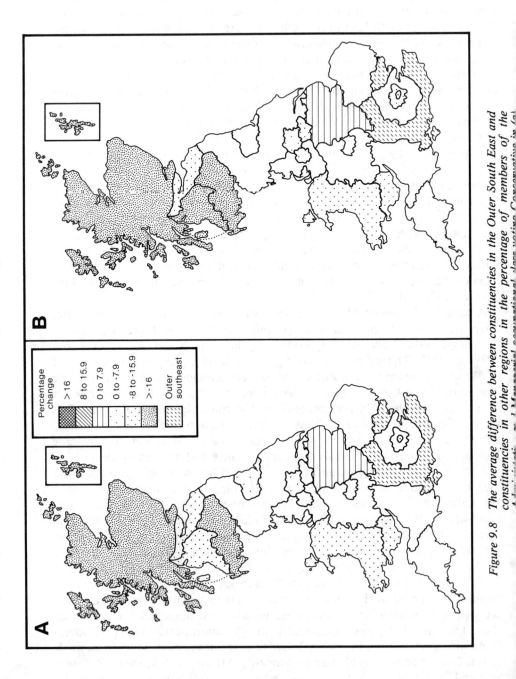

Figure 9.8   The average difference between constituencies in the Outer South East and constituencies in other regions in the percentage of members of the

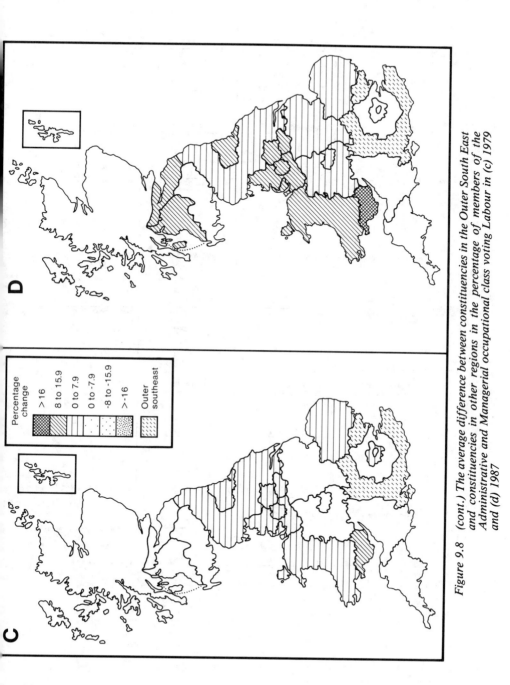

Figure 9.8 (cont.) The average difference between constituencies in the Outer South East and constituencies in other regions in the percentage of members of the Administrative and Managerial occupational class voting Labour in (c) 1979 and (d) 1987

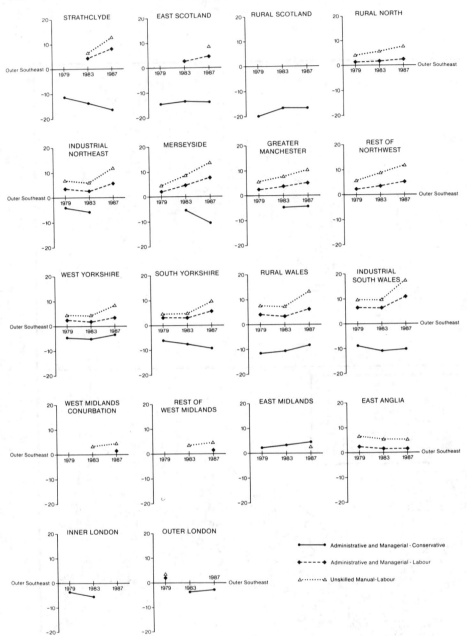

Figure 9.9 Trends in inter-regional differences in voting 1979–1987, by geographical region. The trend lines show the significant differences between each region and the pattern of voting in the Outer South East

shifted away from the Conservative Party this trend was not a characteristic of the more affluent areas, which swung the other way relative to trends in the Agricultural areas. In the Unskilled Manual occupational class, only two regions reported significant differences in voting Conservative across all three elections: the Old Industrial/Mining region (averaging 2.7 percentage points less voting Conservative than in the Agricultural region) and the Poorest Domestic Conditions region (averaging 6 percentage points less).

If the pattern of voting Conservative by class did not vary significantly between functional types of place, the same was not true for Labour and Alliance. With regard to Labour voting among the Administrative and Managerial occupational class, only 7 of the 30 regions did not have a significantly-larger Labour vote than was the case in the Agricultural region (Poorest Immigrant, Poor Inner City, Scottish Rural, Resort and Retirement, Recent Growth, Rapid Growth and Prosperous/No Industry). All but Recent Growth similarly showed no significant differences in Labour voting for the Unskilled Manual occupational class. Thus, compared to the rural areas, both classes gave more votes to Labour in the majority of the other functional regions. This occurred with the differences between geographical regions held constant, indicating that the geography of Labour voting was ordered according to both aspects of the country's economic and social geography. The pattern changed very little between 1979 and 1987, however, with a substantial increase in the difference in only a small number of regions. Thus the increased spatial polarization indicated for the geographical regions was not matched by an increased polarization for the functional types of place.

Although there were very few significant differences among the geographical regions in the percentage of the Professional occupational class voting Alliance, there were significant differences among the functional regions, with a majority of them reporting substantially lower percentages voting Alliance than was the case in the Agricultural region. Furthermore, in most of these the difference was larger in 1987 than 1979 (Figure 9.10), indicating the growing strength of the Alliance in rural areas relative to many other parts of the country.

This section has thus provided very clear evidence of the nature, extent and change in the spatial polarization in voting patterns in Great Britain, by occupational class, over the period 1979–87. With constituency characteristics held constant, the percentages voting Conservative were much lower, and the percentages voting Labour much higher, in many of the geographical regions than in the Outer South East. Further, the difference between that area and most of those in northern Britain and Wales increased over the period, providing clear evidence of a widening north-south divide. Similarly, the percentages voting Labour in most functional types of place were significantly greater than in the Agricultural region, without any clear increase in the difference. The percentage voting Alliance within the Professional occupational class was significantly smaller in many of those regions than in the Agricultural, and increasingly so. Thus the regional structure of the country is a major influence on voting patterns, it seems, and in terms of geographical regions voting patterns for Conservative and Labour are becoming increasingly polarized.

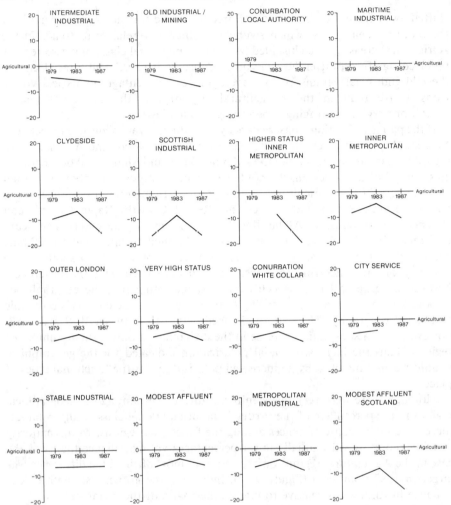

*Figure 9.10 Trends in inter-regional differences in voting Alliance by the Professional
occupational class, 1979–87, by functional region. The trend lines show the
significant differences between each region and the pattern of voting in the
Agricultural region.*

Towards an explanation

How are these patterns and trends to be accounted for? The traditional model
of voting behaviour in Great Britain clearly ties support for the Conservative and
Labour Parties to the occupational-class cleavage, accepting the arguments of
Pulzer (1967) and Bogdanor (1983) that knowledge of a person's occupational-
class position is a satisfactory predictor of vote. The data presented here clearly
contest that view: people in the same class position vote differently, and
increasingly so, in different geographical contexts. Why should this be the case,
when the world is becoming increasingly integrated into an economic whole, the

main focus of ideology is at the level of the State (Taylor, 1982), and parties campaign on national issues and through the national media?

A feature of voting behaviour in Britain in recent years has been the increasing volatility of the electorate, with a growing proportion prepared to shift allegiance between elections. Various accounts of how people decide which way to vote have been presented, focusing on their evaluation of party policies, performances and leaders. Of these, it seems that perceptions of recent economic trends and likely trends in the near future are the most influential (see, for example, Sanders, Ward and Marsh, 1987, on the relative impact of the 'Falklands factor' in 1983). Part of this involves what is called *retrospective voting*: people reflect on the trends in both the national economy and their personal economic experiences in recent months, and if they are relatively satisfied they are more likely to vote for the incumbent government (rewarding it for its economic stewardship) than if they are dissatisfied. Similarly, there is also a process of *prospective voting*: people who are optimistic about the future (both nationally and personally) are more likely to vote for the party in power than are those who are pessimistic.

This thesis of the importance of retrospective and prospective voting can be linked to our results regarding the spatial polarization of the British electorate. If there is a north-south divide in economic and social well-being, as argued in the other contributions to this book, and if it is widening, then that could be reflected in people's interpretations of the economic situation. Those in the relatively depressed areas will be less satisfied and more pessimistic than will those in the 'booming' areas, who are more likely to be satisfied with recent trends and who are more likely to be optimistic about the near future. If, then, the more satisfied/optimistic are more likely to vote for the party in power than the less satisfied/pessimistic, the geography of voting can be clearly linked to the geography of evaluation of government performance.

This hypothesis is tested here using data from the surveys conducted by Gallup for the BBC at each of the three general elections. In the 1983 and 1987 surveys, respondents were asked whether they thought both the national economy and their individual financial circumstances had 'got better', 'stayed about the same' or 'got worse' over the previous twelve months. They were also asked whether they thought either would 'get better', 'stay about the same' or 'get worse' over the next twelve months. The 1979 sample was asked the retrospective question only about personal circumstances.

In analysing these data, the respondents have been grouped into five major geographical regions: London, South, Midlands, North Urban and Scotland/Wales (the small numbers in rural constituencies in northern England and in Devon and Cornwall were excluded). Further subdivision into more regions could not be supported by the data, so we are able to portray broad trends only.

Figure 9.11 shows the Better/Worse ratios for the respondents in each region on each of the four questions. The greater the ratio, the greater the proportion of satisfied/optimistic relative to dissatisfied/pessimistic respondents. The top two graphs refer to the national situation. With one exception (North Urban respondents to the prospective question) they show greater satisfaction and

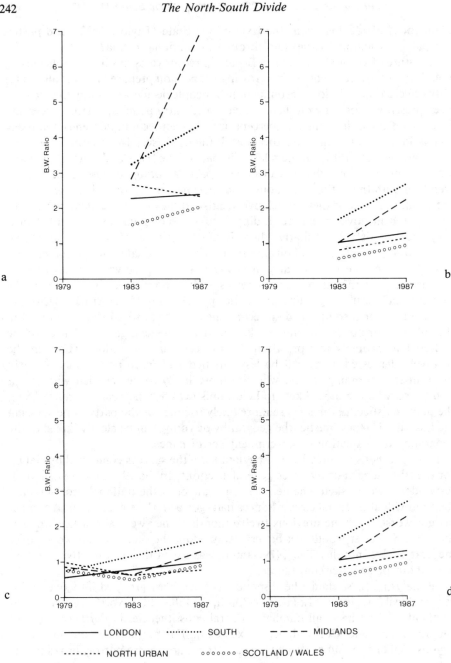

Figure 9.11 Trends in the Better/Worse ratio, by region, with regard to: (a) the national economic situation over the last 12 months; (b) the national economic situation over the next 12 months; (c) personal economic situation over the last 12 months; (d) personal economic situation over the next 12 months

optimism in 1987 than 1983, as well as marked regional variation at both dates. People in the South were most satisfied with the performance of the national economy over the previous twelve months; people in Scotland and Wales were least satisfied. Similarly, Scottish and Welsh respondents were least optimistic about the future; Southerners were the most optimistic in 1983, but Midlanders were in 1987. Overall, optimism about the future was greater than satisfaction with the recent past.

The same conclusions can be drawn with respect to the evaluations of personal economic circumstances shown in the lower pair of graphs, for 1983 and 1987 if not for 1979. In the first year of the sequence, people in the northern regions were more satisfied with their experience under the incumbent Labour government than were people in the south, although in all regions more people were dissatisfied than were satisfied. Again, people were much more optimistic about the future than they were satisfied with the past.

What of the voting patterns of people with different evaluations of the economic situation? Figure 9.12 shows the trends in support between 1983 and 1987 for those with the three evaluations of the national situation over the previous twelve months. In each year, the Conservative Party obtained a majority of the votes from those who said things had got better, in every region, but it lost support substantially among the satisfied in London and Scotland/Wales, while gaining in the Midlands. In 1983, almost half of those who thought things had stayed about the same voted Conservative in every region except Scotland/Wales, whereas Labour won less than one fifth of the votes. Four years later, the Labour vote had virtually doubled in all regions, but was still much lower in the South, whereas the Conservative vote fell. Of those who thought things had got worse Labour won a plurality of votes in every region except the South in 1983, when it came second to the Alliance. Labour support among the dissatisfied increased substantially in all regions between 1983 and 1987, while Conservative and Alliance voting fell.

Turning from retrospective to prospective voting, Figure 9.13 shows very similar trends. Thus we can conclude the following:

1. There was a clear north-south divide in people's perceptions of recent economic changes, with people in the South and Midlands much more satisfied and optimistic than people in North Urban, Scotland and Wales. (People in London were generally less satisfied and optimistic than people elsewhere in the South.)
2. People who were satisfied/optimistic were most likely to vote Conservative in 1983 and 1987 whereas those who were dissatisfied/pessimistic were most likely to vote Labour.
3. Combining these two findings, the greater level of satisfaction/optimism in the South and Midlands can account for part of the north-south divide in voting.
4. In 1987, people who were dissatisfied/pessimistic were much more likely to vote Labour than was the case in 1983, and this can help to account for the growing north-south divide.
5. In addition, however, there were clear inter-regional differences that were

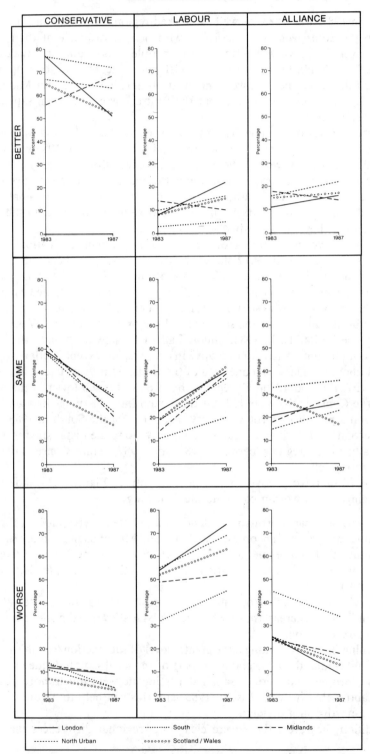

Figure 9.12 Voting trends among people who thought national economic conditions had 'got better', 'stayed about the same' and 'got worse' over the previous 12 months

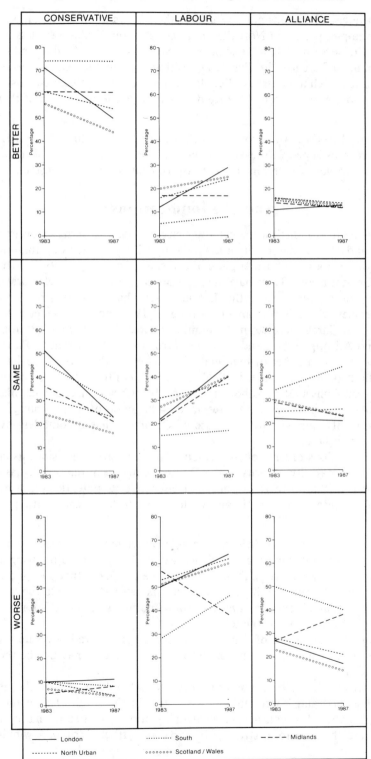

Figure 9.13 Voting trends among people who thought national economic situations would 'get better', 'stay about the same' and 'get worse' over the next 12 months

independent of these trends. Whatever their views of the national economy, for example, people in North Urban, Scotland and Wales were less likely to vote Conservative than residents of South and Midlands, undoubtedly reflecting differences in class composition among the regions, as well as constituency characteristics. People who were dissatisfied/pessimistic were much more likely to vote Alliance if they lived in the South than if they lived elsewhere.

In sum, therefore, the growing north-south divide is linked to differences between regions in people's level of economic satisfaction and optimism and their willingness to vote for the incumbent government party as a consequence.

And the implications?

The growing inter-constituency heterogeneity in voting patterns by occupational classes, and the spatial polarization in support for each party that this has produced, are not just a further piece of evidence of growing regional differences within Great Britain. They have also produced a major new electoral arena. Basically, in relative terms, the Labour Party has become stronger in the constituencies where it was already strong in 1979, and weaker elsewhere (as shown by the large increase in the number of lost deposits in 1983: Johnston, Pattie and Allsopp, 1988), and the same is true of the Conservative Party. As a consequence, the number of marginal seats involving the two parties has fallen substantially (Curtice and Steed, 1986). The growth of the Alliance since 1979 has not replaced Conservative:Labour marginals by either Conservative:Alliance or Labour:Alliance marginals. As a result, the likelihood of major changes in the distribution of seats within the House of Commons has become less over the period studied here.

The implications of this for the Labour Party are profound, since its chances of winning a majority of seats in the House, again, seem remote. It has a very strong base in the northern regions, but elsewhere its potential for winning is slight. The options open to it appear to be as follows, each with attendant problems:

1. To hope for a collapse in the economic buoyancy in at least some of the currently more-affluent regions, which would produce a major swing against the Conservatives there. Labour could not be confident that it would benefit from that, however. The Alliance (or its successor) could be a major beneficiary, and it could be that substantial numbers of voters would swing to the right rather than to the left.
2. To hope for a collapse of confidence in the Conservative leadership – similar to that in Labour's leadership in 1983. Again, Labour may not be the main beneficiary.
3. To alter the focus of its appeal, so as to win over many of the affluent working-class and lower middle-class voters in the south. This could mean dropping the 'class-conflict' element of its appeal, and so alienating its left wing and their electoral strength in parts of northern Britain – winning the

south could involve losing the north (but to whom?).

4. To develop policies aimed at a wider social spread of voters, in the same way that the New Zealand Labour Party has done (Johnston and Honey, 1988). Again, this risks alienating the left and the north to win in the south.

5. To enter a pact with the successors to the Alliance, whereby each agrees to abstain from putting up a candidate in certain constituencies to promote the electoral chances of the other. This would be tantamount to an admission that Labour could not win on its own, and would risk alienating Labour support in the constituencies where the party withdrew. Even if it worked, in the long term the Alliance could be the major beneficiary, since it would become a party of government for the first time.

6. To embrace electoral reform. Once more, this would be an admission of an inability to win a majority of seats again, and would be unlikely to help it defeat the Conservatives.

The increasing spatial concentration of Labour's votes presents it, therefore, with a major set of electoral problems. For the Alliance (now the Social and Liberal Democrats) the problem is the opposite: its vote-winning is spatially too diffuse to provide many opportunities for potential victory, and as a consequence it has to develop strategies that will deliver a plurality, if not a majority, of votes in a large number of constituencies. For the Conservative Party, there is no immediate problem – its majority in the House looks relatively secure. But the party is clearly intent on invading the Labour strongholds, as shown by its inner-city, local government and industrial restructuring policies. It wants to win more, everywhere.

Whatever the strategies the parties develop, the new electoral geography means that they must work in the new arena. The north-south divide not only represents an electoral polarization of Great Britain: it is also requiring the development of new political agenda.

Notes

1. The data for occupations in the census are for employed persons only, so it has to be assumed that the class structure of each constituency is exactly reflected in the occupational structure. The data are taken from the 1981 census, and have to assume no relative change in a constituency's occupational structure between 1979 and 1987.

2. The 1979 election was fought in different constituencies from 1973 and 1987. A BBC/ITN (1983) study estimated what the voting would have been if the 1979 election had been held in the 1983–7 constituencies.

REFERENCES

Abel-Smith, B. (1964) *The Hospitals, 1800–1948*, Heinemann, London.

The Accountant (1986) 'Touche and Spicers surge in boom year for all firms', 26 June, pp. 14–16.

The Accounting Bulletin (1983) 'Big firms on the move', August, pp. 8–9.

Alexander, I. (1979) *Office Location and Public Policy*, Longman, London.

Alexander, S. (1987) 'Lawyers on the mark', *Financial Times Survey*; *Bristol as a Financial Centre*, 26 November, p. 7.

Armstrong, H. (1987) 'The "north-south" controversy and Britain's regional problem', *Local Economy*, Vol. 2, pp. 93–105.

The Banker (1981) 'Foreign banks with offices outside London', November, p. 113.

The Banker (1986) 'Foreign banks with offices outside London', November, p. 74.

Barnett, C. (1972) *The Collapse of British Power*, Eyre & Methuen, London.

Bassett, K. (1988) *Economic Change in the Sun-belt: Service Sector Growth and Employment Change in the Swindon Economy*, Department of Geography, University of Bristol (mimeo).

Bateman, M. (1985) *Office Development: A Geographical Analysis*, Croom Helm, Beckenham.

Bavishi, V. B. and Wyman, H. E. (1983) *Who Audits the World?*, School of Business Administration, University of Connecticut.

BBC/ITN (1983) *The BBC/ITN Guide to the New Parliamentary Constituencies*, Parliamentary Research Services, Chichester.

Beech, R., Challah, S. and Ingram, R. (1987) 'Impact of cuts in acute bed services on services to patients', *British Medical Journal*, Vol. 294, pp. 685–8.

Bennett, R. J. (1980) *The Geography of Public Finance*, Methuen, London.

Bertrand, O. and Noyelle, T. J. (1986) *Changing Technology, Skills and Skill Formation in French, German, Japanese, Swedish and US Financial Service Firms: Preliminary Findings*, Report to the Center for Educational Research and Innovation, OECD, Paris and New York.

Beveridge, W. H. (1944) *Full Employment in a Free Society*, George Allen & Unwin, London.

Beyers, W. B., Tofflemeire, J. M., Stranahan, H. A. and Johnson, E. G. (1986) *The Service Economy; Understanding Growth in the Central Puget Sound Region*, Central Puget Sound Economic Development District, Seattle, Wash.

Birch, A. (1975) 'Economic models in political science', *British Journal of Political Science*, Vol. 5, pp. 69–82.

Blaug, M. (1984) 'Education vouchers – it all depends on what you mean', in J. Le Grand and R. Robinson (eds.) *Privatisation and the Welfare State*, Allen & Unwin, London.

Boddy, M., Lovering, J. and Bassett, K. (1986) *Sunbelt City?: A Study of Economic Change in Britain's M4 Growth Corridor*, Clarendon Press, Oxford.

Bogdanor, V. (1983) *Multi-Party Politics and the Constitution*, Cambridge University Press.

Bohdanowicz, J. (1984) *Who Audits the UK?*, Financial Times Business Information, London.

Bradford, M. G. (1988) 'Educational change in the city', in D. Herbert and D. M. Smith (eds.) *Social Problems and the City*, (2nd edn), Oxford University Press.

Bradford, M. G. and Burdett, F. J. (1989) 'Spatial polarisation of private education in England', *Area*, in press.

Bramley, G. and Paice, D. (1987) *Housing Needs in Non-Metropolitan Areas*, Association of District Councils, London.

Breheny, M., Hall, P. and Hart, D. (1987) *Northern Lights: A Development Agenda for the North in the 1990s*, Derrick, Wade & Waters, Preston and London.

Breheny, M., Hart, D. and Hall, P. (1986) *Eastern promise?: Development Prospects for the M11 Corridor*, Derrick, Wade & Walters, London.

BSA (1981) *BSA Bulletin of Information,* No. 25, January.

BSA (1987) *BSA Bulletin of Information,* January.

BSA/DoE (quarterly) 'Five per cent sample survey of building society mortgage completions', *BSA Bulletin of Information.*

Buiter, W. H. and Miller, M. H. (1983) *The Macro-Economic Consequences of a Change in Regime: The UK under Mrs Thatcher*, Discussion Paper 179, Centre for Labour Economics, London School of Economics and Political Science.

Business (1987) 'Across the north-south divide', September, pp. 45–58.

Butchart, R. L. (1987) 'A new U.K. definition of the high technology industries', *Economic Trends*, Vol. 400, pp. 82–9.

Butler, D. E. and Sloman, A. E. (1980) *British Political Facts*, Macmillan, London.

Butler, D. E. and Stokes, D. (1969) *Political Change in Britain*, Macmillan, London.

Butler, D. E. and Stokes, D. (1974) *Political Change in Britain* (2nd edn), Macmillan, London.

Cambridge Econometrics and the Northern Ireland Economic Research Centre (1987) *Regional Economic Prospects, Analyses and Projections to the Year 2000*, Cambridge Econometrics (1985) Ltd, Cambridge.

Central Statistical Office (1988) 'Regional accounts 1986, Part 2', *Economic Trends*, Vol. 410, pp. 100–5.

Champion, A. G. (1987) 'Recent changes in the pace of population deconcentration', *Geoforum*, Vol. 18, pp. 379–401.

Champion, A. G. and Green, A. E. (1985) *In Search of Britain's Booming Towns*, Discussion Paper No. 72, Centre for Urban and Regional Development Studies, University of Newcastle upon Tyne.

Champion, A. G. and Green, A. E. (1987) 'The booming towns of Britain: the geography of economic performance in the 1980s', *Geography*, Vol. 72, pp. 97–108.

Champion, A. G. and Green, A. E. (1988) *Local Prosperity and the North-South Divide: Winners and Losers in 1980s Britain*, Institute for Employment Research, University of Warwick.

Champion, A., Green, A. and Owen, D. (1987) 'Housing, labour mobility and unemployment', *The Planner*, Vol. 73, no. 4, pp. 11–16.

Champion, A., Green, A. and Owen, D. (1988) 'House prices and local labour market performance: an analysis of building society data for 1985', *Area*, Vol. 20, pp. 253–63.

Champion, A. G., Green, A. E., Owen, D. W., Ellin, D. J. and Coombes, M. G. (1987) *Changing Places: Britain's Demographic, Economic and Social Complexion*, Arnold, London.

Charlton, J., Hartley, R., Silver, R. and Holland, W. (1983) 'Geographical variation in mortality from conditions amenable to medical intervention in England and Wales', *The Lancet*, 26 March, pp. 691–6.

Cheshire, P., Carbonaro, G. and Hay, D. (1986) 'Problems of urban decline and growth in E.E.C. countries: or measuring degrees of elephantness', *Urban Studies*, Vol. 23, pp. 131–49.

Chesshyre, R. (1987) *The Return of a Native Reporter*, Viking, London.

Chesterton Research Department (1988) 'The explosion in provincial office rents', *Perspectives*, February/March, pp. 8–9.

The City Directory (1984–5), Woodhead Faulkner, London.

Coates, B. E. and Rawstron, E. M. (1971) *Regional Variations in Britain: Studies in Economic and Social Geography*, Batsford, London.

Coffey, W. J. and Polese, M. (1987) 'Trade and location of producer services: a Canadian perspective', *Environment and Planning A*, Vol. 19, pp. 597–611.

Commission of the European Communities (1987) *Third Periodic Report on the Social and Economic Situation and Development of the Regions of the Community*, Commission of the European Communities, Brussels.

Conservative Party (1979) *1979 Election Manifesto*, Conservative Party Central Office, London.

Cooke, P. (1986) 'The changing urban and regional system in the United Kingdom', *Regional Studies*, Vol. 20, pp. 243–52.

Cooke, P. (1987) 'Britain's new spatial paradigm: technology, locality and society in transition', *Environment and Planning A*, Vol. 19, pp. 1289–301.

Cooke, P. (ed.) (1989) *Localities*, Hutchinson, London.

Cooke, P., Morgan, K. and Jackson, D. (1984) 'New technology and regional development in austerity Britain; the case of the semi-conductor industry', *Regional Studies*, Vol. 18, pp. 277–89.

Coombes, M. G., Dixon, J. S., Goddard, J. B., Openshaw, S. and Taylor, P. J. (1982) 'Functional regions for the population census of Great Britain', in D. T. Herbert and R. J. Johnston (eds.) *Geography and the Urban Environment: Progress in Research and Applications*, Vol. 5, Wiley, Chichester, pp. 63–112.

Coopers & Lybrand (undated) *Relocation Trends in the Financial Services Sector*, Hampshire Development Corporation, Winchester.

Cox, B., Blaxter, M., Buckle, A., Fenner, N., Golding, J., Gore, M., Huppert, F., Nickson, J., Roth, M., Stark, J., Wadsworth, M. and Whichelow, M. (1987) *The Health and Lifestyle Survey*, Health Promotion Research Trust, Cambridge.

Crawford's Directory of City Connections (1986), Economist Publications, London.

Crewe, I. (1986) 'On the death and resurrection of class voting', *Political Studies*, Vol. 34, pp. 620–38.

Crewe, I. and Denver, D. (eds.) (1985) *Electoral Change in Western Democracies*, Croom Helm, Beckenham.

Crewe, I. and Fox, A. (1984) *British Parliamentary Constituencies: A Statistical Compendium*, Faber & Faber, London.

Crewe, I. and Payne, C. (1976) 'Another game against nature', *British Journal of Political Science*, Vol. 6, pp. 43–81.

Crewe, I., Sarlvik, B. and Alt, J. (1977) 'Partisan de-alignment in Britain, 1964–1974', *British Journal of Political Science*, Vol. 7, pp. 129–90.

Crichfield, R. (1987) 'Britain: a view from the outside', *The Economist*, 21 February, pp. 1–26.

Crouch, C. (1985) 'Can Socialism achieve street credibility?', *Guardian*, 14 February, p. 13.

Crouch, C. S. (1982) 'Comment: trends in unemployment'. *Area*, Vol. 14, pp. 56–9.

Crouch, C. S. (1989) 'The economic geography of the UK in recession: the early 1980s and historical perspectives', unpublished PhD thesis, University of Durham.

Crum, R. E. and Gudgin, G. (1977) *Non-production activities in UK manufacturing industry*, Commission of the European Communities, Brussels.

Curtice, J. (1986) 'Political partisanship', in R. Jowell, S. Witherspoon and L. Brock (eds.) *British Social Attitudes: The 1986 Report*, Gower, Aldershot.

Curtice, J. and Steed, M. (1982) 'Electoral choice and the production of government', *British Journal of Political Science*, Vol. 12, pp. 249-98.

Curtice, J. and Steed, M. (1986) 'Proportionality and exaggeration in the British electoral system', *Electoral Studies,* Vol. 5, pp. 209-25.

Damesick, P. J. (1979) 'Office location and planning in the Manchester conurbation', *Town Planning Review*, Vol. 50, pp. 436-60.

Damesick, P. J. (1987) 'Regional economic change since the 1960s', in P. J. Damesick and P. A. Wood (eds.) *Regional Problems, Problem Regions, and Public Policy in the United Kingdom*, Oxford University Press.

Damesick, P. J. and Wood, P. A. (eds.) (1987) *Regional Problems, Problem Regions, and Public Policy in the United Kingdom*, Oxford University Press.

Daniels, P. W. (ed.) (1979) *Spatial Patterns of Office Growth and Location*, Wiley, Chichester.

Daniels, P. W. (1982) *Service Industries: Growth and Location*, Cambridge University Press.

Daniels, P. W. (1985) *Service Industries: a Geographical Appraisal,* Methuen, London.

Daniels, P. (1987) 'The geography of services', *Progress in Human Geography*, Vol. 11, pp. 433-47.

Daniels, P. and Thrift, N. (1987) *The Geographies of the UK Service Sector: A Survey*, Working Papers on Producer Services, University of Bristol and University of Liverpool.

Danson, M. (ed.) (1986) *Redundancy and Recession*, Geo Books, Norwich.

Darling-Hammond, L. and Kirby, S. N. (1988) 'Public policy and private choice: the case of Minnesota', in T. James and H. M. Levin (eds.) *Comparing Public and Private Schools*, Falmer Press, London.

Day, P. and Klein, R. (1985) 'Towards a new health care system', *British Medical Journal*, Vol. 291, pp. 1291-3.

Dennison, S. R. (1984) *Choice in Education*, Institute of Economic Affairs, London.

Denver, D. T. (1987) 'The British general election of 1987: some preliminary reflections', *Parliamentary Affairs*, Vol. 40, pp. 449-57.

Department of Employment (1987) '1984 Census of Employment and revised employment estimates', *Employment Gazette*, Vol. 95, pp. 31-7.

Department of Health and Social Security (1976) *Sharing Resources for Health in England: The Report of the Resources Allocation Working Party*, DHSS, London.

Department of Health and Social Security (1987) *Independent Sector Hospitals, Nursing Homes and Clinics in England*, DHSS, London.

Department of Trade and Industry (1985) *The Balance of Trade in Manufactures*, Cmnd. 9697, HMSO, London.

Department of Trade and Industry (1986) *UK Regional Development Programme, 1986-90*, Submission to the European Regional Development Fund (17 vols.).

Department of Trade and Industry (1988) *DTI - the Department for Enterprise*, Cmnd. 278, HMSO, London.

Draper, P., Smith, F., Stewart, W. and Hood, N. (1988) *The Scottish Financial Sector*, Edinburgh University Press.

Duffy, H. (1987) 'Regional development', *The Financial Times*, 19 January, Survey p. I.

Dunleavy, P. (1979) 'The urban basis of political dealignment', *British Journal of Political Science*, Vol. 9, pp. 409-43.

Dunleavy, P. (1987) 'Class dealignment in Britain revisited', *West European Politics*, Vol. 10, pp. 400-19.

Dunleavy, P. and Husbands, C. T. (1985) *British Democracy at the Cross-roads*, Allen & Unwin, London.

The Economist (1987a) 'North-South: Britain - a touch of class', 7 February, p. 63-4.

The Economist (1987b) 'Scotland's canny market', 19 December, pp. 84-85.

Edwards, J. (1988) 'Focus on the dumb-bell', *Financial Times Weekend*, 30 April, p. 5.

Employment Institute (1988) *How much has Unemployment Fallen?*, Economic Report, Vol. 3, no. 7, Employment Institute, London.

Euromoney (1987) 'The power league', February, pp. 85–95.

Euromoney (1988) 'Scotland: a step ahead', *Euromoney Supplement*, April.

Evans, A.W. (1973) 'The location of the headquarters of industrial companies', *Urban Studies*, Vol. 10, pp. 387–95.

Facey, M. and Smith, G. (1968) *Offices in a Regional Centre: A Study of Office Location in Leeds*, Location of Offices Bureau, London.

Farmbrough, H. and Jenkins, I. (1987) 'Big Bang starts the age of legal giants', *Financial Weekly*, 5 February, p. 7

Fennell, E. (1987a) 'High-fliers look to the North', *The Times*, 7 May.

Fennell, E. (1987b) 'All aglow in Glasgow', *The Times*, 9 April.

Fennell, E. (1987c) 'Looking for a top lawyer?', *The Times*, 12 March.

Feuchtwanger, R.J. (1968) *Disraeli, Democracy and the Conservative Party*, Oxford University Press.

The Financial Times (1987) 'Thatcher says north of England thriving', 4 January, p. 6.

Financial Weekly (1987) 'Professional melt-down', 25 June, pp. 28–35.

Fitz, J., Edwards, T. and Whitty, G. (1986) 'Beneficiaries, benefits and costs: an investigation of the Assisted Places Scheme', *Research Papers in Education*, Vol. 1, pp. 169–93.

Fitzgerald, T. (1983) 'The New Right and the family', in M. Loney, D. Boswell and J. Clarke, (eds.) *Social Policy and Social Welfare*, Open University Press, Milton Keynes.

Flynn, N. (1986) 'Performance measurement in public sector services', *Policy and politics*, Vol. 14, pp. 389–404.

Fogarty, M.P. (1945) *Prospects of the Industrial Areas of Great Britain*, Methuen, London.

Foley, P. (1986) 'House price boom or bust', *Lloyds Bank Economic Bulletin*, Vol. 93, September.

Foley, P. (1987) 'Two nations?', *Lloyds Bank Economic Bulletin*, Vol. 101.

Fothergill, S. and Gudgin, G. (1982) *Unequal Growth: Urban and Regional Employment Change in the UK*, Heinemann, London.

Fox, A. and Adelstein, A. (1978) 'Occupational mortality: work or way of life?', *Journal of Epidemiology and Community Health*, Vol. 36, pp. 938–45.

Fox, A. and Goldblatt, P. (1982) 'Socio-demographic mortality differentials from the OPCS longitudinal study, 1971–1975', OPCS, HMSO, London.

Fox, A., Jones, D., Moser, K. and Goldblatt, P. (1985) 'Socio-demographic differentials in mortality 1971–1981', *Population Trends*, Vol. 44, pp. 10–16.

Fox, I. (1985) *Private Schools and Public Issues*, Macmillan, London.

Franklin, M.N. (1985) *The Decline of Class Voting in Britain*, Clarendon Press, Oxford.

Gamble, A. (1987) 'Thatcherism and the politics of inequality', paper given at the Institute of British Geographers Annual Conference, Portsmouth, 6–9 January.

Gardner, M. (1984) 'Mapping cancer mortality in England and Wales', *British Medical Bulletin*, Vol. 40, pp. 320–8.

Gardner, M., Winter, P., Taylor, C. and Acheson, E. (1983) *Atlas of Cancer Mortality in England and Wales (1968–1978)*, Wiley, Chichester.

Giddens, A. (1979) 'The anatomy of the British ruling class', *New Society*, Vol. 50, no. 88, pp. 8–10.

Gillespie, A.E. and Green, A.E. (1987) 'The changing geography of producer services employment in Britain', *Regional Studies*, Vol. 21, pp. 397–412.

Gilmour, I. (1977) *Inside Right*, Hutchinson, London.

Glass, G.V., Cahen, L.S., Smith, M.L. and Filby, N.N. (1982) *School Class Size: Research and Policy*, Sage, Beverley Hills, Calif.

Goddard, J.B. and Champion, A.G. (eds.) (1983) *The Urban and Regional Transformation of Britain*, Methuen, London.

Goddard, J.B. and Smith, I.J. (1978) 'Changes in corporate control in the British urban system, 1972–1977', *Environment and Planning A*, Vol. 10, pp. 1073–84.

Green, A.E. (1988) 'The north-south divide in Great Britain: an examination of the evidence', *Transactions, Institute of British Geographers*, New Series, Vol. 13, pp. 179-98.

Griggs, C. (1985) *Private Education in Britain*, Falmer Press, London.

Gudgin, G., Crum, R. and Bailey, S. (1979) 'White-collar employment in UK manufacturing industry', in P.W. Daniels (ed.) *Spatial Patterns of Office Growth and Location*, Wiley, Chichester.

Halifax Building Society (1987), *Regional Bulletin* No. 12, January.

Hall, P. (1975) *Urban and Regional Planning*, Penguin, Harmondsworth.

Hall, P., Breheny, M., McQuaid, R. and Hart, D. (1987) *Western Sunrise: The Genesis and Growth of Britain's High Technology Corridor*, Allen & Unwin, London.

Halsey, A.H., Heath, A.F. and Ridge, J.M. (1980) *Origins and Destinations*, Clarendon Press, Oxford.

Hamilton Fazey, I. (1987a) 'Local firms thrive among the internationals', *Financial Times Survey: Sheffield*, 13 March, p. 4.

Hamilton Fazey, I. (1987b) 'Financial and professional services: centre of gravity in Manchester', *Financial Times Survey: North West England*, 29 October, p. 3.

Hamilton Fazey, I. (1987c) 'Financial and professional services: a remarkable growth of strategic importance', *Financial Times Survey: Yorkshire and Humberside*, 29 July, p. 5.

Hamilton Fazey, I. (1987d) 'Behind the nappies', *Financial Times Survey: Northern England*, 30 November, p. 3.

Hamilton Fazey, I. (1987e) 'Venture capital: many players in a growing game', *Financial Times Survey: Yorkshire and Humberside*, 29 July, p. 3.

Hamilton Fazey, I. (1987f) 'Japanese investment: banks give a boost', *Financial Times Survey: North West England*, 29 October, p. 4.

Hamnett, C. (1983) 'Regional variations in house prices and house price inflation 1969-81', *Area*, Vol. 15, pp. 97-109.

Hamnett, C. (1984) 'The postwar restructuring of the British housing and labour markets: a critical comment on Thorns', *Environment and Planning A*, Vol. 16, pp. 147-61.

Hansen, N.M. (1981) 'Development from above: the centre-down development paradigm', in W.B. Stöhr and D.R.F. Taylor (eds.) *Development from Above or Below?*, Wiley, Chichester.

Harris, D. (1988) 'British MBOs still thriving', *Euromoney Supplement*, April, pp. 25-6.

Harrison, R.T. and Mason, C.M. (1986) 'The regional impact of the small firms loan guarantee scheme in the UK', *Regional Studies*, Vol. 20, pp. 535-49.

Harvey, D. (1987) 'Flexible accumulation through urbanization: reflections on "post-modernism" in the American city', *Antipode*, Vol. 19, pp. 260-86.

Hattersley, R. (1987) *Choose Freedom: The Future for Democractic Socialism*, Michael Joseph, London.

Hausner, V.A. (1987) (ed.) *Urban Economic Change: Five City Studies*, Clarendon Press, Oxford.

Healey, M.J. and Watts, H.D. (1987) 'The multi-plant enterprise', in W.F. Lever (ed.) *Industrial Change in the United Kingdom*, Longman, London.

Healey, N. (1987a) 'The widening price of a house' *Town and Country Planning*, Vol. 56, pp. 328-9.

Healey, N. (1987b) 'Housing and the north-south divide', *Housing Review*, Vol. 36, pp. 189-90.

Heath, A., Jowell, R. and Curtice, J. (1985) *How Britain Votes*, Pergamon Press, Oxford.

Heath, A., Jowell, R. and Curtice, J. (1987) 'Trendless fluctuation: a reply to Crewe', *Political Studies*, Vol. 35, pp. 256-77.

Heath, E. (1965) *The Great Divide*, Conservative Political Centre, London.

Heath, E. (1985) 'North-south: the other common crisis', speech to Sunderland Conservative Association, Sunderland, 14 January.

Henley Centre for Economic Forecasting (1988) 'Forecasts of house prices prepared for the Household Mortgage Corporation', Henley Centre for Economic Forecasting.

Heseltine, M. (1987) quoted in an interview in *Marxism Today*, March.

Hillier Parker (1987a) *Industrial Rent and Yield Contours*, Hillier, Parker, May & Rowden, London.
Hillier Parker (1987b) *Office Rent and Yield Contours*, Hillier, Parker, May & Rowden, London.
Hirschman, A.O. (1958) *The Strategy of Economic Development*, Yale University Press, New Haven, Conn.
Hirschman, A.O. (1970) *Exit, Voice and Loyalty*, Harvard University Press, Cambridge, Mass.
HM Government (1987) 'Employment', *House of Commons Parliamentary Debates (Written Answers), Hansard*, Vol. 108, no. 33, pp. 286-7, HMSO, London.
Hodson, R. (1988) 'The professionals' arrival will change the skyline', *Financial Times Survey: Swindon*, 11 May, p. 3.
Hogarth, T. (1987) 'Long distance weekly commuting', *Policy Studies*, Vol. 8, part 1, pp. 27-43.
House of Commons Social Services Committee (1988) *First Report, Session 1987-1988: Resourcing the NHS - Short Term Issues* (House of Commons Paper HC-264), HMSO, London.
House of Lords (1985) *Report*, House of Lords Select Committee on Overseas Trade, Session 1984-5, Cmnd. 238-I, HMSO, London.
Howells, J. and Green, A.E. (1988) *Technological Innovation, Structural Change and Location in UK Services*, Gower, Aldershot.
Hudson, R. and Williams, A.M. (1986) *The United Kingdom*, Harper & Row, London.
Hunt, E.M. (1973) *Regional Wage Variations in Britain, 1850-1914*, Clarendon Press, Oxford.
Hunter, D. (1983) 'The privatisation of public provision', *The Lancet*, 4 June, pp. 1264-8.
Incomes Data Services (1984) *Private Health Insurance*, IDS Report no. 317, Incomes Data Services, London.
Incomes Data Services (1988) *Skill Shortages in the South East*, Labour Market Supplement no. 2, Incomes Data Services, London.
The Independent (1987), 14 December, p. 7.
Investors Chronicle (1987) 'New merchant bank breaks the mould', *Investors Chronicle Survey: Greater Manchester*, 9 October, p. 16.
Jack, I. (1987) *Before the Oil Ran Out: Britain 1977-87*, Martin Secker & Warburg, London.
Jenkins, P. (1987) *Mrs Thatcher's Revolution: The Ending of the Socialist Era*, Jonathan Cape, London.
Jensen-Butler, C. (1987) 'The regional economic effects of European integration', *Geoforum*, Vol. 18, pp. 213-27.
Jessop, B., Bonnett, K., Bromley, S. and Ling, T. (1984) 'Authoritarian populism, two nations and Thatcherism', *New Left Review*, Vol. 147, pp. 32-60.
Johnston, R.J. (1978) *Multivariate Statistical Analysis in Geography*, Longman, London.
Johnston, R.J. (1981) 'Regional variations in British voting trends, 1966-1979: tests of an ecological model', *Regional Studies*, Vol. 15, pp. 23-32.
Johnston, R.J. (1985) *The Geography of English Politics*, Croom Helm, Beckenham.
Johnston, R.J. (1986a) 'A space for place (or a place for space) in British psephology', *Environment and Planning A*, Vol. 19, pp. 599-618.
Johnston, R.J. (1986b) 'The neighbourhood effect revisited', *Environment and Planning D: Society and Space*, Vol. 4, pp. 41-55.
Johnston, R.J. (1987a) 'The rural milieu and voting in Britain', *Journal of Rural Studies*, Vol. 3, pp. 95-103.
Johnston, R.J. (1987b) 'A note on housing tenure and voting in Britain, 1983', *Housing Studies*, Vol. 2, pp. 112-21.
Johnston, R.J. and Hay, A.M. (1982) 'On the parameters of uniform swing in single-member constituency electoral systems', *Environment and Planning A*, Vol. 14, pp. 61-74.
Johnston, R.J. and Honey, R. (1988) 'The 1987 general election in New Zealand and the demise of electoral cleavages', *Political Geography Quarterly*, Vol. 7, pp. 363-8.

Johnston, R.J. and Pattie, C.J. (1987) 'A dividing nation? An initial exploration of the changing electoral geography of Great Britain, 1979-1987', *Environment and Planning A*, Vol. 19, pp. 1001-13.

Johnston, R.J. and Pattie, C.J. (1988) 'Are we all Alliance nowadays? Discriminating by discriminant analysis', *Electoral Studies*, Vol. 6, pp. 27-32.

Johnston, R.J. and Pattie, C.J. (1989) 'A growing north:south divide in British voting patterns, 1979-1987', *Geoforum*, Vol. 20.

Johnston, R.J., Pattie, C.J. and Allsopp, J.G. (1988) *A Nation Dividing?* Longman, London.

Jones Lang Wootton (1986a) *50 Centres: A Guide to Office and Industrial Rental Trends in England and Wales*, June, Jones Lang Wootton, London.

Jones Lang Wootton (1986b) *The Decentralisation of Offices from Central London*, Jones Lang Wootton Technical Paper, London.

Jones Lang Wootton (1987a) *The Decentralisation of Offices from Central London*, Jones Lang Wootton Technical Paper, London.

Jones Lang Wootton (1987b) *50 Centres: A Guide to Office and Industrial Rental Trends in England and Wales*, June, Jones Lang Wootton, London.

Joseph, K. and Sumption, J. (1980) *Equality*, Murray, London.

Keeble, D.E. (1976) *Industrial Location and Planning in the United Kingdom*, Methuen, London.

Keeble, D.E. (1977) 'Spatial policy in Britain: regional or urban?', *Area*, Vol. 9, pp. 3-8.

Keeble, D.E. (1987) 'Entrepreneurship, high technology and regional development in the United Kingdom: the case of the Cambridge phenomenon', paper given at a Seminar on Technology and Territory: Innovation Diffusion, the Regional Experience of Europe and the USA, University of Naples, February.

Kennedy, C. (1988) 'Industrial journey: Manchester and Sussex', *The Director*, March, pp. 54-7.

King, D.S. (1987) *The New Right: Politics, Markets and Citizenship*, Macmillan, London.

Kinnear, M. (1981) *The British Voter: An Atlas and Survey Since 1885*, Batsford, London.

Kooiman, J. and Eliasson, K.A. (1987) *Managing Public Organisations*, Sage, London.

Labour Party (1918) *Labour and the New Social Order*, Labour Party, London.

Labour Party (1935) *A Nation without Poverty: Labour's Plan for Organising a Prosperous Society*, Labour Party, London.

Langman, M. (1987) 'Efficiency savings or financial cuts: some evidence from Birmingham', *British Medical Journal*, Vol. 295, pp. 902-3.

Lash, S. and Urry, J. (1987) *The End of Organised Capitalism*, Polity Press, Cambridge.

Law, C.M. (1985) 'The spatial distribution of offices in metropolitan areas: a comparison of Birmingham, Glasgow and Manchester', *Manchester Geographer*, New Series, Vol. 6, pp. 33-41.

Law, C.M. (1986) 'The uncertain future of the city centre: the case of Manchester', *Manchester Geographer*, New Series, Vol. 7, pp. 26-43.

Leat, D. (1986) 'Privatisation and voluntarisation', *Quarterly Journal of Social Affairs*, Vol. 2, pp. 285-320.

Lee, C.H. (1979) *British Regional Employment Statistics, 1841-1971*, Cambridge University Press.

Lee, C.H. (1980) 'Regional structural change in the long run: Great Britain 1841-1971', in S. Pollard (ed.) *Region and Industrialisation*, Vandenhoeck & Ruprecht, Gottingen.

Lee, C.H. (1984) 'The service economy, regional specialisation and economic growth in the Victorian economy', *Journal of Historical Geography*, Vol. 10, pp. 139-55.

Lee, C.H. (1986) *The British Economy since 1700: A Macro-Economic Perspective*, Cambridge University Press.

Le Grand, J. (1982) *The Strategy of Equality*, Allen & Unwin, London.

Le Grand, J. and Robinson, R. (1984) *Privatisation and the Welfare State*, Allen & Unwin, London.

Levitas, R. (ed.) (1986) *The Ideology of the New Right*, Polity Press, Cambridge.

Leyshon, A., Daniels, P. and Thrift, N. (1987) *Large Accountancy Firms in the UK: Operational Adaption and Spatial Development*, Working Papers in Producer Services no. 2, St David's University College, Lampeter, and University of Liverpool.

Leyshon, A., Thrift, N. and Daniels, P. (1987) *Large Commercial Property Firms in the UK: The Operational Development and Spatial Expansion of General Practice Firms of Chartered Surveyors*, Working Papers in Producer Services no. 5, University of Bristol and University of Liverpool.

Lloyd, P.C. (1987) 'Seeking regional advantage from recent trends in business organisation: some observations from the North West', paper given at the TCPA Conference on the North-South Divide, December.

MacInnes, J. (1988) *The North-South Divide: Regional Employment Change in Britain 1975–87*, Centre for Urban and Regional Research, Discussion Paper 34, University of Glasgow.

Macleod, I. (1952) *One Nation*, Conservative Political Centre, London.

Macleod, I. and Maude, A. (1950) *One Nation: A Tory Approach to Social Policy*, Conservative Political Centre, London.

McLoughlin, J. (1987) 'Dispelling the north-south myths', *Guardian*, 25 June.

Macmillan, H. (1938) *The Middle Way: A Study of the Problem of Economic and Social Progress in a Free and Democratic Society*, Macmillan, London.

Macmillan, H. (1966) *Winds of Change, 1914–1939*, Macmillan, London.

Macmillan, H., Boothby, R. and Loder, J. de von (1927) *Industry and the State: A Conservative View*, Macmillan, London.

Manchester Evening News (1984) 'Independent schools: havens of stability', 5 June.

Marshall, J.N. (1985a) 'Business services, the regions and regional policy', *Regional Studies*, Vol. 19, pp. 353–64.

Marshall, J.N. (1985b) 'Research policy and review 4. Services in a post-industrial economy', *Environment and Planning A*, Vol. 17, pp. 1155–68.

Marshall, J.N. (ed.) (1988) *Uneven Development in the Service Economy: Understanding the Location and Role of Producer Services*, Oxford University Press.

Marshall, J.N. and Bachtler, J. (1987) 'Services and regional policy', *Regional Studies*, Vol. 21, pp. 471–5.

Marshall, J.N., Damesick, P. and Wood, P. (1987) 'Understanding the location and role of producer services in the United Kingdom', *Environment and Planning A*, Vol. 19, pp. 575–95.

Marshall, M. (1987) *Long Waves of Regional Development*, Macmillan, London.

Martin, R.L. (1982) 'Job loss and the regional incidence of redundancies in the current recession', *Cambridge Journal of Economics*, Vol. 6, pp. 375–96.

Martin, R.L. (1985) 'Monetarism masquerading as regional policy? The government's new system of regional aid', *Regional Studies*, Vol. 19, pp. 379–88.

Martin, R.L. (1986a) 'In what sense a jobs boom? Employment recovery, government policy and the regions', *Regional Studies*, Vol. 20, pp. 463–72.

Martin, R.L. (1986b) 'Thatcherism and Britain's industrial landscape', in R.L. Martin and R.E. Rowthorn (eds.) *The Geography of De-industrialisation*, Macmillan, London.

Martin, R.L. (1987) 'Mrs Thatcher's Britain; a tale of two nations', *Environment and Planning A*, Vol. 19, pp. 571–4.

Martin, R.L. (1988a) 'The Growth and Geographical Anatomy of Venture Capitalism in the UK', Paper presented to the Annual Conference of The Regional Studies Association on the Financial Sector and Regional Development, Policy Studies Institute, London, 18 November.

Martin, R.L. (1988b) 'The new economics and politics of regional restructuring: the British case', in L. Albrechts, P. Roberts and E. Swyngedouw (eds.) *Regional Planning at the Crossroads*, Roger Booth Publishers, Newcastle.

Martin, R.L. and Rowthorn, R.E. (1986) *The Geography of De-Industrialisation*, Macmillan, London.

Marxism Today (1988) 'The Tory opposition', March, pp. 12–19.

Mason, C. (1987) 'Venture capital in the United Kingdom: a geographical perspective', *National Westminster Bank Quarterly Review*, May, pp. 47–59.

Mason, C. and Harrison, R.T. (1987) 'The regional impact of the Business Expansion Scheme', Paper presented at the Tenth National Small Firms Policy and Research Conference, Cranfield Institute of Technology, 19–21 November.

Massey, D. (1979) 'In what sense a regional problem?', *Regional Studies*, Vol. 13, pp. 233–43.

Massey, D. (1984) *Spatial Divisions of Labour: Social Structures and the Geography of Production*, Macmillan, London.

Massey, D. (1985) 'Geography and class', in D. Coates, G. Johnston and R. Bush (eds.) *A Socialist Anatomy of Britain*, Polity Press, Cambridge.

Massey, D. (1986) 'The legacy lingers on: the impact of Britain's international role on its internal geography', in R.L. Martin and R.E. Rowthorn (eds.) *The Geography of De-Industrialisation*, Macmillan, London.

Massey, D. (1987) 'Geography matters', *Geography Review*, Vol. 1, pp. 2–9.

Massey, D. (1988) 'A new class of geography', *Marxism Today*, May, pp. 12–17.

Massey, D.B. and Meegan, R.A. (1982) *The Anatomy of Job Loss*, Methuen, London.

Mays, N. and Bevan, G. (1987) *Resource Allocation in the Health Service: A Review of the Methods of the Resource Allocation Working Party*, Bedford Square Press, London.

Miller, W.L. (1977) *Electoral Dynamics*, Macmillan, London.

Miller, W.L. (1984) 'There was no alternative: the British general election of 1983', *Parliamentary Affairs*, Vol. 37, pp. 364–84.

Minford, P., Peel, M. and Ashton, P. (1987) *The Housing Morass: Regulation, Immobility and Unemployment*, Institute of Economic Affairs, London.

Mohan, J.F. (1984) 'Geographical aspects of private hospital developments in Britain', *Area*, Vol. 16, pp. 191–9.

Mohan, J.F. (1988a) 'Restructuring, privatization and the geography of health care in England, 1983–7', *Transactions, Institute of British Geographers*, New Series, Vol. 13, pp. 449–65.

Mohan, J.F. (1988b) 'Spatial aspects of health care employment change in Britain, 1: aggregate trends', *Environment and Planning A*, Vol. 20, pp. 7–23.

Mohan, J.F. (1988c) 'Spatial aspects of health care employment change in Britain, 2: current policy initiatives', *Environment and Planning A*, Vol. 20, pp. 203–17.

Molle, W. with van Holst, B. and Smit, H. (1980) *Regional Disparity and Economic Development in the European Community*, Saxon House, Farnborough.

Moore, B., Rhodes, J. and Tyler, P. (1986) *The Effects of Government Regional Economic Policy*, HMSO, London.

Morgan, K. (1986a) 'The spectre of "two nations" in contemporary Britain', *Catalyst*, Vol. 2, no. 2, pp. 11–18.

Morgan, K. (1986b) 'Re-industrialisation in peripheral Britain: state policy, the space economy and industrial innovation', in R.L. Martin and R.E. Rowthorn (eds.) *The Geography of De-Industrialisation*, Macmillan, London.

Morris, J. (1986) *The Internationalisation of Banking, Technological Change and Spatial Patterns: A Case Study in South Wales*, Department of Business and Economics, UWIST, Cardiff (mimeo.).

Moser, K., Goldblatt, P., Fox, A.J. and Jones, D. (1987) 'Unemployment and mortality: comparison of the 1971 and 1981 Longitudinal Study sample', *British Medical Journal*, Vol. 294, pp. 86–90.

Moss, M.L. and Dunau, A. (1986) *The Location of Back-offices: Emerging Trends and Development Patterns*, Sylvan Lawrence Research and Data Center, New York University, NY.

Myrdal, G. (1957) *Economic Theory and Underdeveloped Regions*, Duckworth, London.

Nationwide Building Society (1987) *House Prices: The North-South Divide*, August, Nationwide Building Society, London.

Nelson, K. (1986) 'Labour demand, labour supply and the suburbanisation of low-wage office work', in A.J. Scott and M. Storper (eds.) *Production, Work, Territory: The*

Geographical Anatomy of Industrial Capitalism, Allen & Unwin, Boston, Mass.

New Earnings Survey (1985) Department of Employment, London.

Newsom, J. (1968) *The First Report of the Public Schools Commission,* HMSO, London.

Norton, P. and Aughey, A. (1981) *Conservatives and Conservatism,* Temple Smith, London.

One Nation Group of MPs (1976) *One Nation at Work,* Conservative Political Centre, London.

OPCS (1981) *Area Mortality 1969–1973* (OPCS Series DS4), HMSO, London.

OPCS (1986) *General Household Survey, 1984,* HMSO, London.

OPCS (1987a) *Local Authority Vital Statistics, 1986, Series VS3,* OPCS, London.

OPCS (1987b) *OPCS Monitor DH3 87/4: Infant and Perinatal Mortality, 1986,* OPCS, London.

Owen, D.W., Gillespie, A.E. and Coombes, M.G. (1984) '"Job shortfalls" in British local labour market areas: a classification of labour supply and demand trends, 1971–81', *Regional Studies,* Vol. 18, pp. 469–88.

Parsons, D.W. (1986) *The Political Economy of Regional Policy,* Croom Helm, Beckenham.

Parsons, D. (1987) 'Recruitment difficulties and the housing market', *The Planner,* Vol. 73, no. 1, pp. 30–4.

Parsons, G. (1972) 'The giant manufacturing corporation and balanced regional growth in Britain', *Area,* Vol. 4, pp. 99–103.

Pensions Management (1987) 'The survey: fund managers performance – surviving the squall?', *Pensions Management,* December, pp. 51–79.

Penycate, J. (1987) 'The property boom widens the north-south divide', *The Listener,* 13 November, pp. 4–5.

Peston, M. (1984) 'Privatisation of education', in J. Le Grand and R. Robinson (eds.) *Privatisation and the Welfare State,* Allen & Unwin, London.

Pring, R. (1983) *Privatisation in Education,* Right to Comprehensive Education (RICE), London.

Pugh, M. (1985) *The Tories and the People, 1880–1935,* Basil Blackwell, Oxford.

Pulzer, P.G.J. (1967) *Political Representation and Elections in Britain,* Allen & Unwin, London.

Rae, J. (1981) *The Public School Revolution: Britain's Independent Schools 1964–1979,* Faber & Faber, London.

Ramsden, J.A. (1980) *The Making of Conservative Party Policy: The Conservative Research Department since 1929,* Longman, London.

Reed, H.C. (1981) *The Pre-Eminence of International Financial Centres,* Praeger, New York, NY.

Reeves, R. (1987a) 'Financial and legal services: attracting inward investment', *The Financial Times Survey: Norwich,* 9 July, p. 36.

Reeves, R. (1987b) 'Home-grown industry is expanding on all fronts', *The Financial Times Survey: Norwich,* 9 July, p. 33.

Reward Regional Surveys (1987) *UK Regional Cost of Living Report,* Reward Regional Surveys, Stone, Staffs.

Rhodes, J. (1986) 'Regional dimensions of industrial decline', in R.L. Martin and R.E. Rowthorn (eds.) *The Geography of De-Industrialisation,* Macmillan, London.

Roberts, J. and Graveling, P. (1986) *The Big Kill: Smoking Epidemic in England and Wales,* Health Education Council, London.

Rogaly, J. (1987) 'Divided they stand', *The Financial Times,* 31 March.

Rogerson, R., Findlay, A. and Morris, A. (1988) 'A report on quality of life in British cities', Department of Geography, University of Glasgow (mimeo.).

Rose, R. and McAllister, I. (1986) *Voters Begin to Choose,* Sage, London.

Rothwell, R. (1982) 'The role of technology in industrial change: implications for regional policy', *Regional Studies,* Vol. 16, pp. 361–70.

Rowthorn, R.E. (1986) 'De-industrialisation in Britain', in R.L. Martin and R.E. Rowthorn (eds.) *The Geography of De-Industrialisation,* Macmillan, London.

Rowthorn, R.E. and Wells, J. (1987) *De-Industrialisation and Foreign Trade: Britain in a Global Perspective*, Cambridge University Press.

Royal Commission on the Distribution of Income and Wealth (1977) *Third Report on the Standing Reference*, Cmnd. 6999, HMSO, London.

Rubenstein, W.D. (1977) 'The Victorian middle classes: wealth, occupation and geography', *Economic History Review*, Vol. 30, pp. 602-23.

Rubenstein, W.D. (1981) *Men of Property: The Very Wealthy in Britain since the Industrial Revolution*, Croom Helm, Beckenham.

Sanders, D., Ward, H. and Marsh, D. (1987) 'Government popularity and the Falklands war: a reassessment', *British Journal of Political Science*, Vol. 17, pp. 281-313.

Sarlvik, B. and Crewe, I. (1983) *Decade of Dealignment*, Cambridge University Press.

Savas, E.D. (1982) *Privatising the Public Sector*, Chatham House, Chatham, NJ.

Sayer, A. and Morgan, K. (1986) 'The electronics industry and regional development in Britain', in A. Amin and J. Goddard (eds.) *Technological Change, Industrial Restructuring and Regional Development*, Allen & Unwin, London.

Scouller, J. (1987) 'The United Kingdom merger boom in perspective', *The NatWest Review*, April, pp. 14-30.

SEEDS Association (1987) *South-South Divide*, South East Economic Development Strategy, Stevenage.

Shaper, A., Pocock, S., Walker, M., Cohen, N., Wade, C. and Thomson, A. (1981) 'British regional heart study: cardiovascular risk factors in middle aged men in 24 towns', *British Medical Journal*, Vol. 283, pp. 179-86.

Sharpe, L.J. (1982) 'The Labour Party and the geography of inequality: a puzzle', in D. Kavanagh (ed.) *The Politics of the Labour Party*, Allen & Unwin, London.

Smith, D. (1976) 'Codes, paradigms and folk norms: an approach to educational change with particular reference to the work of Basil Bernstein', *British Journal of Sociology*, Vol. 10, pp. 1-19.

Smith, D.M. (1988) 'On academic performance', *Area*, Vol. 20, pp. 3-13.

Solow, R. (1987) 'The Conservative revolution: a round-table discussion', *Economic Policy*, Vol. 5, pp. 181-5.

Southall, H. (1983) 'Regional unemployment patterns in Britain, 1851-1914', unpublished PhD thesis, University of Cambridge.

Southall, H. (1988) 'The origins of the Depressed Areas: unemployment, growth and regional structure in Britain before 1914', *Economic History Review*, Vol. 41, pp. 236-58.

Steed, M. and Curtice, J. (1983) *One in Four: An Examination of the Alliance Performance at Constituency Level in the 1983 General Election*, Association of Liberal Councillors, Hebden Bridge.

Stöhr, W.B. (1981) 'Development from below: the bottom-up and periphery-inward development paradigm', in W.B. Stöhr and D.R.F. Taylor (eds.) *Development from Above or Below?*, Wiley, Chichester.

Storey, D. and Johnson, S. (1987) 'Regional variations in entrepreneurship in the UK', *Scottish Journal of Political Economy*, Vol. 34, pp. 161-73.

Taylor, P.J. (1982) 'A materialist framework for political geography', *Transactions, Institute of British Geographers*, New Series, Vol. 7, pp. 15-34.

Taylor-Gooby, P. (1987) 'Welfare attitudes: cleavage, consensus and citizenship', *Quarterly Journal of Social Affairs*, Vol. 13, pp. 199-211.

TCPA (1987) *North-South Divide: A New Deal for Britain's Regions*, Town and Country Planning Association, London.

Thorns, D.C. (1982) 'Industrial restructuring and changes in the labour and property markets in Britain', *Environment and Planning A*, Vol. 14, pp. 745-63.

Thrift, N. and Leyshon, A. (1988) 'The gambling propensity: banks, developing country debt exposures and the New International Financial System', *Geoforum*, Vol. 19, pp. 55-69.

Thrift, N., Leyshon, A. and Daniels, P. (1987) *Sexy Greedy: The New International Financial System, the City of London and the South East of England*, Working Papers on Producer

Services no. 8, University of Bristol and University of Liverpool.
The Times 1000, 1976-7 (1976) Times Books, London.
The Times 1000, 1986-7 (1986) Times Books, London.
The Times Educational Supplement (1987) 'Accommodating Offers', 15 May.
Titmus, R. (1962) *Income Distribution and Social Change*, Allen & Unwin, London.
Townsend, A.R. (1983) *The Impact of Recession, on Industry, Employment and the Regions, 1976-1981*, Croom Helm, Beckenham.
Townsend, A.R. (1986) 'The location of employment growth after 1978: the surprising significance of dispersed centres', *Environment and Planning A*, Vol. 18, pp. 529-45.
Townsend, A.R. (1987) 'Regional Policy', in W.F. Lever (ed.) *Industrial Change*, Longman, London.
Townsend, A.R. and Peck, F.W. (1985) 'The geography of mass redundancy in named corporations', in M. Pacione (ed.) *Progress in Industrial Geography*, Croom Helm, Beckenham.
Townsend, P., Davidson, N. and Whitehead, M. (1988) *Inequalities in Health: The Black Report and the Health Divide*, Pelican, Harmondsworth.
Townsend, P., Phillimore, P. and Beattie, A. (1988) *Health and Deprivation: Inequality and the North*, Croom Helm, Beckenham.
van Dinteren, J.H.J. (1987) 'The role of business-service offices in the economy of medium-sized cities', *Environment and Planning A*, Vol. 19, pp. 669-86.
von Tunzelman, N. (1981) 'Britain 1900-45: a survey', in R. Floud and D. McCloskey (eds.) *The Economic History of Britain since 1500*, Cambridge University Press, Vol. 2.
Veitch, A. (1987) 'Two nation gap widens', *Guardian*, 29 January.
Walton, R.J. and Trimble, D. (1987) 'Japanese banks in London', *Bank of England Quarterly Bulletin*, November, pp. 518-24.
Warde, A. (1986) 'Space, class and voting in Britain', in K. Hoggart and E. Kofman (eds.) *Politics, Geography and Social Stratification*, Croom Helm, Beckenham.
Watson, A., Reynolds, R. and Jardine, C. (1987) 'The Business guide: Manchester', *Business*, April, pp. 109-18.
Watts, H.D. (1972) 'Further observations on regional growth and large corporations', *Area*, Vol. 4, pp. 269-73.
Watts, H.D. (1981) *The Branch Plant Economy*, Longman, London.
Watts, H.D. (1987) 'Producer services, industrial location and uneven development', *Area*, Vol. 19, pp. 353-5.
Watts, H.D. (forthcoming) 'Industrial expansion and dereliction: the changing geography of UK manufacturing industry', in T.P. Bayliss-Smith and S. Owens (eds.) *The Geography of Britain from the Air, Volume 3, Landscape Change, Resources and Conservation*, Cambridge University Press.
Weatherall Green and Smith (Chartered Surveyors) (1986) *International Rent Survey*, Autumn, Weatherall Green and Smith, London.
Webber, R. and Craig, J. (1978) *Socio-Economic Classifications of Local Authority Areas*, OPCS studies in Medical and Population Subjects, No. 35, HMSO, London.
Webster, C. (1988) *The Health Services since the War, Vol. 1.: Problems of Health Care, 1948-1957*, HMSO, London.
Wells, J. (1986) *Financial Services in Scotland: Working Paper 2, Locational Trends*, Jones Lang Wootton Technical Paper, London.
Westaway, J. (1974) 'Contact potential and the occupational structure of the British urban system 1961-1966: an empirical study', *Regional Studies*, Vol. 10, pp. 57-73.
White, D. (1985) 'Tilting Britain onto its side' *New Society*, 14 June, pp. 383-5.
Whitehead, M. (1987) 'The health divide', in P. Townsend, N. Davidson and M. Whitehead, *Inequalities in Health: The Black Report and the Health Divide*, Pelican, Harmondsworth.
Whiteley, P. (1982) 'The decline of Labour's local party membership and electoral base, 1945-79', in D. Kavanagh (ed.) *The Politics of the Labour Party*, Allen & Unwin, London.
Whiteley, P. (1983) *The Labour Party in Crisis*, Methuen, London.
Whiteley, P. (1986) 'Predicting the Labour vote in 1983', *Political Studies*, Vol. 34, pp. 82-98.

Williams, B., Nicholl, J., Thomas, K. and Knowelden, J. (1984) 'Contribution of the private sector to elective surgery in England', *The Lancet*, 14 July, pp. 88-92.

Wilsher, P. and Cassidy, J. (1987) 'Two nations: the false frontier', *The Sunday Times*, 11 January.

Wilson, A.G. (1970) *Entropy in Urban and Regional Modelling*, Pion, London.

AUTHOR INDEX

Facey, M. 158
Farmborough, H. 149
Fennel, E. 134
Feuchtwagner, R.J. 60
Financial Times, 2, 3, 4, 21, 59
Findlay, A. 96
Fitz, J. 194
Fitzgerald, T. 199
Flynn, N. 196
Fogarty, M.P. 22
Foley, P. 61, 98
Fothergill, S. 7, 62
Fox, A. 176, 179, 215
Fox, I. 194, 197, 198, 200
Franklin, M.N. 42, 214

Gamble, A. 53
Gardner, M. 177, 178
Gaskell, E. 59
Giddens, A. 198
Gillespie, A.E. 62, 64, 114, 154, 168
Gilmour, I. 47
Glass, G.V. 198
Goddard, J.B. 62, 63, 158
Green, A.E. ix, 4, 15, 41, 61, 62, 96, 98, 100, 114, 119, 154, 166, 168
Griggs, C. 194, 195, 198
Gudgin, G. 7, 62, 158

Hall, P. 4, 22, 62, 84, 95, 96
Halsey, A.H. 198
Hamilton Fazey, I. xiii, 132, 134, 143, 149, 150
Hamnett, C. ix, 17, 62, 97
Hansen, N.M. 6
Harris, D. 150
Harrison, R.T. 54, 149
Harvey, D. 28
Hattersley, R. 51
Hausner, V.A. 121
Hay, A.M. 219
Hay, D. 62
Healey, M.J. 159
Healey, N. 64, 98
Heath, A. 198, 214
Heath, E. 21, 49
Hirschman, A.O. 6, 201
Hodson, R. 154
Hogarth, T. 98
Honey, R. 247
Hood, N. 142
Howells, J. 62, 114
Hudson, R. 7
Hunt, E.M. 25
Hunter, D. 189

Husbands, C.T. 200, 214

Independent, The, 59, 98, 157, 164

Jack, I. 2,3
Jackson, D. 153
Jenkins, P. 2
Jensen-Butler, 7
Jessop, B. 53, 187
Johnson, M. 54
Johnston, R.J. x, 4, 6, 202, 213, 214, 219, 226, 227, 246, 247
Joseph, K. 58
Jowell, R. 214

Keeble, D.E. 7, 31, 50
Kennedy, C. 143, 145
King, D.S. 192, 193
Kinnear, M. 59
Kirby, S.N. 195
Kooiman, J. 192

Labour Party, 48
Langman, M. 186
Lash, S. 28
Law, C.M. 159, 167
Leat, D. 194
Lee, C.H. 24, 25, 26
Le Grand, J. 196, 197
Levitas, R. 192
Lewis, J. xii, 1
Leyshon, A. x, 4, 11, 114, 119, 131, 133, 135, 136, 149, 155
Ling, T. 53, 187
Lloyd, P.C. 61
Loder, J. de von, 60
Lovering, J. 42, 126, 144, 145, 152

Macleod, I. xiii, 20, 48, 60
McAllister, I. 214
McLoughlin, J. 61, 95
Macmillan, H. 47, 60
Marsh, D. 241
Marshall, J.N. 7, 62, 158
Marshall, M. 23
Martin, R.L. x, 6, 8, 15, 20, 30, 31, 53, 54, 61, 62, 164
Mason, C. 54, 149
Massey, D. 4, 8, 22, 23, 42, 128, 151
Maude, A. 48
Mays, N. 185
Meegan, R.A. 8
Miller, W.L. 214, 219, 226
Minford, P. 98
Mohan, J.F x, 175, 188, 190

SUBJECT INDEX